OCCULT RUS

"In *Occult Russia,* Christopher McIntosh, master historian of the esoteric, presents a panoramic view of a Russia few people in the West know about or even suspect exists. From its very beginnings, Russia has been a nation of magic, mysticism, and profound spirituality, and its people the bearers of a deep inner life. For most Westerners, Russia means either the dark days of the Soviet Union or the more recent tumultuous times following the USSR's collapse. But long before Lenin reached the Finland Station, a heady brew of pagan, Christian, and occult beliefs—and not Marx—informed Russia's turbulent, apocalyptic heritage. 'Occult,' we know, means hidden, and in this painstakingly researched and finely written work, Christopher McIntosh brings this hidden side of Russian history, too long kept in the shadows, into the light."

GARY LACHMAN, AUTHOR OF *THE RETURN OF HOLY RUSSIA*

"Insightful, meticulously researched, and timely in so many ways, *Occult Russia* is a passionate journey to the heart and soul of Russia. Christopher McIntosh, author of many groundbreaking books, masterly uncovers the 'hidden history' of the vast northern land, introducing an amazing cast of dramatic and colorful characters, from shamans to commissars, artists to conspirators, mystics to messiahs. . . . This book may hold the key to understanding Winston Churchill's observation, Russia is 'a riddle, wrapped in a mystery, inside an enigma.' You'll not find a more fascinating or wonderfully written study of occult Russia and the powerful spiritual energies emanating from that enigmatic nation. I heartily recommend this book."

DAVID P. JONES, *NEW DAWN* MAGAZINE

"This book of marvels might easily have been called *The Spirit of Russia,* or *The Spirit in Russia,* for that is its true trajectory. Christopher McIntosh wants to show us an unknown country with an immensely varied culture based on spiritual awareness of God or divine powers in humankind and in the natural world that brings us life. We cross the threshold from nature to super-nature with remarkable ease with the assistance of the uniquely Russian sensibility. It is enormously helpful to see this range of knowledge brought to bear with such vivid focus on a single country. That country is today one of the most controversial in the world. We hear much about Russia—or think we do. What we do *not* hear, and what I fear the prevailing mentality of our dominant news media *does not want us to hear*—you will find beautifully and simply expressed in this vital book. If 'occult' is taken in its true meaning of 'something hidden,' this book is indeed about an occulted Russia, hidden from the eyes of the West, which has so much to learn from it. This is a vital, engaging, always surprising text for anyone who wants to understand this massive neighbor of East and West, and who has the courage to build on the courage of those who have, against the odds, worked and suffered and died to maintain and promote spiritual consciousness in Russia. Christopher's book also shows where spirituality can be harnessed to some rather unspiritual objectives. We see the beauty, and the warts, but all in all: a must-read. *Occult Russia* is sober, informed, provocative, clear, and important."

Tobias Churton, Britain's leading scholar of
Western Esotericism and author *Deconstructing Gurdjieff:
Biography of a Spiritual Magician*

"*Occult Russia* is a study of the mystical, artistic, and neo-pagan ideals that are transforming Russia. This book is lively and urbane because Christopher McIntosh is deeply informed about the inspiring contemporary scene in the post-Soviet era. Many believe a huge spiritual revival is happening. Deliciously detailed, he describes a building wave of enchantment, exciting magic, and mystery that is awakening deep in the Russian soul. People inspired by Tolstoy's ideals—pacifism, vegetarianism, and the use of potent folk medicine for vibrant health—are moving back to the land to live in communities. American New Age readers will be amazed to see that current Russian idealism is very much like their own! This book is a gem for anyone who has found deep richness in Russian culture and wonders what is going on now since the fall of communism. Thoroughly entertaining, informative, and deeply meaningful—a page-turner!"

Barbara Hand Clow, author of *Awakening the
Planetary Mind* and *The Pleiadian Agenda:
A New Cosmology for the Age of Light*

"*Occult Russia* is a superb introduction to hidden aspects of Russian spiritual life, full of striking reflections and themes. To explore the richness of Russian spirituality, you can't do better than this book."

Arthur Versluis, author of *The Secret History
of Western Sexual Mysticism* and *Sacred Earth*

OCCULT RUSSIA

PAGAN, ESOTERIC, AND MYSTICAL TRADITIONS

CHRISTOPHER McINTOSH

Inner Traditions
Rochester, Vermont

Inner Traditions
One Park Street
Rochester, Vermont 05767
www.InnerTraditions.com

Text stock is SFI certified

Cataloging-in-Publication Data for this title is available from the Library of Congress

ISBN 978-1-64411-418-6 (print)
ISBN 978-1-64411-419-3 (ebook)

Printed and bound in the United States by Lake Book Manufacturing, LLC.
The text stock is SFI certified. The Sustainable Forestry Initiative® program
promotes sustainable forest management.

10 9 8 7 6 5 4 3 2 1

Text design by Priscilla Harris Baker and layout by Kenleigh Manseau
This book was typeset in Garamond Premier Pro with Heirloom Artcraft and
Pineforest.
Artwork by courtesy of Wikimedia Commons unless otherwise noted.

Because hyperlinks do not always remain viable, we are no longer including URLs
in our resources, notes, or bibliographic entries. Instead, we are providing the
name of the website where this information may be found.

To send correspondence to the author of this book, mail a first-class letter to
the author c/o Inner Traditions • Bear & Company, One Park Street, Rochester,
VT 05767, and we will forward the communication. Contact information is also
included on the author's website: **www.ozgard.net.**

To all my Russian friends

A Note on Transliteration

Most Cyrillic letters can be fairly simply transliterated one-to-one into the Roman alphabet, but some require two or more Roman letters. For example the Cyrillic letters e and ë are commonly transliterated as "ye" and "yo" respectively. Some Cyrillic letters have a soft and a hard form, and there are words that have two different meanings depending on whether a letter is soft or hard. In certain cases I use a diacritical apostrophe to indicate the soft sign—thus *t'*. However, complete consistency is virtually impossible to achieve, and certain incorrect transliterations have become the accepted norm. For example, the name of the Russian medieval hero who defeated the Teutonic Knights is almost invariably spelt in Roman letters as Alexander Nevsky, although Nyevsky would be correct. In such cases I have opted for the commonly used form.

Contents

Acknowledgments

Among the many people within and outside of Russia who have assisted me during the writing of this book, I owe a special debt of gratitude to Dana Makaridina, artist and art curator of St. Petersburg, with whom I was kindly put in touch by my friend Zhenya Gershman of Los Angeles, artist and creator of the project Aesthetics of Western Esotericism (AWE). Dana went through the text with a fine-tooth comb and made numerous corrections and constructive suggestions based on her wide knowledge of the esoteric and spiritual scene in Russia. Ekaterina Petoukhova also made important comments on the text. My friend Gary Lachman, author of the excellent study *The Return of Holy Russia,* helped me with book recommendations and valuable contacts. One of those contacts was David Jones, editor of the Australian magazine *New Dawn,* who has published much material on Russia and has a strong connection with the country. He generously supplied me with material and referred me to Yuri Smirnov, an activist in the Ringing Cedars movement and organizer of tours to sacred sites in Russia. Yuri in turn was unstintingly generous with his time and assistance, allowing me the use of images from his rich photographic collection and sharing with me his thoughts on the Ringing Cedars movement and Russia's spiritual path. Further, I am grateful to the artist Alexander Uglanov for allowing me to publish his beautiful painting of a Slavic pagan ritual, to Kumar Alzhanov for permission to reproduce his painting of Anastasia, and to all the owners and copyright holders of the various images reproduced in the book as well as to the authors and publishers of quoted passages. My wife, Dr. Donate McIntosh, gave me loving support, encouragement, and useful feedback during the writing process and helped to keep my spirits and motivation high. Last but not least I must thank Jon Graham, Acquisitions Editor of Inner Traditions International, for taking on the book, as well as Patricia Rydle, Assistant to the Editor in Chief, the book's editor Renée Heitman, the copy editor Beth Wojiski, the Publicity Manager Ashley Kolesnik, Publicist Manzanita Carpenter Sanz, and all of their colleagues who were involved in the book in various ways.

 INTRODUCTION

Russia's Mystical Quest

Upon hearing the word "Russia," you may think of military parades in Red Square, the war in Ukraine, the annexation of Crimea, gangsters, internet hackers, assassinations of journalists, and imprisonment of opposition politicians. This book is not about those things but about a different Russia that is invisible to many people in the west—namely, the inner Russia, the Russia of mysticism, myth, magic, the esoteric, and the spiritual. The time is ripe for an investigation of Russia from this perspective. Like a vast river, long ice-bound, the spiritual force deep in the Russian soul is moving again. In the wake of the collapse of communism, the Russian people are seeking new—or often old— ways of giving meaning to their lives. This search has given rise both to a revival of ancient spiritual traditions and to a plethora of new movements, cults, sects, -isms, and -ologies, most of which would have been banned in the Soviet era. Out of this ferment exciting things are emerging, and the intention of this book is to make them known to western readers and to attempt to uncover the deeper significance that I believe underlies these developments.

The German philosopher Friedrich Nietzsche wrote the following about Russia in his book *Beyond Good and Evil*:

The strength to will, and to will something for a long time, is somewhat stronger already in Germany . . . considerably stronger in

1

England, Spain and Corsica . . . but strongest and most astonishing of all in that gigantic empire-in-between, where Europe as it were flows back into Asia, namely in Russia.[1]

I imagine Nietzsche would say much the same about the Russia of today, and he might go on to say that, in comparison, the peoples of the western world have essentially lost their vital will, as is shown in countless ways: the dominance of a global capitalism that wants to turn the world into the image of a suburban shopping mall full of docile consumers, the loss of pride in one's nation and local community, the erosion of tradition and inherited values, the betrayal of beauty in the arts and architecture, the falling birth rates, the decline of religion and the failure to put anything meaningful in its place, the dumbing down of the language we use, the banality of most public debate. He might add that, in addition to losing our vital will, we have lost the strength to dream—to imagine a better and more beautiful world—and that we have largely forgotten how to celebrate the realm of myth, symbol, mystery, and magic, except perhaps by escaping into computer games or fantasy films or the works of J. K. Rowling or J. R. R. Tolkien.

In a word, we are suffering from what the German sociologist Max Weber called "disenchantment" (*Entzauberung,* literally "removing the magic"). Weber used this much-quoted word in a lecture that he gave in 1917, which was published two years later as a booklet. He speaks of disenchantment as the price we pay for rationality, scientific thinking, and progress. As he recognizes, something precious gets lost in this process, and he mentions an observation of Tolstoy: that for us in the modern world, death is deprived of any real meaning on account of the notion of continual progress. We die with the sense of something perpetually unfinished, whereas the ancients could, if they lived long enough, die with a feeling of satisfaction, of having drunk fully of life and completed their own cycle within the greater cycles of the universe.

After disenchantment comes a longing for "re-enchantment," which has become a buzzword since around the beginning of the twenty-first century with the appearance of numerous books calling for or describing a re-enchantment of the world, of art, of nature, of politics, of everyday life—in fact, of everything under the sun. Of course there are numerous ways that enchantment can be found in the West, ranging from institutional religion to the world of esoteric and neo-pagan groups and from Disneyland to fantasy fiction and films. But the condition of disenchantment remains a salient feature of modern western society.

Here we can take a leaf out of the Russian book. In Russia the quality of enchantment is still vital and is present in multiple facets of Russian life including religion, art, literature, politics, and much else. One aspect of this is a millenarian view—the expectation of a coming New Age—which crops up again and again in Russian history.

The Soviet Union collapsed in 1991 almost at the end of the second millennium. But a further significant event came at the start of the new millennium. As the chimes of the great Kremlin clock announced the beginning of the year 2000, Vladimir Putin was taking over from Boris Yeltsin as acting president of the Russian Federation. These things might appear to have been mere coincidence, but not if you believe that nations are destined to pass through a cycle—a rise, fall, and final golden age—and that these phases are accompanied by signs and portents in the world. This way of thinking, which goes right back to the book of Revelation or Apocalypse in the New Testament, is deeply woven into the religious history of Russia and partly accounts for the temporary success of Marxism with its doctrine that history moves in a preordained sequence, leading finally to pure communism.

Some people might say that what we are dealing with here is merely myth, but myths can drive history in undeniable ways. I would argue that nations, like certain people, can consciously or unconsciously act out the script of an epic drama. Think of how the lives of leading figures in history repeatedly follow a certain pattern that closely corresponds to the great heroic epics of literature. The leader emerges in response to a crisis and gathers a following; there ensues a struggle, initial failure, and often exile or imprisonment; then the hero returns, rallies the followers, and finally triumphs. This pattern is seen in the lives of many national heroes, such as King Robert the Bruce of Scotland, Simon Bolivar, Mao Tse Tung, and the Russian medieval hero Alexander Nevsky, Prince of Novgorod, who lived for a period in exile before returning to win his famous battle on the ice against the Teutonic Knights, so dramatically portrayed in Eisenstein's 1938 film *Alexander Nevsky*.

Similarly, there are certain patterns on the collective level of the tribe or the nation that mirror apocalyptic prophecies. One particularly influential prophetic tradition goes back to the twelfth-century Calabrian monk Joachim of Fiore, who spoke of history unfolding in three ages, corresponding to the three persons of the Trinity: Father, Son, and Holy Spirit. Thus Joachim set out a threefold historical process that proved to have a lasting appeal and has reappeared repeatedly in different guises. Over time this Joachite scenario became mingled with other prophetic traditions such as those stemming from the Sybilline books, a set of Greek prophetic writings that were kept in Rome from the fifth century BCE. Norman Cohn, in his book *The Pursuit of the Millennium,* describes how such prophecies could mobilize vast numbers of people in medieval Europe, unleashing rebellions, crusades, and bizarre movements like the flagellants, who would pour into a city and stand in the marketplace flogging themselves for hours on end in order to purge themselves for the coming of the Third Age, which they believed to be imminent.[2]

Typical of the prophetic texts described by Cohn is the *Pseudo-Methodius,* a Christian work imitating the Sybilline books. It describes a future time of tribulation when the Christians suffer terrible persecution by the Ishmaelites. Just when the situation has become unbearable there arises a great emperor, known as the Emperor of the Last Days, who defeats the Ishmaelites and ushers in an era of peace and joy. This is temporarily interrupted when "the hosts of Gog and Magog break out bringing universal devastation and terror, until God sends a captain of the heavenly host who destroys them in a flash."[3] After a further interval the Emperor dies, and the reign of the Antichrist begins. He in turn is defeated and killed when Christ returns to carry out the Last Judgment. Here we have again a basic threefold scheme, if we begin with the advent of the Emperor of the Last Days: first an age of relative peace and harmony under a great leader, then the reign of an evil power (the Antichrist or the Beast of Revelation), and finally a new millennium, destruction of the evil power and salvation for the chosen.

Looking back over the past two centuries, it struck me that Russia's recent history could be divided into these three phases: first Russia under the Tsar (the "Emperor of the Last Days"), then the Bolshevik reign (the Antichrist or the Beast), and finally the new Russia, born close to the millennium. I should mention, however, that a variation of the millenarian theory says that Russia is still under the reign of the Antichrist.

The Apocalyptic theme was already in the air at the beginning of the twentieth century. One of those who attached a deep significance to the new century was the prominent symbolist poet, playwright, and philosopher, Vyacheslav Ivanov (1866–1949). In an essay of 1910 entitled "On the Russian Idea," he wrote:

Agrippa of Nettesheim [the sixteenth-century German polymath and occultist] taught that 1900 will be one of the great milestones in history, the beginning of a new period of universality. Hardly anyone in our present society knew about the calculations of such ancient sorcerers, but there is no doubt that, precisely on the threshold of the new astral era, sensitive souls have become aware of new tremors and vibrations in the inter-psychic field surrounding us. . . . Ideas are spreading themselves, refracted through the prism of apocalyptic eschatology. . . . The mystics of East and West agree that at this moment in time a certain torch has been handed to Russia. Will our people hold it up or drop it? This is a question on which the fate of the world will depend.[4]

Ivanov, who fled Soviet Russia in 1924, might say, were he alive today, that the torch was temporarily extinguished during the communist years but is now once again alight.

Today's spiritual quest in Russia covers an enormous spectrum. Millions are turning or returning to the Orthodox Church, and thousands of new churches are being built. At the same time, the postcommunist period has been marked by serious rifts within the Orthodox community. One such rift occurred in 2016 when a group of believers broke away from the main church on account of a meeting in Cuba between the Pope and the Moscow Patriarch Kirill and a resulting joint declaration, which the group considered heretical. Members of the break-away movement call themselves Non-Mentioners (*Nyepominayushchie*) because they refuse to mention Kirill's name during their services. An even more serious rift happened in 2018 when a community of Orthodox Churches in Ukraine was recognized as independent from Moscow by the Patriarchate of Constantinople, causing the Moscow Patriarchate to sever connections with Constantinople (as Istanbul is still referred to by the Orthodox).

As for alternative forms of spirituality, many people are turning to doctrines such as Theosophy, Anthroposophy, and the teachings of Nikolai and Helena Roerich. Another group is turning back to the pre-Christian gods of Russia or to shamanism, often of the variety practiced by the urban intelligentsia. Meanwhile the indigenous pagan communities such as the Mari and the various shamanic peoples of Siberia are enjoying a new lease of life. In Russia the shamanic and pagan traditions have long existed side by side with the Orthodox religion—if not always in peaceful coexistence, at least in a modus vivendi that the Russians call *dvoeverie* (dual faith). And this, I believe, offers a positive way forward both in Russia and elsewhere.

I have mentioned how history can be driven by mythical motifs, and this perhaps applies particularly strongly to Russia. One useful term for such a motif is the word "meme," coined by the British biologist Richard Dawkins in his 1976 book *The Selfish Gene*. Originally used in the biological context, it has come to mean an idea or notion that spreads like a message through a society, transmitted from person to person or through the media.

A phenomenon with some similarities to the meme, but operating at a deeper level, is that of the egregore, a collective thought-form on the invisible plane, created by many people focusing on the same ideas and symbols. Deriving from a Greek word meaning "watcher," an egregore can take an infinite variety of forms—an angel or demon, a god or goddess, a hero or heroine, an object of special veneration, a sacred place, or a compelling narrative such as the millenarian one just mentioned. The concept of the egregore overlaps to some extent with the notion, developed by the psychologist Carl Gustav Jung, of the archetype, an inherited motif in the collective unconscious of humanity.

In exploring Russia's mystical quest we shall find various powerful memes, egregores, and archetypes at work. The theme of the millennium is one of them. Others include the following:

Holy Russia

The notion of Holy Russia is searchingly explored by Gary Lachman in his book of that title. Deeply engrained in the Russian collective soul is the conviction that Russia has a special spiritual mission. This is reflected in the powerful mystique of the Orthodox Church and the concept of the "Third Rome"—the first Rome being the city on the Tiber, the second being Constantinople, and the third and final one being Moscow. All of this has given rise to an egregore of enormous vitality, which has enabled the Orthodox religion to flourish anew after the communist era.

The Warrior Hero

An early example of this figure is the semilegendary Ilya Muromets, who features in various Russian epics as well as in films, novels, and art. He is described as one of the *bogatyr,* a group of elite knights similar to those of King Arthur's court. Probably a composite of various different people, he appears as a defender of Kievan Rus in the tenth century, and in later incarnations he fought the Mongols and saved the Byzantine Emperor from a monster. He eventually became a saint of the Orthodox Church. The role of the warrior hero has also been played by certain real historical figures such as Prince Alexander Nevsky, who defeated the Teutonic Knights in the thirteenth century, Tsar Peter the Great, and even Joseph Stalin.

The Never-Never Land

This motif crops up repeatedly in Russian history in various forms and under various names: Byelovodye (Land of the White Waters); Opona, the utopia of peasant folklore; and Hyperborea, the vanished promised land in the North. This egregore is still very much alive, as we shall see in chapter 2. The never-never land is also thought of as the source of an ancient wisdom tradition that has the power to transform human life if one could only access it.

The Rustic Sage

This figure is typified by Tolstoy's character of Platon Karataev, the wise peasant who is a fellow prisoner of the hero Pierre Bezukhov in *War and Peace.* Tolstoy himself adopted this persona in his later years.

The Holy Fool

Alternatively "fool for Christ," this term is applied to someone who adopts an apparently mad way of life, marked by great austerity and extreme piety. It can overlap with the concept of the *starets,* the independent, god-illuminated holy man or woman. It has been pointed out to me by my correspondent Dana Makaridina that there are two kinds of holy fool, namely the *blazhennyi* ("blessed") and the *yurodviy* ("foolish"). The distinction is subtle. The former are characterized by a state of saintly bliss, whereas the latter are conspicuous by their craziness and weird, antisocial behavior. Both are associated with freedom, being unconstrained by any social norms and able to communicate directly with God. Dana Makaridina mentions a friend who has had the nickname *blazhennyi* since childhood because of his strange, otherworldly behavior. She writes that "now he is an extravagant rock musician and performance artist dealing with topics of freedom and death."

The New Messiah

Prophets and Messiah figures have abounded in Russian history, overlapping somewhat with the starets and the fool for Christ, and they continue to appear in the present day. A typical example is the case of Sergei Anatoljewitsch Torop, an artist and jack-of-all-trades who, in 1991, proclaimed himself to be Jesus Christ returned. Adopting the name Vissarion, he founded a community called the Church of the Last Testament, gathered several thousand followers, and established an ecospiritual settlement in Siberia. At the time of writing he is in prison facing a charge of extorting money from his followers and subjecting them to emotional abuse.

The Woman Clothed with the Sun

This figure originates in a passage in chapter 12 of the book of Revelation in the New Testament. To quote the King James Bible:

And there appeared a great wonder in heaven; a woman clothed with the sun, and the moon under her feet, and upon her head a crown of twelve stars:

And she being with child cried, travailing in birth, and pained to be delivered.

And there appeared another wonder in heaven; and behold a great red dragon, having seven heads and ten horns, and seven crowns upon his heads.

And his tail drew the third part of the stars of heaven, and did cast them to the earth: and the dragon stood before the woman which was ready to be delivered, for to devour her child as soon as it was born.

And she brought forth a man child, who was to rule all nations with a rod of iron: and her child was caught up unto God, and to his throne.

And the woman fled into the wilderness, where she hath a place prepared of God, that they should feed her there a thousand two hundred and threescore days.

And there was war in heaven: Michael and his angels fought against the dragon; and the dragon fought and his angels,

And prevailed not; neither was their place found any more in heaven. And the great dragon was cast out, that old serpent, called the Devil, and Satan, which deceiveth the whole world: he was cast out into the earth, and his angels were cast out with him.

And I heard a loud voice saying in heaven, Now is come salvation, and strength, and the kingdom of our God, and the power of his Christ: for the accuser of our brethren is cast down, which accused them before our God day and night.

This image of the woman clothed with the sun, combined with the millenarian theme, crops up repeatedly in Russian prophetic writings.

Another key factor for understanding Russia, but one which

is rarely dealt with by western commentators, is the Russian language, which I was fortunate enough to study at the United Nations Language School in New York. A language is not just a means of communication but also a mode of thinking, a way of perceiving the world, and potentially a magical instrument. Each language carries its own energy, accumulated over time, which affects the user and listener in very tangible ways. For example, the deep chanting of the priests in the Orthodox liturgy would not have the same power and resonance in, say, French or Italian. The structure of the language also gives it special possibilities of expression in poetry or prose. In a chapter on this topic I attempt to convey something of the richness of Russian in terms that will be understandable to nonspeakers of the language.

A further aspect of mystical Russia that I examine is the domain of the arts—literature, painting, and the performing arts. Some discussion of this area was included in my book *Beyond the North Wind,* and here I explore it in greater detail.

I should emphasize that I do not turn a blind eye to some of the darker aspects of Russian religious and spiritual history, such as the periodic outbreaks of anti-Semitic and anti-Masonic hysteria and the machinations of people like the Orthodox mystic Sergey Nilus (1862–1929) who, more than anyone else, was responsible for the dissemination of the anti-Semitic forgery, the *Protocols of the Elders of Zion.* Nor do I attempt to deny that there are xenophobic elements in some of the Russian neopagan groups. The portrait of Russia that I present is a portrait with "warts and all."

Whatever faults Russia may have, it possesses a quality of spiritual depth that is hard not to sense. One traveler who experienced it was the Austrian poet Rainer Maria Rilke, who made two trips there, in 1899 and 1900, and came to regard Russia as his spiritual homeland. Rilke described Russia as "that broad land in the east, the only one through which God is still connected to the earth." He was not referring specifically to Orthodox Christianity, because he also wrote positively about the dual Christian and pagan belief *dvoeverie*. He went on to say that, while the western nations pursue a wasteful way of life, the Russians "are storing up all their energies, as though in granaries, in preparation for some new beginning not yet arrived, when the peoples of impoverished nations will leave their homelands with hungry hearts."[5]

My own perception of Russia has been through different stages. As far as I can remember, the country meant little to me until 1953, when I was nine years old and one morning at breakfast my father picked up the newspaper and remarked that Stalin had died. I may have asked who Stalin was and been told that he had been the leader of our powerful eastern ally during the Second World War. Later I absorbed the cold war propaganda. Russia came to mean the suppression of the Hungarian uprising, defectors from the West like Burgess and Maclean, Khrushchev banging his shoe on the table at the United Nations General Assembly, the Cuban missile crisis, the crushing of the Prague Spring, the persecution of dissidents. At the same time I was fascinated enough by Russia to start learning the language when I was nineteen years old, a process that I resumed in my fifties, by which time I had witnessed the advent of Gorbachev and perestroika, shortly to be followed by the breakup of the Soviet empire and the collapse of communism itself. While these tumultuous changes were going on, I visited Russia for the first time in 1991 with an American contingent of very amiable born-again Christians, whose tour group I was able to join through the facilitation of an acquaintance.

A particularly vivid memory of that trip was visiting a Russian Orthodox seminary near St. Petersburg. On entering the building I found myself transported into another world, marked by candlelit icons, the fragrance of incense, and an atmosphere of still reverence. There was a quiet dignity about the priests and seminarists moving about in the dim corridors. One of them, looking startlingly like the photographs I had seen of the wild-eyed prophet Rasputin, was a young man with long black hair and a solemn expression, dressed all in black in a sort of peasant's tunic, trousers, and boots. We were shown to the chapel of the seminary where a service was held, and I began to understand why Madame Blavatsky, non-Christian though she was, always vehemently defended the Orthodox Church.

A striking feature of any Orthodox church is the iconostasis, a screen, crowded with icons, hiding an inner sanctuary, where the sacrament of the Eucharist is celebrated out of sight of the congregation. This element of concealment and mystery at the heart of Orthodox worship is one of the things that gives the liturgy its enormous vitality and strength. More icons are placed around the church, and members of the congregation can pray and light candles to them. The icons themselves—images depicting Christ, the Virgin Mary, the saints, or scenes from the Bible—are believed to be charged with numinous energy. Usually painted on wood, they typically have a gold leaf background and the figures are traditionally depicted in a flat, stylized manner, although a less stylized and more realistic form was introduced from the seventeenth century. For the iconographers, the making of them is a sacred act for which they prepare themselves through prayer and fasting. Certain icons are said to have appeared out of thin air, conjured forth by holy men with special powers, or just miraculously sent from heaven and found by ordinary people, sometimes in a moment of collective need. Such icons are the objects of special veneration and are considered able to perform miracles.

Orthodoxy came to Russia in the year 988 when Prince Vladimir I, ruler of Kievan Rus, converted from paganism to Byzantine Christianity and took the country with him. The religion had many qualities that suited the Russians. It spoke to their mystical and otherworldly strain, it had the warmth and emotional resonance they needed, and it provided a way of coming to terms with the suffering with which they

Fig. I.1. The Maria Ascension Church in Astrakhan, showing the screen known as the iconostasis, concealing the inner sanctum from the congregation
(See also color plate 1)
WIKIMEDIA COMMONS, PHOTOGRAPH BY MARK VOORENDT

were so often afflicted. By the seventeenth century it permeated every aspect of their lives. As Robert Massie writes in his book about the life of Peter the Great:

> In Peter's time the Russian believer exhibited a piety of behavior as complicated and rigorous as his piety of belief was simple and profound. His calendar was filled with saints' days to be observed, and with innumerable rites and fasts . . . Before sleeping with a woman, a man would remove the crucifix around her neck and cover all the icons in the room . . . Thieves on the point of theft bowed to icons and asked forgiveness and protection.[6]

For such a deeply and conservatively religious people it was a profound shock when, in the late seventeenth century, after a bitter controversy, a series of reforms was introduced in the Church. One such reform was that henceforth worshippers should cross themselves with three fingers (symbolizing the Trinity) rather than with two fingers as previously done (symbolizing the dual nature of Christ). To the modern secular mind such disputes seem trivial, but to the Russian believer of that time they were matters of vital importance. The reform program was in fact seen by many as an evil of apocalyptic magnitude, and no wonder, since it happened around the year 1666—the number 666 being that of the Beast of the apocalypse. Opponents of the reforms created a splinter movement called the Old Believers (*Starovery*), and resisted all efforts to bring them back into the main fold of the Church. Thousands faced torture and death at the stake rather than yield, and thousands more fled to remote areas or to foreign countries. Nothing could force them to recant, and they remain a force to be reckoned with today.

At the present time, in the wake of the collapse of communism, the Orthodox religion is once again playing a central role in the life of the nation. But not everyone is happy with the current situation, and some of the initial post-perestroika religious enthusiasm is waning. Many believers oppose what they see as an increasing tendency toward a merger of state and Church, while people of other persuasions do not want Orthodox Christianity to be imposed on the population.

A striking example of a church-state initiative is the Cathedral of the Military Forces, located in Patriot Park near Moscow. The site has a special significance, being the place where the German invaders were turned back in the Second World War, and the whole complex forms a sort of shrine to the heroism of the Soviet armed forces, with a war museum and a reconstruction of the battlefield. The Cathedral itself is one of several such religious buildings in Russia commemorating military victories. It was completed in 2020, marking the seventy-fifth anniversary of Russia's victory in the Great Patriotic War, as they call it. Built of khaki-green metal, it has six towers topped by domes of shining, gold-colored titanium. The main tower is seventy-five meters high, one meter for each year from the end of the war to the completion of the building, and its dome, resembling the helmet of Prince Alexander Nevsky, is 19.45 meters in diameter, referring to the victory year 1945. The Archangel Michael, the dragonslayer, is shown in relief on the east and west sides of the tower, symbolically defending the homeland and driving back the invader. The whole building abounds in reliefs, mosaics, and stained-glass panels depicting military scenes and heroes from various periods of Russian history, especially from the Second World War. As an architectural and engineering feat the Cathedral could qualify as one of the wonders of the world, but some believers say that it does not speak of Christianity but rather of some hybrid new cult of military victory.

The very fact that this debate can take place with such intensity is a measure of how deeply engrained is the religiosity of the Russian people. To quote Robert Massie again, "Russians are preeminently a pious, compassionate and humble people, accepting faith as more powerful than logic and believing that life is controlled by superhuman forces, be they spiritual, autocratic or even occult."[7]

Next to the seminary that I visited was an asylum for the mentally ill—a Dickensian place in which shabbily clad inmates with pale faces and absent expressions shuffled around in great gloomy halls. At a meeting with the doctors—all of them extremely dedicated—we were told how important it was for them to have the spiritual support of the priests from the neighboring seminary. We were also told that in Russia the insane are not looked down upon but regarded as holy, like Prince Mishkin in Dostoyevsky's novel *The Idiot*. However, this view has to be qualified. In Soviet times there existed what was called "punitive psychiatry," and among those who lived under the Soviet regime there is still a great fear of being seen as crazy. Many of them are afraid even to consult a psychotherapist, let alone a psychiatrist, for fear of ruining their reputation. In this respect members of the younger generation are totally different and speak openly about their mental health problems, in tune with international tendencies.

Visiting Russia reinforced my view that it has a special destiny, as many prophets have predicted. One of them, the German writer Oswald Spengler, wrote in an essay entitled "The Two Faces of Russia" (1922):

> The bolshevism of the early years has thus had a double meaning. It has destroyed an artificial, foreign structure, leaving only itself as a remaining integral part. But beyond this, it has made the way clear for a new culture that will some day awaken between "Europe" and East Asia. It is more a beginning than an end.[8]

Fig I.2. A 1930s cartoon by Olaf Gulbransson, caricaturing the German historian Oswald Spengler. The woman in the background riding a bear symbolizes Spengler's prediction that a new culture will come out of Russia. (See also color plate 2)

Collection of Olaf Gulbransson Museum, Tegernsee, photograph courtesy of VG Bild-Kunst, Bonn 2022

Thirteen years later Spengler's vision for Russia was illustrated in a cartoon by the artist Olaf Gulbransson, which appeared in 1935 in a literary-satirical journal originally produced in Munich under the name *Simplicissimus,* but by then published in exile in Prague under the title *Simpl.* The cartoon, entitled *Melancholia,* is a parody of Albrecht Dürer's famous engraving known under the same title. In the foreground sits a melancholy Spengler, quill pen in hand, beside an even more melancholy dog and various other objects including an obstetric forceps, perhaps indicating that the New Age in Russia will have a difficult birth. In the background is an image of the New Age itself in the form of a naked young woman riding a rather complacent-looking bear, both framed in a large rising sun.

In the present world climate of renewed cold war, there are high tensions between Russia and the West. Politicians and the media eagerly seize on Russia as a scapegoat for all manner of things from an unwelcome election result to an aircraft crash. Russia is frequently described as a "kleptocracy," a "criminal state," and the like. While not wishing to idealize the country nor to deny that abuses of power happen there, as they do everywhere else, I hope to show that there is something to be learned at the spiritual level from the Russian experience. To understand this experience it is helpful to know where the country is coming from in terms of its spiritual trajectory. Therefore I begin with the "Silver Age" before the Revolution of 1917, an era of great spiritual quest and experiment, which was curtailed by the revolution, although many mystical and esoteric groups continued well into the Bolshevik years, as I describe. I go on to explore the postperestroika spiritual revival in its many different forms, and finally I attempt to come to certain conclusions about what the rest of the world might learn from Russia, which I suggest has much to do with the quality of enchantment.

I come back to Oswald Spengler's prediction, illustrated in Olaf Gulbransson's cartoon of 1935, which appeared during a troubled time.

Germany had been through a military defeat, followed by the ravages of inflation and depression and then by the Nazi seizure of power in 1933. In Russia the Bolsheviks ruled. Another war was on the horizon. But Gulbransson pictured a bright future coming from the direction of Russia, symbolized by the maiden riding the bear. Between then and now there are certain parallels; the present era is also marked by conflicts, crises, and catastrophes. But the maiden riding the bear still carries a hopeful message.

ONE

Twilight

Let us imagine that we have been transported back in time to St. Petersburg in, say, the autumn of the year 1910, in what is often called Russia's Silver Age (c. 1890–1920), an age rather too troubled to be golden but silver on account of the rich cultural and intellectual life that flourished in those years. Stepping into a faded sepia photograph, we marvel at the breathtaking stretches of palatial buildings, their frothy facades reflected in the dreaming canals and the vast expanse of the river Neva. In the elegant Nevsky Prospect, a few motor vehicles jostle with the horse-drawn carriages and the pavements throng with shoppers, beggars, *boulevardiers* in top hats, and military officers in smart uniforms. Little do they know that in faraway Paris a Damoclean sword hangs over Russia in the form of a young Russian exile with a bald head and narrow eyes that give his face a look of cunning, a man whose real name is Vladimir Ilich Ulyanov, but whom the world will know as Vladimir Lenin when he returns to Russia to seize power. Meanwhile it's business as usual in Nevsky Prospect. A short distance away, in Senate Square, stands the bronze equestrian statue of Tsar Peter the Great who, two centuries earlier, had built the city as his new capital, conjuring it out of a swamp at the cost of thousands of lives in a rehearsal of Stalin's labor camps. Peter's drive to modernize the country come what may marked a traumatic caesura in Russia's history, which has left opinion still divided as to how his legacy should be judged. St. Petersburg became symbolic of his attempt to turn the country toward the West, but Moscow remained the unofficial capital of the old Russia and the tension between the worlds they represent has continued to the present day.

Not far away from the statue is the Winter Palace, residence of the Tsar, a reminder of the events of Bloody Sunday in 1905 when several thousand demonstrators, demanding reforms, marched toward the Palace from the outskirts of the city only to be mown down by the sabers of Cossack cavalrymen and the bullets of infantry soldiers—an event that precipitated nationwide strikes and helped to pave the way for the coming revolution. The same year saw a humiliating Russian defeat in a war against Japan. Tsarist Russia was beginning to crack at the foundations, while the Tsar himself played the Emperor of the Last Days, sitting in the Winter Palace, foreseeing much but unable to alter it.

DANCE TO A TICKING BOMB

It is a curious feature of civilizations in crisis that they are often marked by a sudden flourishing of creativity and intellectual exploration. This was the case in France around the collapse of the Second Empire and in fin de siècle Vienna, and the same phenomenon was seen in Russia in the troubled years before the First World War and the revolution. The cultural and intellectual scene at this time included an upsurge of interest in the esoteric and the occult, which was reflected in the work of a remarkable constellation of writers, artists, and thinkers.

In Nevsky Prospect we might notice a square-faced young man with a pince-nez and a pensive expression, called Pyotr Demianovich Ouspensky, later to become known as a leading exponent of the Gurdjieff teaching. He is strolling along, thinking about the fourth dimension. Noticing a passing horse-drawn vehicle, he reflects that the horse is only an atom of some "great horse," just as each human being is an atom of the "Great Man," only visible in the fourth dimension.[1]

Ouspensky had come from Moscow and settled in St. Petersburg, attracted by the vibrant esoteric scene in the imperial capital. In Moscow he had worked as a newspaper journalist, but during office hours, bored by the work, he had devoured books like A. P. Sinnett's *The Occult World* and Eliphas Lévi's classic, *Dogme et Rituel de la Haute Magie*.[2] In these books he found a new kind of truth. As he later wrote:

> I had been living in a desiccated and sterilized world, with an infinite number of taboos imposed on my thought. And suddenly these strange books broke down all the walls round me and made me think and dream about things of which for a long time I had feared to think and dream. Suddenly I began to find a strange meaning in old fairy-tales; woods, rivers, mountains, became living beings; mysterious life filled the night.[3]

At the corner of Nevsky Prospect and Pushkin Street was an apartment that was one of three properties owned by Ouspensky's guru, George Ivanovich Gurdjieff, then in the early stages of building his remarkable career as a promoter of his idiosyncratic teaching, the essence of which was that most human beings are kept in a kind of sleep.[4] The Gurdjieff system or "the Work," as he called it, was designed to wake people up through a variety of mental and physical exercises and challenges. Gurdjieff was in fact Greco-Armenian rather than Russian, but he was an important part of the remarkable constellation of spiritual teachers and thinkers in Russia at that time. Later he was impelled by the revolution to leave the country and continue his work elsewhere.

A mile or so to the northwest of Nevsky Prospect there still stands a magnificent neoclassical apartment building on the corner of Tavrichesky and Tversky streets—all turrets, mansard roofs, pilasters, decorative stonework, and wrought iron balconies. At the corner, resembling an enormous hinge, is an imposing domed tower, which earned the building the name of the House with the Tower. In a flat on one of the upper floors lived the poet, dramatist, and philosopher Vyacheslav Ivanov who, in his magnum opus *The Hellenic Religion of the Suffering God* (1904), ingeniously managed to combine a celebration of the ecstatic cult of Dionysus with a profound Christian faith.*

Ivanov and his second wife Lydia ran a weekly salon from their aerie in the House of the Tower, which became a favorite venue for the St. Petersburg intelligentsia. After Lydia's death in 1907 the distraught Ivanov leaned increasingly in a mystical and occult direction. Consolation came in the form of Anna Rudolfovna Mintzlova, a formidable grande dame of the esoteric scene in St. Petersburg and later in Moscow, who became Ivanov's mentor and possibly lover. This many-faceted, multilingual and highly educated woman had, among other things, made the first complete Russian translation of Oscar Wilde's novel, *The Picture of Dorian Gray.* Enthused by all things esoteric, she had attended the London Theosophical Conference of 1905 and a series of Rudolf Steiner's lectures in Paris. She could hold forth on everything from Rosicrucianism to the mystical state of samadhi. In the words of her contemporary, the artist and poet Margarita Sabashnikova, she presented "a shapeless figure with an excessively large forehead . . . and bulging blue eyes, very short-sighted, which nevertheless always seemed to be looking into immense distances. Her reddish hair with a straight parting, curled in waves, was always in disarray. . . . Her most distinctive feature was her hands—white, soft, with long narrow fingers. When greeting someone she held their extended hand longer than usual, shaking it slightly . . . her voice lowered almost to a whisper, as if hiding strong excitement."[5]

In 1910 Anna Mintzlova suddenly disappeared without trace.

---

*For the influence of esotericism on Ivanov and other literary figures of his era, see Николай А. Богомолов (Nikolai A. Bogomolov), *Русская литература начала XX века и оккультизм. Исследования и материалы* (*Russian Literature of the Early 20th Century and Occultism*).

Whether she committed suicide or entered some enclosed mystical order remains to this day an unsolved mystery.[6] As a transmitter of esoteric ideas, she deserves more than a footnote in the history of Russia's mystical quest.

Three years after her disappearance Ivanov married his stepdaughter Vera, who had already borne him a son. The gatherings in the House of the Tower continued, but in 1920 Vera tragically died at the age of thirty. Ivanov moved away from St. Petersburg and a few years later left Russia altogether.

Another popular haunt of literati, artists, and esotericists in St. Petersburg was the Stray Dog Café in Michaelovsky Square, a semi-basement hostelry (now reopened since 2001). Ouspensky was one of its habitués, and another person who probably went there was the poet and novelist Andrei Biely, also a member of the Tower circle. He was best known for his extraordinary novel *Petersburg,* which vividly evokes the feverish atmosphere of anxiety and terrorist conspiracy that characterized Russia at that time. The main character is a young man called Nikolai Apollonovich Obleukhov, who becomes involved with a group of revolutionary terrorists. He is given a time bomb and the task of placing it in the study of a prominent Tsarist official, who happens to be his father. As the time bomb ticks away, he frantically seeks distraction in foolish ways such as by attending a masked ball dressed in a red domino mask and cape. The story moves relentlessly to an unexpected and slightly comical climax. A similarly feverish atmosphere pervades Biely's novel *The Silver Dove* (1909) about a murder in a prerevolutionary Russian religious cult resembling the Khlysty.

Biely was a leading exponent of the symbolist school of literature, which had originated among French poets but soon spread to fiction, visual arts, and even music. Instead of simply portraying phenomena in a literal way, the symbolists sought to use the things they portrayed as metaphors or pointers to ideas, states of mind, metaphysical concepts, or perceptions of a reality beyond the mundane. In Russia, as elsewhere, the movement proved attractive to those of an esoteric

Fig. 1.1. Andrei Biely, writer and esotericist, as portrayed by Leon Bakst. Biely's extraordinary novel *Petersburg* captures the feverish atmosphere of prerevolutionary Russia. (See also color plate 3)

turn of mind, and Biely was no exception. Biely combined the role of spiritual seeker with the persona of a character from one of his novels. Handsome, temperamental, elegantly dressed, and a womanizer, he led a restless life, traveling widely through Europe and North Africa, attracting attention everywhere with his eccentric behavior (dancing wildly in a Berlin nightclub like some whirling dervish), on account of which he gained the nickname *Yurodivii* ("Holy Fool").

Much of Biely's work is an attempt to give the written word a musical quality, since he believed that "the eternal is closest to us and most accessible in music."[7] As a boy in the 1890s he had come under the influence of the mystical philosopher Vladimir Solovyov, author of a visionary work called *Short Story of the Antichrist,* in which he predicted the Antichrist's imminent coming. That figure would in due course be vanquished, the woman clothed with the sun would appear in the heavens, and Christ would descend, resurrect the dead, and reign with them for a thousand years, as predicted in the book of

Revelation.[8] Solovyov was therefore firmly in the Russian millenarian tradition. Biely's belief in this prophecy is reflected in his work. Here for example is a quote from his complex "musical" novel *The Dramatic Symphony,* first published in 1901: "And the ascetic cried out along the nocturnal avenues: 'Lo! We shall raise up against the beast the *woman clothed with the sun* as our sacred, snowy-silver banner!'"[9]

Here again we have the ubiquitous "woman clothed with the sun" as in Gulbransson's cartoon *Melancholia,* featuring a young woman riding on a bear against a rising sun, as mentioned in the Introduction.

There is something strikingly Russian in the fact that Biely was both a highly avant-garde writer and an apocalyptic visionary. Not surprisingly he became drawn to theosophy and its offshoot, anthroposophy. Theosophy was founded in 1875 by a Russian woman, Madame Helena Petrovna Blavatsky, not in Russia but in New York, and later spread to many countries and established a headquarters in India. Eventually it made its way to Madame Blavatsky's homeland, and a St. Petersburg branch of the Theosophical Society was founded in 1908. Anthroposophy was established in 1912 by the former theosophist Rudolf Steiner and also gained a following in Russia. Biely stayed for a time in Steiner's community at Dornach in Switzerland and helped in the construction of the first Goetheanum, a sort of anthroposophical temple, named after the poet Johann Wolfgang von Goethe, whom Steiner revered.

Biely's works are dotted with theosophical and anthroposophical references, as in the novel *Petersburg,* when the main character Nikolai Apollonovich is described as "setting off on a distant astral journey, or sleep (which, let us note, is the same thing)."

The passage goes on: "The door opened onto the measureless immensity of the cosmos."[10]

The term "astral journey" refers to the theosophical notion of the astral body, a kind of spirit body that can leave the physical body during sleep or in a trance and move about freely. In such a state one has access to "the measureless immensity of the cosmos."

Fig. 1.2. The artist and explorer Nikolai Roerich, promoter of the Shambhala legend.
WIKIMEDIA COMMONS

Another person influenced by theosophy, who was also living in St. Petersburg at the time, was the painter Nikolai Roerich (1874–1947), who was also Director of the Art School run by the Society for the Encouragement of the Arts. Having undergone formal training as a painter in St. Petersburg and Paris, he had developed his own style, strongly influenced by folk art and often portraying vernacular, historical, or religious scenes, marked by bold lines, distinct patches of clear color, and an indefinably serene quality. One only has to look at his paintings to see that he regarded the artist as having a sacred mission to uplift and inspire. His work included set designs for the impresario Sergei Diaghilev, art patron, publisher, organizer of exhibitions, and creator of the famous Ballet Russe. Roerich designed, among other things, the stage set for the ballet *The Rite of Spring,* choreographed by Vaslav Nijinsky and featuring the music of Igor Stravinsky.

Roerich had a great respect for both ancient Slavic and Indian culture. He and his wife Helena both avidly studied the writings of Ramakrishna and Vivekananda and the classics of Indian spirituality such as the *Bhagavad Gita*. As Jacqueline Decter writes in her biography of the artist:

> Roerich's belief that modern man had much to learn from ancient, prehistoric man undoubtedly drew him to a fundamental tenet of Eastern philosophy—that the history of the universe is cyclical rather than linear. The Eastern concept of a "perennial philosophy, an ageless wisdom, revealed and re-revealed, restored, lost and again restored through the cycle of the ages" was much closer to Roerich's vision than the relatively recent Western view of history as an ever-progressing phenomenon.[11]

This raises a vital point. The linear view of history, which has dominated western thinking for many centuries, has had many damaging consequences for our society. Starting as a paradigm of the monotheistic religions, which teach a continuous progression toward the Second Coming, the Last Judgment, the Earthly Paradise, or some other distant goal, this notion became transferred to secular domains such as the arts and architecture with the result that traditional notions of beauty were thrown overboard in the name of progress and modernity. This is a theme to which I shall return later in the book. I shall also return to the Roerichs on account of their journeys in the 1920s through Central Asia in search of the fabled land of Shambhala.

DECADENCE AND SPIRITUALISM

While St. Petersburg had its Roerichs, Ivanovs, and Bielys, Moscow had its own coterie of literary figures interested in occultism.

One of them was the prominent poet, novelist, translator, and critic, Valerii Bryusov (1873–1924), who was deeply involved in spiritualism. He began attending séances at about the age of nineteen in the early 1890s, when the fashion for spiritualism was spreading rapidly in Russia, having spilled over from America, and carefully recorded them in his diary, where some of the entries reveal a degree of hubris. On March 4, 1893, he wrote:

> To be honest, talent, even genius, will only bring tardy success, if at all . . . It is too little for me. I have to choose something else. Without dogmas one can sail everywhere. To find a guiding star in the fog. And I see them: decadence and spiritualism. Yes! One can say they are false, they are laughable, but they are moving forward, they are developing, and the future will belong to them, especially if they find a worthy leader. And I shall be that leader! Yes, I![12]

At the early sessions he took the opportunity afforded by the darkness of the room to make amorous advances to the female participants. On February 6, 1893, he wrote: "Yesterday I was at a séance. I became impudently daring with Yelena Andreevna."[13]

His account of the actual spiritualistic phenomena became more detailed as the happenings became more extraordinary. At a meeting in March of the same year various objects were placed on different tables: a musical box, a whistle, rattles, and a guitar. As the séance proceeded the main table began to swing, and the participants felt something touching them on the hands, the cheek, the hair. One of them felt the soft contact of a child's hand. The table moved around the room. A box containing pencils rose into the air and knocked against a wall. The guitar floated above the table while playing a tune and flew up to the ceiling when one of the women tried to grasp it. A box of cigarettes on the mantelpiece disgorged its contents, which rained down on those present.

Over the next few years Bryusov became a noted expert on spiritualism and was a contributor to the St. Petersburg journal *Rebus*, which specialized in such subjects. *Rebus* was launched in 1881 and continued until 1918, when it was shut down by the new communist regime. In the 1930s it was withdrawn from libraries and the copies destroyed, but some issues survived elsewhere, and today the journal is a valuable source of reference on mediumship, spiritualism, and the paranormal in Russia in the late nineteenth and early twentieth centuries. In issue number 30 in 1900 Bryusov published an article entitled "The Method of Mediumship" in which he grappled with the subject in a very searching and interesting way.

In the article Bryusov argues that mediumistic phenomena cannot be assessed using the methods of physics and chemistry, as scientists have often tried to do: "All phenomena studied by science . . . are conceivable only in three-dimensional space. With the assumption of multidimensional space, the first axiom of natural science falls: the law of conservation of energy."[14]

If one posits a fourth dimension, many spiritualistic phenomena become explicable and not merely table-turning. He also points out that the scientific study of the mind involves the notion of sequential time—that is, that causes come before effects. But this law is violated when, for example, a noise causes one to wake up and remember a dream in which the noise was the final part of the dream sequence—as though the noise worked backward in time, causing the dream. In mediumship, he says, we are often confronted with extratemporal manifestations such as predictions of future events and the appearance of long-dead people in the same form, even in the same clothes, as during their lifetimes.[15]

The atmosphere of a Russian séance is vividly captured by the poet Boris Alexeevich Leman (who wrote under the pseudonym Boris Dix) in his poem "Séance,"* which opens as follows:

---

*My translation.

In a cozy room at a round table
Six have sat down and clasped hands with each other.
The light is extinguished. Silence. Then come the
  scurrying knocks.
And again the silence hangs there stonily.

The table swayed, and above it, flickering,
A dim light appeared and vanished again.
The medium fell into a trance, his breathing grew
  heavy.
Suddenly all were alert, anticipating success.

As though a dam had broken, the surroundings
Were filled with repeated noises, crackling, dry and
  distinct.
And, as if answering the waves of knocks,
The table came to life, making a full turn on the
  floor.[16]

ESOTERICISM AND THE AVANT-GARDE

From the figures mentioned so far, it will be apparent that Russia's cultural and intellectual sphere was in many ways markedly different from that of the western world. Modernity in the West has come to mean liberation from tradition and the absence of any spiritual perspective (with some notable exceptions), whereas in Russia spirituality and the avant-garde often go hand in hand, as with Biely and Roerich. Their equivalent in the sphere of music was the composer and pianist Alexander Scriabin (1872–1915), who was deeply influenced by theosophy and eastern spirituality.

In 1910 Scriabin was living in Moscow writing an epic piece

of music entitled *Prometheus: Poem of Fire.* The work came about through his friendship with the Belgian artist, poet, and theosophist Jean Delville, whom he met in Brussels. The story is told by the Irish poet and theosophist James Cousins:

> Scriabine [sic] noticed something in Delville that he himself lacked: Scriabine was groping towards some kind of comprehension of life. He asked Delville . . . what was behind his attitude to life, and how he, the questioner, could reach a similar attitude. Delville produced two large volumes and put them before Scriabine. "Read these—and then set them to music," he said. Scriabine read the books—*The Secret Doctrine.* He went on fire with their revelation. The result was his immortal masterpiece, "Prometheus." . . . While Scriabine composed the Symphony, he came excitedly at intervals into Delville's drawing-room and played for the painter the musical ideas that were crowding in on him.[17]

When the piece was published Delville created a beautiful image for the cover, showing the fiery face of Prometheus combined with a lyre, presumably implying the Promethean quality of music. Scriabin also planned an even more ambitious creation called *Mysterium,* a total work of art incorporating music, poetry, drama, dance, colored lighting effects, and even perfumes. Joscelyn Godwin writes about this project as follows:

> It was to be held in a hemispherical temple in India containing an artificial lake, so that the audience or congregation would seem to be enclosed in a perfect sphere. The effects of the Mystery were to exceed by far any Platonic or Wagnerian ambitions: beginning with the enlightenment of its beholders, it would spread worldwide to bring about the apocalypse and usher in the New Age.[18]

Mysterium was therefore yet another example of the Russian millenarian worldview. Instead of Christ's second coming it was going to be a concert to end all concerts that would summon the new world. The choice of India—and specifically the Himalayas—is also fascinating, as it ties in with the whole mythos of Shambhala, Agartha, and Madame Blavatsky's Mahatmas. Sadly, Scriabin died in 1915 at the age of thirty-eight before he had even completed the score of the work. After his death his work for a time went out of favor but is now once again widely admired and performed.

While Scriabin, Biely, Roerich, and others turned to theosophy in their spiritual search, others turned to freemasonry in its various different forms. Freemasonry came to Russia in 1731, when an English Provincial Grand Lodge was established at St. Petersburg, and the movement grew steadily, with rivalries developing between different national obediences—English, French, Prussian, and Swedish—and between the main Masonic bodies and various more exotic systems such as the German Rosicrucian order, the Golden and Rosy Cross, and the French rite called the Chevaliers Bienfaisants de la Cité Sainte, also known as the Rectified Scottish Rite or the Lyons System. There were also periods of persecution and prohibition from the government, the monarchy, and the Orthodox Church. One prominent eighteenth-century Mason was Nikolai Novikov, writer, publisher, philanthropist, and one of the great figures of the Russian Enlightenment. Novikov, a member of the Golden and Rosy Cross and the Lyons System, was imprisoned for a time on the orders of the Empress Catherine the Great but was released when she died and her son Paul I came to the throne. Among the esoteric currents linked with Freemasonry that came to Russia was the movement known as Martinism, based on the ideas of Louis Claude de Saint-Martin (1743–1803), who professed a Manichean worldview in which human beings are trapped in a state of darkness and suffering from which they can only be released by contacting a source of light outside the material world.

In the nineteenth century freemasonry had an unsteady existence in Russia. Bans were imposed, lifted, and then reimposed. For western-leaning, democratically minded Russians, freemasonry was attractive—those who joined it in the early part of the nineteenth century included the writer Alexander Pushkin and the father of Leo Tolstoy—but to those of a conservative outlook it was a foreign body that promoted dangerous and subversive ideas. Some, like Tsar Alexander I, were torn between these two points of view. Alexander had himself been initiated as a Mason, but finally he bowed to conservative forces and in 1822 ordered a fresh ban on freemasonry.[19] From that date it was suppressed in Russia for many decades, except for those lodges that met in secret. Meanwhile it continued to be a target for conspiracy theorists and anti-Semites. The "Judeo-Masonic conspiracy" became a favorite bête noire of this faction. As a result of the preliminary revolution of 1905 the Craft was once again permitted, and in 1906 lodges were founded in St. Petersburg and Moscow under the aegis of the French grand lodge, the Grand Orient de France.[20]

DIRE PROPHECIES

These lodges were soon followed by others of a more mystical and esoteric bent, where the talk was often of Rosicrucianism, theosophy, astrology, alchemy, Kabbalah, magic, the tarot, and suchlike. Information about these subjects came to a large extent from abroad through writings like the *Doctrine and Ritual of High Magic* by the French magus Eliphas Lévi and Madame Blavatsky's *Secret Doctrine,* which had been published in English but then translated into Russian. There were also emissaries from abroad such as the Frenchman Papus (alias Dr. Gérard Encausse), a prolific author on esoteric subjects, who had founded his own version of Martinism in 1884.

In 1905 Papus visited Russia with his mentor, the healer Master Philippe of Lyons. The sensational events of this visit were later recorded in an article in the *Revue des deux mondes* by Maurice-Georges Paléologue, who was ambassador to the Russian court at the time of the visit.[21] He describes how the whole country was marked by "revolutionary troubles, bloody strikes, and scenes of pillage, massacre and arson," with the Emperor living "in a state of cruel anxiety." Summoned to the Imperial Palace, Papus proceeded to organize "a grand ritual of incantation and necromancy" in which he summoned up the ghost of the Tsar's father, Alexander III. The latter urged his son to crush the revolution at all costs but warned that it would return one day with even greater force. Papus then performed a ritual of exorcism to banish the impending catastrophe, after warning that the efficacy of the exorcism would cease after his own death.

An article by Marina Aptekman relates:

In 1911 Papus met the famous publisher and critic Ivan Antoshevsky, and together they established an occult magazine, *Isida,* which was intended to serve as a rival to the major magazine of the spiritualist movement, *Rebus.* . . . Between 1908 and 1912 A. V. Troianovsky translated all of Papus's major works, which were immediately published in *Isida* and subsequently in book form.[22]

In 1910 a lodge of Papus's Martinist order was established in St. Petersburg and Grigorij Ottonovich Mebes, a teacher of mathematics and French and a prominent Freemason, became its head.[23] Mebes also founded an Initiation School of Western Esotericism, with an outer and an inner circle, the latter reserved for carefully chosen students. The wide-ranging course on occultism was structured around the tarot. Mebes and his school were crushed during the Bolshevik terror. Mebes was sent to a Gulag in the far north and died a few years later. The course material was preserved in the form of students' notes and was assembled by Mebes's followers in the Russian diaspora into an encyclopedia of occultism, which has appeared in Portuguese, Russian, and more recently in a two-volume English edition (see Bibliography). The work has influenced authors on the tarot such as Mouni Sadhu and Valentin Tomberg.

In 1911 Papus's journal *L'Initiation,* in its January issue, reported that in Russia, "Martinist and occult movements are taking on immense proportions. . . . Through the teachings expounded in the works of Papus, Eliphas Lévi, Stanislas de Guaita and Saint-Yves d'Alveydre, the ideas of these Masters are manifesting themselves to an extraordinary degree."[24]

The above-named Joseph Alexandre Saint-Yves d'Alveydre (1842–1909), who used the title Marquis, was a fascinating figure. His influence in Russia was no doubt helped by the fact that he was married to a strikingly beautiful Russian woman, the Countess Marie-Victoire de Riznitch-Keller. After a stormy childhood and youth, Saint-Yves became a traditionalist of sorts and developed a political philosophy involving a Christian theocratic and monarchical system that he called Synarchy—from the Greek *syn* (together) and *archy* (rulership), thus the opposite of anarchy (without rulership)—which he set out in books such as *Mission actuelle des Souverains* (1882) and *Mission des Juifs* (1884). The system involved three ruling councils: one for religious and intellectual life, another for political and legal matters, and a third for economic matters. Saint-Yves's vision is difficult to place on the political spectrum, as it combines both authoritarian and egalitarian features. As the word "Synarchy" implies, its aim was to unite rather than divide society. In some ways he anticipated future developments. For example, he advocated free movement of goods and people throughout Europe, which came later with the European Union.

Synarchy, he claimed, had once been the universal system in a previous golden age, but now it only remained in a place called Agarttha (now usually spelled Agartha), a fabled underground kingdom somewhere in the Himalayas, whose inhabitants practiced Synarchy and possessed a level of scientific knowledge far beyond anything in the West.[25] His pronouncements on this subject had a strong influence on the explorer Alexander Barchenko, whom we shall encounter again in the next chapter. Curiously, Saint-Yves was also versed in marine biology and published a treatise on the uses of marine algae, *De l'utilité des algues marines* (1879).

Interestingly, Saint-Yves placed great hopes in Russia. In his book *Mission de l'Inde,* written in 1886 but not published until a posthumous edition of 1910, he wrote: "The deeply religious sentiment of the Russian masses, their instinctive occultism, their language, their legends, their prophecies, and the Hermetic interpretation that some sects keep of the sacred scriptures, are all so many ties indicative of an intellectual and social alliance with Asia."[26]

Furthermore, he wrote an open letter to the Tsar, advising the latter as follows on Russian policy in central Asia: "Sire, have caution when touching Afghanistan and do not advance into the territory of these amphictyons* without pronouncing the ancient password of the Kingdom of God. . . ."

He added that "The peoples of Central Asia feel great sympathy toward Russia and toward its sovereign."[27]

Apart from the esoteric groups I have mentioned, others operating in Russia around this time included the Society of the Sphinx, the Order of the Knights of the Grail, and the Society for the Revival of Pure Knowledge, founded in 1916.[28]

There were also those who looked to the eastern religions for enlightenment, especially Buddhism. These divided basically into three groups. There were the indigenous Buddhists of Mongolian descent—such as the Buryats, Yakuts, and Kalmyks—who practiced the Tibetan form of Buddhism with its elaborate rites, rich symbology, and admixture of elements from the pre-Buddhist Bon religion. Then there were Buddhists from the Asian countries who were resident in Russia. These tended to follow the more austere Theravada Buddhism, which emphasized

---

*A term referring to representatives of ancient Greek states forming a council. Here Saint-Yves has applied the term to the rulers of Agartha.

Fig. 1.3. The Buddhist temple in St. Petersburg, built just before the revolution
(See also color plate 4)

WIKIMEDIA COMMONS

self-perfection and purification of the mind. Finally there were members of the westernized intelligentsia who had picked up Buddhism via influences coming from places like London and Paris, often along with theosophy. These people were sometimes referred to as "Theosopho-Buddhists."[29]

In 1906 the Tsar granted an audience to the prominent Tibetan Lama Agvan Dorjiev, an emissary of the then thirteen-year-old Dalai Lama, at which Dorjiev for the second time requested permission for a Tibetan Buddhist temple or *datsan* to be built in St. Petersburg. No decision was taken at the time, but three years later the Tsar gave his permission, remarking that "Buddhists in Russia should feel as if they were under the wing of the mighty eagle" (a reference to Russia's heraldic emblem). The decision was undoubtedly connected with the Great Game, the struggle between Russia and Britain for control of central Asia. In 1903–4 a British force under Col. Francis Younghusband had invaded Tibet and forced the Dalai Lama to flee to Mongolia. It was therefore understandable that Dorjiev would prefer to throw in his lot with the Russians, who had an interest in keeping the goodwill of the Dalai Lama.[30]

Great care and considerable expense went into the construction of the temple. It was oriented toward the north, the direction of the mythical land of Shambhala, and in the north wall of the prayer hall stood the main altar with a gilt alabaster statue of Buddha, about nine feet high. The entrance facade was decorated with traditional Buddhist emblems such as the eight-spoked Wheel of Dharma. The exterior walls were clad with tiles of granite, ashlar, and glazed brick in various different colors, and everything had an art nouveau touch—a deliberate decision on Dorjiev's part to make the building and Buddhism in general attractive to the Russian public. The decoration of the interior was carried out in 1914–15 under the supervision of the painter Nikolai Roerich, aided by some native Buryat artists.[31] In short, the temple was a thing of great beauty and one of the wonders of St. Petersburg. In the Stalinist period it was dreadfully vandalized, as I shall mention in

Fig. 1.4. Grigori Rasputin, who exerted a fateful influence over the royal family

a later chapter, but after the collapse of communism it was carefully restored and is now back in full use as a place of worship.

By the time the temple was complete the Bolshevik Revolution and the end of the Silver Age were close at hand and, as the days of the monarchy moved toward their tragic conclusion, a curious holy man, part maniac, part saint, and (some said) more than part demon, managed to become a close confidant of the Tsar and Tsarina. His name was Grigori Rasputin (1871–1916), often called the "holy devil" (*sviatoi tchort*), and he played a fateful role in the events leading up to the removal and execution of the royal family. In order to understand the hold that he established over the Tsar and his wife, it is necessary to know something about his background and the religious tradition out of which he came.

Essentially Rasputin belonged to the tradition of the *staretsy*, God-illuminated hermits and pilgrims, who were credited with special powers of prophecy and healing. Growing up in a pious family in Siberia, as a young man he was fired by religious fervor and came under the influence of an old starets called Makari, who predicted an important future for him. While already married and with a growing family, Rasputin pursued a restless existence, going on a pilgrimage to Mount Athos in Greece and for a time joining a strange sect called *Khlysty* or Men of God, the name taken from the Russian word *khlyst,* meaning a whip, on account of the intense flagellation sessions that they held. The *Khlysty* believed that the Holy Spirit could inspire young virgins to become "begetters of Christs." At their meetings the participants were divided into three grades: Christ-bearers, Christs, and candidates. Stephen Graham, an expert on Russian religion, writes about the *Khlysty* as follows:

> The chief mass was a *radenie* or "fervour," in which all danced round a jar of water heating by a stove in the center. The participants were in white cotton and the virgins held wands of twigs rolled in towels with which they beat the dancers, urging them to go faster and faster until they fell in hysteria. It was alleged that the hysteria was

followed by promiscuous copulation, but this has not been proved. The task of the Christ-bearers [literally God-bearers, *Bogoroditsi*] was to inculcate the gift of prophecy, to teach the technique of healing though prayer and to learn how to expel demons, in all of which Grigori Rasputin became proficient. He also accepted the heretical dogma that to repent one must first commit sin.[32]

Flagellation, as a means of inducing altered states of consciousness, is one of the techniques used by shamans in many parts of the world. Arguably, therefore, Rasputin can be seen as a kind of shaman, and we shall find other instances of shamanic practices cropping up in various forms of Russian spirituality. Apparently there were survivals of the *Khlysty* sect active up to the late twentieth century.

Rasputin's involvement with the *Khlysty* landed him in trouble with the Church, but after a time he returned to Orthodoxy and became a *strannik,* a wandering preacher, cutting an arresting figure with his long dark hair and beard, striking features, and piercing eyes. Everywhere he drew large crowds, attracted by his powerful charisma and his undoubted skills as a healer. Soon he came to the attention of Bishop Theophan of St. Petersburg, who introduced him to the Grand Duke Nikolai and his wife Anastasia. The Grand Duke in turn, deeply impressed by Rasputin, presented him to Tsar Nicholas II and the Tsarina Alexandra.

Earlier the Tsarina had given birth to a son, Alexis, who suffered from hemophilia, a hereditary disease that prevents blood from clotting. This meant that even the slightest wound could be life-threatening. Only Rasputin was able to stop the bleeding. Here he evidently applied one of the methods he had learned from Siberian folk healers. Paul Kourennoff, an expert on Russian folk medicine, describes the practice of treating ailments with the human voice:

In the course of sonic-therapy studies it has been discovered that sounds profoundly affect the physiological functions of the human

body, particularly, but not exclusively, of the nervous system.
Dr. Alexander Dogel has conducted a special study of the folk medicine "talking away" methods, and discovered that certain timbres of
voices not only deadened pain, but so lowered the cardiac activity
as to stop external hemorrhaging. The case of the infamous Grigori
Rasputin instantly comes to mind . . . Rasputin . . . had been practicing folk medicine in Siberia before coming to St. Petersburg.[33]

Rasputin quickly became indispensable to the royal family not
only as healer, but also as prophet and spiritual guide. Soon he was also
exerting influence in political matters. Rivals began to intrigue against
him, and scandalous rumors circulated about his sexual exploits—
women found him irresistible, and there are photographs of him surrounded by hordes of female devotees.

In the winter of 1916 a faction surrounding Prince Felix Yussopov
decided that Rasputin would have to go. The Prince, having feigned
friendship with Rasputin, invited him to a banquet. Cakes were provided, which Yussopov had instructed a doctor to impregnate with
poison. Evidently the doctor had cold feet at the last minute because
Rasputin eagerly wolfed down the cakes with no ill effect. Yussopov
and his co-conspirators then shot and wounded their victim, tied him
up, and dumped him into the frozen Neva through a hole in the ice.
According to some accounts he was still alive at that moment. When
his body was found, his right hand was against his chest with the
thumb, forefinger, and middle finger pressed together. Evidently he
had died making the sign of the cross.[34]

Rasputin had predicted that if he fell, the monarchy would fall as
well. His prophecy was soon to be fulfilled.

TWO

Fabled Lands

Uncountable are the inhabitants of Shambhala. Numerous are the splendid new forces and achievements which are being prepared there for humanity.

NIKOLAI ROERICH, SHAMBHALA.

While some waited for Christ or the "woman clothed with the sun" to vanquish the Antichrist and usher in the New Age, others focused their gaze on some never-never land, far away or long ago—and here we have yet another example of a powerful egregore. One such place that came to have a magnetic appeal for thousands, perhaps millions, of people in Russia, was Byelovodye, the "Land of the White Waters," which to this day remains a compelling legend, inspiring writers and painters and giving rise to a popular drama series on television.

How the legend of Byelovodye arose is an extraordinary story.[1] News of the place reached St. Petersburg in 1807 when a man from Siberia named Bobilev presented himself at the Ministry of the Interior and reported that he had visited a community of Old Believers living on the shore of a lake in a place called Byelovodye close to the Chinese border. There they had their churches, where they held their ceremonies according to the old liturgy, and where they baptized their infants, carried out weddings and prayed, crossing themselves with two fingers.

They paid no tribute to anyone. The population of Byelovodye numbered 500,000 or more. After delivering his report, Bobilev said he was willing to go to Byelovodye and follow instructions. The Ministry gave him 150 rubles and ordered him to report to the governor general of Siberia, but Bobilev failed to show up and disappeared without trace.

It was not so surprising that the Ministry officials believed Bobilev's account, as rumors about Byelovodye had apparently reached them before, and they knew that there were many communities of Old Believers who had fled to places far and wide on the fringes of the Russian state, some of them not shown on any map, as the maps of that time still had many blank spots. The authorities had an ambivalent attitude toward these fugitives. Officially they were religious outlaws, but on the other hand they played a useful role in colonizing previously uninhabited territories.

After the great schism of the seventeenth century. the Old Believers had split into a number of subsects who squabbled over fine points of doctrine but basically shared a millenarian worldview. One of the most radical of these was a sect called the Fugitives or Runners (*Byeguni*), who had appeared in the second half of the eighteenth century. They were millenarians with a difference because they believed that the Antichrist had already arrived and taken over the Russian state. To some extent they prefigured Marxism by rejecting private property and class division. Their agenda was not just to escape from mainstream society, but to actively fight against it and its ruler, the Antichrist. Hence, they waged a propaganda war through the writings that they circulated. One of these, which went through numerous copyings and variations, was called the *Traveler* (*Puteshestvennik*), and it was this document, more than any other, that established the Byelovodye legend. In it there are numerous references to Byelovodye as a place that is safe from the Antichrist. The document found a ready audience among the sixteen to eighteen million Old Believers and members of heterodox sects at the time.

Whether or not Byelovodye ever existed as a real place, it soon took on a mythical quality and was passionately sought and longed for. Information about its actual location was vague. One group of people was said to have reached it by sea via the Arctic Ocean. Alternatively there was reputed to be a southern sea route, presumably via the Indian Ocean and the Pacific. There were also those who were reported to have found it by land. The *Traveler,* in its various versions, is confusing about the location, placing it behind high mountains at the edge of the earth or on the shore of the sea, or on seventy large islands.[2] Significantly, the *Traveler* states that only those who are determined to break all ties with the past will be able to reach it. This is a motif that appears again and again in accounts of otherworldly places. In Tibetan Buddhism there is the notion of *beyul,* hidden lands that only the spiritually enlightened can enter.[3] The motif appears again in Gurdjieff's account of his journey, blindfold in the final stage, to the monastery of the Sarmoung Brotherhood, reached via a perilous rope bridge over a chasm.[4] It also appears, as we shall see, in accounts of the hidden Himalayan kingdom of Shambhala.

The legend of Byelovodye continues to capture the imagination of Russians today, as shown by the works of art that the theme has inspired. A painting by the artist Vsevelod Ivanov shows a lake and on the bank a lone, robed figure with a staff and a tired looking yak beside him. He is gazing across the lake to a region of gloomy, jagged mountains. At first you wonder whether he has journeyed in vain in search of Byelovodye. Then you notice, just visible over the crest of the hill on the far bank, a white citadel, caught by a few rays of sunshine from a break in the clouds.

One of the most striking works inspired by Byelovodye is an enormous mural, thirty meters high, painted on the side of a tower block in the Siberian city of Omsk, one of a series of murals celebrating Russian life and traditions. Where half a century ago the same wall would have displayed a communist slogan and a vast hammer and sickle or perhaps

Fig. 2.1. Mural of the fabled land of Byelovodye on an apartment block in Omsk
(See also color plate 5)

a striding figure of Lenin, now it shows an idyllic otherworldly scene: in the background, a mountain, rising above the clouds, with three bearded faces carved out of tree trunks, a temple, a waterfall, and a rainbow; in the foreground is a shining city built on a circular island in a lake; and across the middle of the mural is written, in Old Church Slavonic letters, the word "Byelovodye." The work was made by a local arts cooperative called Astraea-Garant Omsk. It must surely be uplifting to the residents to see such an image every time they approach the building. In contrast, the mural art that one sees in west European and American cities, while often technically skilled, seems calculated to startle and provoke rather than to uplift.

There is also a television drama series called Byelovodye. The main hero is Kyril Andreev, a young Moscow journalist. He finds a fern-like plant with a flower that has magical power and enables him and his friends to enter another world containing enormous destructive forces that erupt into the everyday world, causing terrifying results. It has little to do with the original Byelovodye and the Old Believers who searched for it, but it makes for good television.

SEARCHING FOR HYPERBOREA

While the theme of Byelovodye is of relatively recent origin, there is another legend that goes back to antiquity, namely the legend of Hyperborea, the name coined by the ancient Greeks for the land beyond Boreas, the north wind.[5] This was said to be a warm, fertile place, a sort of oasis in the icy north, inhabited by an advanced civilization. Over the centuries the notion of Hyperborea took on a powerful mystique. It became a popular motif among writers and poets, and an important journal and later publishing house in the Silver Age was called *Hyperborea*. There was also much speculation about the exact location of the place.

One who did more than speculate was Alexander Barchenko (1881–1938), writer, esotericist, archaeologist, explorer, and scientist whose expeditions to the far north of Russia and his later attempts to organize an expedition in search of Shambhala are described by Alexander Andreyev in his book *Occultist of the Soviet Country: the Secret of Doctor Barchenko* (English translation of the Russian title). Barchenko was, as Andreyev writes, "one of those who believed in the possibility of building a new Russia on the basis of a union of science and socialism and who worked to that end."[6]

Like many of the same ilk, he was eventually crushed by the Bolshevik tyranny and executed in 1938, but for a time he was able to work freely and even enjoyed the support of certain people within the security forces.

Barchenko was a many-faceted man. Born the son of a notary in the town of Yelets, located about half a day's drive to the southwest of Moscow, he studied medicine and then switched to jurisprudence but curtailed his studies for financial reasons. He married, moved to St. Petersburg with his wife and young son, and began a successful career as a writer of popular novels about exotic places and the paranormal. He also experimented with telepathy, extrasensory perception, and the like.

While at university Barchenko had been introduced by one of his professors to the writings of the French esotericist Alexandre Saint-Yves d'Alveydre, who was mentioned in the previous chapter, and the Frenchman's works made a profound impression on him. The concept of Synarchy appealed to him, and he was convinced about the existence of Agartha (or Agartta, as Saint-Yves spelled it), which at some point came to overlap with the myth of Shambhala. What especially fascinated him was the idea that in such places an ancient, secret tradition of knowledge was preserved and that, if this knowledge could be recovered, it would be of immense value to Russia.

Barchenko had long been preoccupied with the subject of energy, especially the solar "radiant energy," as he called it, which was so crucial for life on Earth but also, as he speculated, for life on other planets such as Mars, and could be harnessed within the human brain, given the right techniques. He was also concerned with the related concept of ether. In an essay entitled "The Spirit of Nature" he wrote: "Experts have come to the conclusion that the whole universe is filled with a substance so fine that it penetrates freely into the interstices between even the smallest visible objects."[7]

Given his preoccupation with energy, it is not surprising that he knew of the work of G. I. Gurdjieff, who was living in St. Petersburg in the years leading up to the revolution. Barchenko's close friend Peter Shandarovsky was a pupil of Gurdjieff and told Barchenko about the system.[8] It is even possible that Barchenko and Gurdjieff met at some point. They would certainly have found much to talk about, as a central element of Gurdjieff's system was the mutual interaction of human and cosmic energy.

Could it be, Barchenko asked himself, that the secret of universal energy was preserved by a group of initiates in some hidden sanctum over the hills and far away? Apart from Gurdjieff's mysterious Sarmoung Brotherhood and Madame Blavatsky's Mahatmas in their center somewhere in the mountains of Tibet, there was talk of a "northern Agartha" in Lapland, more specifically in the region of the Kola peninsula, located in the far north of Russia between the White Sea and the Barents Sea. Barchenko decided to go there and was provided with a justification for the expedition by the prominent psychologist Vladimir Bekhterev, a pioneer in the study of hypnosis and suggestion, who had a particular interest in collective psychological phenomena. Bhekterev was intrigued by reports of an outbreak of mass hysteria among the native Sami or Lapp population, and Barchenko was charged with investigating the phenomenon.

Accordingly, as a freshly accepted member of Bhekterev's research institute and with the backing of the Soviet scientific establishment, Barchenko set off for Lapland in the spring of 1921, accompanied by a small team including his wife, Natalia, and his assistant, Julia

Strutinska.[9] Later they were joined by the astronomer Alexander Kondiain, who found Barchenko busy treating a young man who was in danger of dying from tuberculosis, instructing him to sunbathe in the open air while it was still frosty from the night air. The method appeared to have worked, because the patient was soon able to walk and travel on his own to Crimea to continue being treated.

Barchenko spent two years in Lapland carrying out various scientific investigations, including studying the local vegetation for its potential as cattle fodder. It is unclear whether he was able to throw any light on the mass hysteria among the Lapps, or Sami as they are usually called, but in other ways he learned a great deal about them. While officially Orthodox, they continued to practice their traditional ways, worshipping the old gods and offering bloodless sacrifices at their menhirs. Central to their ancestral religion, which had a shamanistic core, was the worship of the sun.

In the summer of 1922 Barchenko and his team went into the depths of the Kola peninsula in the heart of Russian Lapland, an area that had hardly ever been visited by explorers. From a young woman named Anna Vasilievna, who was a shaman, he learned something of the local folklore. A long time ago, he was told, the Sami had fought with a foreign tribe and driven them away. The foreigners disappeared under the earth, except for two of their leaders who galloped away on horseback, collided with a rock face, and remained there forever. The Sami called them "the Old Ones." The same woman cured Barchenko of a heart attack. While he lay on the ground, she whispered something in his ear then pointed a dagger at his heart, making stabbing, pointing movements. His heart pain grew intense and he felt close to death, but instead he fell into a deep sleep. When he woke up the next morning the heart pain was gone and never came back.[10]

Exploring the interior of the peninsula, Barchenko's team found some remarkable things: an island covered with reindeer horns that was a sacred place for the Sami, an ancient, paved road about one and a half kilometers long, stone pyramids, fallen columns, and a rock face with the dark silhouette of a gigantic human figure—perhaps one of the horsemen who had ridden into the cliff.[11]

Barchenko returned to Petrograd, as it was now called, in 1923. As to what he had discovered in the "northern Agartha," explorer of the region Valerii Dyomin states: "Barchenko gained very important information, now unfortunately lost, about the ancient universal knowledge and Russian culture, the sources of which lay in the north. In the archives of the former KGB are preserved some thirty related files, to which nobody to this day has access."[12]

Back in Petrograd, Barchenko returned to his old, somewhat Bohemian social and intellectual milieu, which was still flourishing six years after the revolution, although its days were numbered. Still nourishing the dream of an ideal society, he founded an organization called the United Work Brotherhood, inspired partly by Gurdjieff's project (referred to by its followers as "the Work") and partly by Saint-Yves d'Alveydre's Synarchy. He also began trying to gain support for another expedition. Having explored the "northern Agartha" he was eager to venture to the eastern one, which by now had become conflated with the mythical Buddhist kingdom of Shambhala, believed to be located somewhere in the mountains of central Asia. In this regard, a key event was his meeting in 1923 with Agvan Dorjiev, the prominent Buryat lama who represented Tibet and Mongolia in Russia and had been instrumental in the building of the Buddhist temple. Also present at the meeting were Dorjiev's deputy Badma Ochirov as well as the Mongol Khayan Khirva and the Tibetan Naga Navyen. With the last two he had further meetings at the temple, where he lived for several months, and they educated him about the "secret knowledge" possessed by the Buddhists of their region and about the Kalachakra Tantra, a powerful esoteric and prophetic tradition within Buddhism, which was said to be carefully preserved in Shambhala.[13]

What was the Kalachakra Tantra, and what was the secret

knowledge that it contained? Tantrism is a tradition that overlaps with both Hinduism and Buddhism but is believed by some to be older than either of them. Whereas other mystical traditions involve a distancing of oneself from the world of the senses, the tantric works deliberately *through* the senses, which can include sexuality, to achieve transcendence. The Indian scholar Benjamin Walker writes:

> The sources of Tantrism are obscure. In one tradition it originated outside India, in a region somewhere in the north-west, near Afghanistan, or further north in a place known by different names, such as Urgyan, Uddiyana, Shambhala and Agharta, around which fabulous legends have grown . . . A hoary tradition survives in India about this mysterious region of Uddiyana, which produced its own semimythical rulers and its beautiful princesses, and the extraordinary rites of sex mysticism to which they were devoted.

So here again we have the notion of the mysterious, faraway, half-hidden land that crops up under so many different names. In describing the nature of the tantric path, Walker writes:

> The chief deity in Tantrism is the female principle, personified as the goddess Shakti. Her name means "Power" and she stands for the primal energy underlying the cosmos . . . The rites involved in Tantrism include magic circles (mandalas), spells (mantras), gestures (mudras), breath control (pranayama), internal alchemy (rasavada), physical culture, heliotherapy or obtaining vigor through the worship of the sun, the activation of the chakras or subtle centers of the body, and the use of bells, incense and other paraphernalia of the occultist's craft.[14]

What would have appealed to Barchenko and his ilk about tantra was the notion that the human mind and body contain forces that can be linked with the cosmos to create tides of immense power, provided that one knows how to make the links. It was essentially this knowledge that was contained in the Kalachakra Tantra. The name Kalachakra is made up of two Sanskrit words: *kala* (time) and *chakra* (wheel). Hence the name means "Wheel of Time," that is to say the cyclical movements of the stars and planets. And herein lies the key to the Kalachakra system. The adept studies the planetary configurations that occur at various regular intervals and is able to link each configuration with a particular chakra or center in the body.*

All of this was probably conveyed to Barchenko by the Tibetan and Mongolian lamas at the Petrograd temple, making him all the more eager to set off for central Asia, and for much of the 1920s he was preoccupied with trying to secure official backing for an expedition. To begin with he made encouraging headway with support from a surprising quarter, namely from Gleb Bokii, a high-ranking official of the secret police (the OGPU, as it was called at that time). Bokii facilitated a meeting with a committee of the OGPU in Moscow, headed by its chief Felix Dzerzhinsky. The committee approved Barchenko's project, which involved research into neuropsychology and telepathy as well as investigating what might be gleaned from Shambhala and the Kalachakra about eastern psychological techniques. Barchenko was brought to Moscow and set up in a laboratory on a generous stipend. Soon he was giving lectures in private apartments to various friends and members of the communist establishment. The lectures, as Andrei Znamenski writes, were "a smorgasbord of Western esotericism and bits and pieces of Tibetan Buddhism he had learned from his Mongol and Tibetan contacts."[15]

At first everything seemed to augur well for Barchenko's planned expedition, but what put an end to it was the opposition of the

---

*For further information on the Kalachakra Tantra and on Tantrism in general see, inter alia: Geoffrey Ashe, *The Ancient Wisdom*; Arthur Avalon (Sir John Woodroffe), *Shakti and Shâkta*; and Oscar Marcel Hinze, *Tantra Vidya*.

Tibetologist Sergei Oldenburg, whose negative reports caused the Commisariat for Foreign Affairs to blackball the project.[16] Barchenko somehow struggled on over the next decade, as Bolshevik repression worsened following Lenin's death in 1924 and Stalin's rise to power. Finally in 1937 he was arrested on a trumped-up charge of subversion, and the following year he was shot. His former benefactor Bokii had suffered the same fate the previous year.

THE GREAT GAME

I return to the theme of Shambhala, which was destined to play a bizarre role in Soviet foreign policy in the context of what has been called the Great Game, the struggle between Russia and Britain for control of central Asia. These powers realized that, in order to win the game, they would have to gain the support of the indigenous populations of the region, and the Russians attempted to do this by invoking the Shambhala mythology. This mythology presented Shambhala as a stronghold of the Buddhist religion and a bulwark against Muslim invaders and said that one day a powerful king would arise in Shambhala and sally forth at the head of a great army to crush the enemies of Buddhism. The Russian strategy was to exploit the Shambhala mystique as a way of bringing the region under Bolshevik control. Thus Bolshevik agents and their indigenous collaborators were active in the region, often posing as Buddhist pilgrims and presenting communism as the natural bedfellow of Buddhism and the fulfillment of the Shambhala prophetic tradition.

Now we must come back to Nikolai and Helena Roerich, as they played a key role in what subsequently unfolded. The whole extraordinary story of the Roerichs and Shambhala has been expertly told by Andrei Znamenski in his book *Red Shambhala,* but I shall summarize it here.* Roerich was born in St. Petersburg in 1874, where he became

*On the Roerichs see also Decter, *Nicholas Roerich*.

prominent as an artist, as mentioned in the previous chapter. He and his wife Helena left Russia just before the revolution and spent some years in the United States where they were closely involved with theosophy and similar movements. Helena had clairvoyant powers and channeled a series of writings, which she and Nikolai believed to come from the theosophical master Morya. Through these communications Morya revealed that they were destined to carry out a great plan, namely to bring about the earthly manifestation of Shambhala in the form of a vast country in central Asia, a kind of eastern Grail kingdom that would send messages out into the world, propagating beauty and spreading peace and harmony. Central to the Roerichs' message was the doctrine of agni yoga, the yoga of fire, named after the Hindu fire god Agni. What they meant by fire was a subtle, universal energy, like chi or prana and very similar to the universal energy that Barchenko was looking for. This energy, they believed, was going to transform the world.

On their way to central Asia to realize the great plan, the Roerichs stopped off in Paris and stayed at the Hotel Lord Byron where a mysterious package was delivered to them. It contained a small box inscribed with the letter "M" repeated four times, which of course they took to stand for Morya. Inside the box was piece of black aerolite stone. The significance of this was immediately apparent. In the medieval epic *Parzival* by Wolfram von Eschenbach the Holy Grail is described as a stone that had fallen from a star. The Roerichs believed that this stone resided in Shambhala—all but a fragment that had become detached and circulated throughout the world. They were sure that it was this fragment that they now beheld, and they believed it to be the Chintamani Stone, a wish-fulfilling stone famous in Buddhist tradition and often shown in Tibetan iconography.[17]

In the years 1925–1928 the Roerichs and their son George carried out an astonishing expedition, starting in Kashmir and traveling in a vast loop through the Himalayas, Siberia, and Mongolia, skirting Tibet and returning via India and Ceylon. The expedition was supported partly by American benefactors and partly also by the Bolsheviks with whom Roerich had concluded an agreement during a side trip to Moscow.[18] In 1934–1935 the Roerichs made another expedition, this time through Manchuria and inner Mongolia with the financial backing of Henry A. Wallace, the American Secretary for Agriculture, and with the approval of President Franklin D. Roosevelt. These politicians also helped him to realize the Roerich Pact, an international agreement to preserve works of art and cultural treasures even in wartime, which was signed at the White House in 1935 by the United States and twenty other countries.

Although the Roerichs' plan for the earthly Shambhala was never realized, they have left behind a considerable legacy: the paintings, the writings, the Roerich pact, and the agni yoga teaching, which has many followers today in Russia and elsewhere. Roerich received a posthumous accolade in 1987 when the Russian leader Mikhail Gorbachev held a meeting in the Kremlin with the Roerichs' younger son Svyatoslav (1904–1993), a fine painter in his own right. A second meeting, also in the Kremlin, took place in 1989, when Gorbachev declared that "In the Soviet Union the memory of Nicholas Roerich is cherished with deep gratitude."[19]

A search on the internet will reveal that Shambhala is still a subject of great fascination in Russia, as is the theme of Hyperborea, as shown by the recent expeditions to the region of the Kola peninsula, explored by Alexander Barchenko in the 1920s. In my book *Beyond the North Wind,* I mentioned two expeditions headed by Valerii Dyomin in 1997 and 1998, which led him to conclude that he had found the remains of Hyperborea, or rather one of its outposts. He noted that the Sami were sun worshippers and that Apollo was said to have spent half the year in the north, hence his sobriquet "the Northern Apollo." In his book on the expeditions, Dyomin wrote:

The expedition headed for the very center of the Kola Peninsula . . . to the area of the Lake of Seyd, which is sacred to the Sami. Here, in mountainous terrain and difficult to reach, at an altitude of approximately half a kilometer from the lake level, we found a gigantic megalithic complex with cyclopean structures . . . defensive masonry and geometrically regular slabs carved with mysterious signs . . . Lastly, there were the remains of an observatory—formed out of the rock formations and with a 15-meter gutter aimed at the sky—it distantly resembled a recessed sextant at the famous observatory of Ulugbek near Samarkand.[20]

They also found more than ten labyrinths, laid out in stones, which Dyomin was convinced were the prototypes of the labyrinths found in Crete and elsewhere.

The theme of Hyperborea, which so captivated Barchenko and Dyomin, has given rise to a whole school of painters. One of the most prominent is Alexander Uglanov (born 1960 in Tver) whom I got to know when I was working on my previous book, *Beyond the North Wind*. His Hyperborean works often show dreamlike images of snow-covered northern Camelots, their turrets, domes, pyramids, and ornate facades dreaming in the pale Hyperborean light. Through them move fur-clad human figures, backpacking through the snow or riding on sleighs pulled by reindeer or mammoths. Some of the paintings depict strange flying machines or images of Slavic deities such as Perun, against a vast Arctic sky.

Among the recent seekers drawn by the fabled lands of Hyperborea, Agartha, and Shambhala is a prominent Russian eye surgeon, explorer, and writer named Ernst Muldashev (born 1948) who, in addition to pursuing a distinguished medical career, has written many books about his expeditions to remote places in search of mysterious ancient knowledge. One of these is a work in five volumes entitled *In Search of the City of the Gods* (*V poiskach goroda bogov,* unfortunately currently only available in Russian). Enticed by the mystique of Central Asia, Muldashev has followed in the footsteps of such explorers as the

Roerichs, the intrepid Swede Sven Hedin, the swashbuckling English gentleman Henry Savage Landor, and the five members of the Nazi SS who went to Tibet in 1938–39 to study the geophysical conditions and the flora and fauna but also to look for traces of an ancient Aryan civilization.

Muldashev looked up at the pyramid-shaped sacred mountain, Kailas, source of the four great rivers of the Indian subcontinent, and came to an astonishing conclusion. Kailas did not merely look like a pyramid—it actually *was* a pyramid. Furthermore it was one of about one hundred pyramids forming what in Tibetan legend was called the City of the Gods. On taking measurements of these pyramids, Muldashev and his team found that they formed groups of three, corresponding to the triplets of "letters" in DNA that are arranged in different combinations to yield the twenty amino acids from which proteins are made. In other words the City of the Gods appeared to be what Muldashev has called the Matrix of Life on Earth. In addition some of the pyramids had concave surfaces that evidently could act as time warps in a way similar to the Kozyrev mirrors that we shall encounter later (see fig. 15.1).[21]

Now that we have considered the fabled lands of Agartha, Shambhala, and Hyperborea, the question arises: Is there a connection between them? I would argue that there is much evidence for the affirmative—that they are even all aspects of the same place, namely the ancient northern homeland of an advanced precursor civilization that vanished long ago but left its traces in the civilizations of later times. From the myths, legends, and various reports that have come down to us, we can speculate that the achievements and attributes of this civilization included: a religion of high spiritual level; a harmonious social order; an artistic and cultural life of great refinement; a language of enormous range and subtlety; and an ability to access a universal energy through a connection between the mind-body and the cosmos.

The precise location of this land is the subject of much speculation. Geoffrey Ashe, in his book *The Ancient Wisdom,* makes a convincing case for the area of the Altai Mountains and Lake Baikal in Siberia.[22] Others, as we have seen, place it in Russian Lapland. At any rate, somewhere in Russia appears to be the most likely location. The memory of this place and the yearning to rediscover it lie deep in the collective mind of the Russians. It explains much in their history and has important implications for the future, as we shall see.

THREE

Reign of the Antichrist

For now the Antichrist appears and reigns in the Temple at Jerusalem, deceiving many by his miracles and persecuting those whom he cannot deceive.

NORMAN COHN, *THE PURSUIT OF THE MILLENNIUM*

The Bolshevik seizure of power in October 1917 marked the beginning of an intensely dark period in the spiritual life of Russia. However, the antireligious hurricane unleashed by the revolution did not at first affect the world of esoteric groups as severely as might have been expected—some surprising things have come to light about the survival of such groups after 1917, which I shall come to shortly.

In contrast, the Orthodox Church suffered under the Bolsheviks right from the start. Following Marxist doctrine, Lenin considered religion to be part and parcel of the structure of repression in the system that he wished to sweep away. The Orthodox Church, which had been part of the fabric of Tsarist Russia, was the main target, but all other religions as well were seen as standing in the way of progress toward true communism. During the Russian Civil War (1918–1922) between the "Reds" (Bolsheviks) and the "Whites" (anti-Bolsheviks), the Red Army went on a rampage against clergy and parishioners, committing a series of terrible massacres. A typical incident was at the Monastery of the Caves in Ukraine, where Vladimir, the Metropolitan of Kiev, was tortured and murdered along with his monks. Another massacre took place in Petrograd, when Red troops led by a woman called Alexandra Kollontai seized the Alexander Nevsky monastery to turn it into a military hospital and shot a group of priests and lay people who protested. Afterward she boasted about the action and, significantly, proclaimed herself the "female Antichrist."

By 1920 two thirds of Russia's monasteries had been closed.[1] Still the government held back from an all-out attack on the Church, wishing to avoid antagonizing the great mass of believers at such a precarious time. But in 1922, with the Civil War over, the regime felt able to strike at the Orthodox religion without restraint, destroying churches, confiscating their properties and treasures, executing priests who resisted, and carrying out a propaganda campaign that included opening antireligious museums in many towns and cities. The atheist crusade was also carried out through newspapers and groups such as the League of Militant Atheists (1925–47). By 1939 there was only one functioning church in Moscow and a hundred or so in the entire country, whereas before the revolution there had been fifty thousand.[2] A pause in this orgy of destruction came in 1943 in the middle of the Second World War when Stalin entered into a concordat with the remnant of the Orthodox leadership, realizing that the Church was indispensable to uniting the country against the German invasion.

Essentially, however, the Church remained under siege for most of the communist period. Its survival is proof of the immense strength of religious belief among the Russian people, who found ways to keep their faith alive even in the face of the most ruthless repression. While churches were being closed or destroyed and the clergy deported or shot, thousands of priests and lay people set off, carrying bibles in their rucksacks, and went from house to house preaching the Gospel. And in 1941, when German troops invaded Russia they found numerous hermitages hidden away in the forests, whose inmates were carrying on the tradition of continuous prayer.[3]

It is striking that the bloodthirsty Alexandra Kollontai saw herself as an "Antichrist," a term that was more often used by anticommunists. The Russian historian Yuri Glazov writes: "There was . . . that core of the common populace close to the Russian Orthodox Church and to various Christian sects which disliked Stalin and saw in him the true Anti-Christ. The anticipation of the Anti-Christ is an essential feature of Russian cultural history and Stalin corresponded well to these expectations."[4]

Here again we are in the realm of the interface between mythology and history, and it is tempting to speculate that Stalin and the Bolshevik movement were unconsciously acting out a millenarian role assigned to them by the Russian collective mind.

THE PETROGRAD BUDDHIST TEMPLE

While the regime began by concentrating its fury on the Orthodox Church, other religious communities were also hit, although some managed to hold out longer than others. The Buddhist temple in Petrograd, created by Lama Dorjiev, suffered a sad fate, as did Dorjiev himself and his monks.[5] In 1919, while Dorjiev was away in Kalmykia, Red Army troops vandalized the building, looting anything of value: the ceremonial objects of gold, silver, copper, and bronze, the fine draperies of Chinese brocade, the silk banners, the furniture, and tableware. The big statue of Buddha had its head removed and a large hole made in its chest as the looters searched for hidden treasure. The temple library, containing hundreds of books in eastern and European languages, was completely destroyed, and Dorjiev's personal archive of documents disappeared without trace. Dorjiev rushed back to Petrograd and tried to restore as much as he could, helped by the Foreign Ministry, which feared a backlash from Russia's potential Buddhist allies in the east.

Over the next decade, thanks to Dorjiev's strenuous efforts, the temple enjoyed a new lease of life, its premises becoming a joint Tibetan and Mongolian enclave with diplomatic status. For a time it functioned again as a place of worship and a center for the Buddhist community in Petrograd (renamed Leningrad after Lenin's death in 1924). Meanwhile Dorjiev was attempting to reform the practice of Buddhism in Russia in the hope of making it compatible with communism, but this caused a damaging split in the Buddhist community between the reformists and the conservatives. Nevertheless, for a time the temple thrived. In his book on the temple, Alexander Andreyev writes: "Old Timers recall that in 1930 the datsan was the scene of a most impressive and colorful performance, the mystery dance of Cham (Tsam), devoted to the Kalachakra. For that purpose a large group of monks came to Leningrad from the Aga datsan, one of the largest and oldest in Buryatia, at the invitation of Dorjiev."[6]

Soon after that came the final blow to the temple, which happened as a result of the new agricultural collectivization policy. This was fiercely resisted by large numbers of peasants in the Buryat and Kalmyk regions, and they were supported by many of the Buddhist clergy. The Soviet regime responded by arresting many of the lamas and closing down Buddhist temples and academies in those regions. For a while the Leningrad temple was spared, but in 1933 worship there came to a close, and two years later many of the lamas were arrested and sentenced to hard labor. Dorjiev himself was arrested in Buryatia in 1937 and died in jail a few months later. Meanwhile all the remaining lamas at the temple were arrested and the whole complex was taken over by the state. The furnishings were placed in the anti-religious museum in the former Kazan Cathedral on Nevsky Prospect. Subsequently the temple became a youth physical training center, then a radio station during the Second World War, and finally an experimental laboratory for the Institute of Zoology.

It was not until 1990, after the Gorbachev reforms, that the temple went back to being a place of worship and underwent a thorough restoration. By that time there was again a sizeable Buddhist community in the city (now called by its original name of St. Petersburg), which included Russian converts as well as native Buddhists. "Today," Alexander Andreyev writes, "the Saint Petersburg Datsan is not just a place of worship but also a popular Buddhist educational center . . . A group of ten Buryat lamas resides permanently at the temple . . . Also there are some astrologers and a specialist in Tibetan medicine available for the needs of the community."[7]

Thus the datsan has again become, as Lama Dorjiev intended, a vibrant spiritual center in the Tibetan Buddhist tradition.

THE RED ROSICRUCIANS

Turning to the world of esoteric orders, it is striking how many of these were active until the latter part of the 1930s. In those years, before the Stalinist screw tightened in earnest, Russia must have seemed to many people like a huge laboratory of ideas, where all kinds of exciting experiments in alternative forms of spirituality were going on. This was a brief window of opportunity between the lifting of the Orthodox Church's censorship powers after 1905 and the onset of the Stalinist repression. Ironically, the best source of information on the esoteric scene at that time is found in the archives of the security police, which were carefully sifted by the historian Andrey Nikitin (1935–2005), whose work I have quoted a number of times.

One particularly surprising fact is that in the 1920s the film director Sergei Eisenstein (1898–1948) was a member of a Rosicrucian lodge in Minsk called the Stella.[8] This does not at all fit the usual image of Eisenstein, star director under Stalin and the maker of such propaganda masterpieces as *Alexander Nevsky, Ivan the Terrible,* and *The Battleship Potemkin.* Yet the evidence is indisputable. Eisenstein mentions his membership of this lodge in his memoirs, and he is shown with other members in a photograph taken in 1920 during the Civil War, in which Eisenstein fought on the Red side. The photograph was auctioned in 2019 by the Moscow auction house Twelfth Chair.[9] In the auction catalogue the men in the picture, apart from Eisenstein, are identified as the actor Ivan Frolovich Smolin, the poet Boris Lvovich Pletner, the writer and orientalist Pavel Antonovich Arensky, and the poet and sculptor Boris Mikhailovich Zubakin, who was the founder of the lodge. All are wearing the uniform of the Red Army, except for Zubakin, who is wearing a white robe, stole, and crucifix. The group is seated around a kind of altar upon which are some roses and a bishop's miter. In the background is a banner featuring a hexagram surrounding what looks like the Hebrew letter *yod*.

Fig. 3.1. Sergei Eisenstein (far right) with members of the Stella Rosicrucian lodge in Minsk. Eisenstein later became a star film director under Stalin.

Photograph courtesy of Twelfth Chair Auction House, Moscow

Boris Zubakin (1894–1938) was a colorful character who called himself Bishop Bogori the Second. Eisenstein, in a letter to his mother, called Zubakin "the wandering Archbishop of the Order of the Knights of the Spirit" and described him as "a highly unusual person" who "sees the astral body of everyone and can utter a person's most secret thoughts."[10] The use of the term "astral body" reveals the theosophical influence on Zubakin. The Stella lodge was a revival of the Astra lodge, created by Zubakin back in 1913 in Petrograd. Eisenstein later wrote:

> I shall never forget the venue of the lodge in Minsk. We arrived there, a small group of people . . . The actor Smolin, from a traveling, front-line troupe, stands at the door strumming a balalaika . . . And here, dressed in a white shirt over his uniform, the lanky anarchist [Pletner] strikes three times with a rod and announces: "Bishop Borogi is ready to receive us."

The account goes on:

> There is feet-washing by the consecrated hands of the Bishop himself. He wears a strange brocade miter . . . Some words are spoken. And now, arm in arm, we go past the mirror, which sends a message from our gathering to the astral plane. The balalaika by the door is replaced by an accordion. The Red Army soldiers are already more cheerful. It was waiting for dinner that had made them sad.[11]

Apart from the fact of Eisenstein's inclusion, another striking thing about the group in the photograph is that the four soldiers are all members of the Red Army, when one might have expected members of a Rosicrucian order at that time to be traditionally minded and therefore on the side of the Whites. But it must be remembered that, in conservative and traditional milieux such as the French Catholic or

Russian Orthodox right, freemasonry, Rosicrucianism, and other such forms of alternative spirituality tended to be seen as radical and subversive. By the same token, the Masons and Rosicrucians and their ilk, with certain notable exceptions, would have been quite likely to see themselves on the left side of the political spectrum. A typical example was the French nineteenth-century occultist Eliphas Lévi, who saw himself as a socialist and was twice imprisoned as a dangerous revolutionary. Thus in the early phase of the Russian Revolution men such as the members of the Stella lodge would have hoped that a Red victory would usher in a New Age of spiritual plurality and freedom.

At the beginning of 1920, the lodge moved to Moscow, where it was joined by the theatrical director Valentin Smyshlyaev, the actors Mikhail Chekhov and Yuri Zavadsky, and others. However, soon the knights quarreled with Zubakin and in 1929 expelled him, after which the lodge dwindled to a small handful of the faithful. In 1937, Zubakin was arrested and executed. Smolin and Arensky died in 1938 and 1941 respectively, so it seems likely that they were also killed in the Stalinist terror.[12]

The photograph came from the legacy of the historian Andrei Nikitin, and thereby hangs a tale. He was the son of the theatrical artist Leonid Alexandrovich Nikitin (1896–1942) and his wife Vera (1897–1976). Both parents were members of a group in Moscow called the Order of the Light. This led to their arrest in 1931 on the charge of belonging to an anarcho-mystical organization and conducting anti-Soviet activities. They were released in 1934 and their son Andrei was born in 1935. They lived for a time in Tver and then in Zagorsk. In 1940, Leonid Nikitin was again arrested on the same charge as before and died in custody. After the death of Stalin, mother and son moved back to Moscow, where Andrei graduated from the History Department of Moscow State University.[13] His books are a priceless source of information on the esoteric movements of the early revolutionary period.

What was the Order of the Light and what was anarcho-mysticism? The term seems like a contradiction, but perhaps not if one defines anarchism according to one of its leading exponents, Prince Pyotr Alexeyevich Kropotkin (1842–1921), who believed in an open, decentralized communist society based on self-governing communities and in which enterprises would be worker run. Kropotkin spent half his life in exile but returned to Russia in 1917. Initially he welcomed the revolution but then grew critical of the increasingly centralized form of communism that emerged. He died in 1924, and his old family home in Moscow was turned into a museum in his memory, which became a favorite meeting place for anarchists and anarcho-mystics.*

Anarcho-mysticism was a New Age movement avant la lettre, a heady mixture of revolutionary politics, alternative history, freemasonry, theosophy, anthroposophy, neo-gnosticism, and neo-Templarism. Its main spokesman was the writer and poet Georgy Chulkov. He in turn drew his theory from Vyacheslav Ivanov's philosophy of *sobornost'*— the mystical togetherness of the people. Another leading proponent of anarcho-mysticism was Apollon Karelin (1863–1926), nicknamed "the Beard" because of his abundant facial hair, which was rivaled only by that of his fellow anarchist Kropotkin. Like Kropotkin he had spent much of his life in exile and in Paris had become a Freemason. After returning to Russia he joined the revolutionary assembly, the All-Russian Central Executive Committee, and in parallel played a prominent role in the anarcho-mystic movement. In 1920 he founded the Order of the Templars. The religious basis of the order was a gnostic type of Christianity. It had a system of "chivalric" degrees and set its members two main aims: first, to work on oneself as a way of serving society and humanity; and second, to combine mystical and scientific knowledge.[14]

The Order of the Templars gave rise to a number of offshoots including the Order of Light and the Temple of the Arts, both based

---

*The museum was closed in 1939 on the orders of Stalin, for whom anarcho-mysticism was clearly a thorn in the flesh.

in Moscow, and the Order of the Spirit, based in Nizhny Novgorod. The Order of Light, which was open to both sexes, was founded by the mathematician, poet, and philosopher Alexei Alexandrovich Solonovich (1888–1937). According to the information recorded by the OGPU secret police, the members of the order called themselves knights, and there were ten degrees with appropriate initiation rituals. The symbol of the order consisted of a blue seven-pointed star and a white rose. When a new candidate was admitted there would be a rose lying on a table, while the senior members would each be holding a rose in the hand. The order aimed "to combat the evil powers such as Ialdabaoth."[15]

The OGPU reporter clearly did not know that the figure of Ialdabaoth was taken from Gnosticism, a dualistic religion going back to antiquity, which held that the world we live in is a kind of prison, created by a mischievous god, the Demiurge, to keep us separated from the true spiritual world above with the help of seven beings called archons, the chief archon being Ialdabaoth.

Thus Solonovich, who had become bitterly opposed to the direction that the revolution had taken, saw the tumultuous events of his time as being the manifestation of a cosmic struggle between godly and demonic forces. In his unpublished book *Bakunin and the Cult of Ialdabaoth* he wrote that the Bolsheviks were possessed by the demon of power.

The principle of power has been injected into humanity as a disease similar to syphilis. It is necessary . . . to fight mercilessly against this madness, because the tracks of Ialdabaoth are crawling with larvae, and demonic filth pollutes the souls of people and their lives. . . . Among the most powerful fanatics of power, for whom the end justifies the means, we find Ivan IV, Philip II, Loyola, Torquemada, Lenin, Marx and others. All of them were under the direct control of the angels of Ialdabaoth in one form or another.[16]

Given Solonovich's implacable opposition to the regime, it was inevitable that he would become yet another victim. The order was liquidated in 1930 by the OGPU, and Solonovich, after repeated arrests, died in custody in 1937 having gone on hunger strike.[17]

SAMIZDAT OCCULTISM

By about 1941 the whole alternative spiritual scene in Russia was in ruins, its groups forbidden, untold numbers of its followers executed or imprisoned. One might have thought that it would never recover. But the Russians are nothing if not resilient. After Stalin's death in 1953 new shoots began to appear cautiously, as after a prairie fire. Those who had managed to survive the terror started to pick up the old threads again, and a new generation of seekers emerged. They drew their information partly from classics of western esotericism that had survived in public libraries or private collections and partly from *samizdat* editions of esoteric texts. At first these seekers kept a low profile, pursuing their paths alone or meeting cautiously in libraries or apartments, but from about the late 1960s they grew bolder, and numerous occult and mystical groups and gurus of one kind or another appeared in Moscow, Leningrad, and other cities. Along with meditational practices, there was a certain amount of experimentation with psychedelic drugs. There was also a good deal of synergy with members of the Russian diaspora in other countries in the form of unofficial contacts and the smuggling of esoteric material published by Russian communities abroad.

Once again the names of Blavatsky, Steiner, Roerich, Ouspensky, and Gurdjieff were bandied about in the occult underground along with their writings. The Gurdjieff movement, for example, enjoyed a strong revival. Gurdjieffian system activists came back from the labor camps or their hiding places and began to teach "the Work," as it was called, to a new audience, who included a number of prominent people in the cultural scene such as the writer Arkadii Rovner, the philologist Mikhail Meilakh, and the musician Boris Grebenshchikov (b. 1953). These people spread Gurdjieff's influence further. There was an equally strong revival of interest in eastern spiritual traditions such as Hinduism and Buddhism, helped by the acceptance of these as legitimate areas of study within the academic establishment. Ironically, a favorite meeting place in Leningrad for people in search of esoteric or mystical knowledge was the Museum of the History of Religion and Atheism. There they could have access to abundant literature, forbidden elsewhere, as well the opportunity to meet kindred spirits.[18]

At the same time there was an area of science bordering on the occult that was at various times officially sanctioned, namely research into the paranormal. There was a history of such research in Russia going back to the 1870s when a commission was convened to investigate spiritualism, headed by the distinguished chemist Prof. Dmitri Mendeleev, who first developed the periodic table of the elements. The commission concluded that spiritualism was a form of superstition, but the debate between the skeptics and the believers still continued. In the decades before and after the turn of the century a number of clairvoyants and mediums were busy communicating with the spirits in Russian.[19]

The potential political use of the paranormal became obvious to anyone who read Gustave Le Bon's *Psychology of Crowds* (1895), published in Russian in 1896. Le Bon's ideas on mass hypnosis impressed the author Maxim Gorky, and it may have been Gorky who drew the attention of Lenin and Stalin to the work. At any rate, Le Bon's book is said to have been included among Stalin's favorite reading. It also influenced Mussolini, among other political figures.[20]

After the revolution the Institute of Brain Research in St. Petersburg set up a commission to study mental suggestion. One of its first tests involved a dog, a fox terrier named Pikki. As the parapsychology expert Guy Lyon Playfair writes:

He was the star performer in his owner Vladimir Durov's circus shows, in which Durov seemed to be controlling his dogs not only by the ultrasonic whistle he used, but also by his mind. At Durov's suggestion, the psychologist Vladimir Bekhterev carried out a number of experiments with Pikki (without the whistle), which left him in no doubt that the dog was indeed responding to unspoken orders, as if his consciousness had blended with that of his owner.[21]

In the 1920s there were various groups in both Leningrad and Moscow conducting research into such things as telepathy and the transmission of thoughts and energy. One of these groups was operating in Moscow under the auspices of the security apparatus, the OGPU, and its researchers included Alexander Barchenko, whom we have already encountered in connection with his Hyperborean expedition and his study of the Kalachakra Tantra.

One group within the esoteric community that managed to remain active under the Bolsheviks for a surprisingly long time were the astrologers. In 1929 they held a congress in Moscow, but it was to prove a fateful event. Immediately afterward nearly all the participants were arrested, putting an end to the practice of astrology in Russia for many decades. One of the few (possibly the only one) who escaped arrest was one Sergei Vronsky (1915–1998), an extraordinary and enigmatic figure whose turbulent life deserves a closer look.[22]

RUSSIAN NOSTRADAMUS

Count Sergei Vronksy, to give him his rightful title, was born in Riga, Latvia, in 1915. His father, Alexei, was a general in the Russian army and of Polish aristocratic descent. After the Russian Revolution Alexei worked as a cryptographer for the Russian general staff. In 1923 the family wished to emigrate and received written permission from Lenin to do so, but on the day before their planned departure a troop of the

OGPU secret police arrived at the house and shot Sergei's parents and sister and the five-year-old son of the family's French governess. Evidently they were acting on the orders of the St. Petersburg OGPU chief, Gleb Bokii, who has already been mentioned in connection with the esoteric research of Alexander Barchenko. Bokii must have felt that Alexei knew too much about the military codes. By a stroke of luck Sergei and the governess were out in the garden and so escaped the massacre. It was the first of many narrow escapes that he was to experience in his life.

For a time he lived in Paris with his governess but then was taken under the wing of his maternal grandmother and went to live with her back in Riga. His grandmother, a princess from Montenegro, came from a family of clairvoyants, healers, hypnotists, chiromancers, astrologers, and magicians, and she herself was well versed in these arts and passed them on to her grandson. Early on he became the epitome of the renaissance individual—mastering many languages and various musical instruments, shining academically, and excelling at sports. At seven he was already casting horoscopes for school friends.

At seventeen he graduated with distinction from an aviation academy in Austria and then made his way to Berlin just after Hitler had come to power. There he was chosen for a coveted place at a secretive college run by the Nazis called *Lehranstalt Nr. 25* (Teaching Institute 25), which appears to have been for the teaching of various alternative and exotic healing methods. Each new student had their horoscope cast. The course involved a good deal of foreign travel, and the teaching staff included Tibetan lamas, Indian yogis, and Chinese acupuncturists. Soon Vronsky was hobnobbing with Nazi top brass and also with other astrologers working in Berlin at that time, including Louis de Wohl, who later fled to England, and Karl Ernst Krafft, the quasi-official astrologer of the regime. Astonishingly, in view of what his family had suffered, he secretly joined the Communist Party and soon after his arrival in Germany he began spying for the Soviets, even making a couple of secret trips back to Russia.

Soon his astrological expertise brought him to the attention of the Deputy Führer Rudolf Hess, who became a friend and whom he taught how to cast horoscopes. Together they scrutinized what the stars predicted for the invasion of Russia that Hitler was contemplating. The answer was clear: a disaster for Germany. In May 1941 Hess made his famous flight to Scotland in an attempt to negotiate a peace. Hitler, enraged, ordered a mass roundup of astrologers, but Vronsky somehow escaped arrest. Just over a month later, Germany invaded Russia.

Things were now becoming increasingly risky for Vronsky in Germany, and the following year he got word from Russia that if he returned there, he would receive an honor from the state. He therefore took a bold and extremely risky step. Armed with a diplomatic pass, he travelled to Latvia, made his way to an airfield, and there hijacked a light aircraft by hypnotizing the air force personnel. He then flew over the battle front into Russia, where he was shot down and dragged from the blazing airplane by Russian soldiers. His life hanging by a thread, he was taken to a military hospital where he had the luck to be operated on by a distinguished surgeon named Nikolai Nilowitsch Burdenko, who saved his life.

The expected honor never came. After the Soviet occupation of Latvia he worked for a time in civil aviation and then as director of a school, before being denounced, arrested, and sentenced to twenty-five years in a labor camp, from which he was released after five years because of ill health. In 1963 he resettled illegally in Moscow, where he moved in Bohemian circles and became increasingly popular as a healer and astrologer. Despite periodic difficulties with the authorities, he gradually gained more official recognition. He traveled with the astronaut Yuri Gagarin to the United States where he met Jack and Bobby Kennedy and predicted a tragic death for them and Marilyn Monroe. Despite the official rejection of astrology, there were those in the upper echelons who valued it, including Yuri Andropov, for whom Vronsky cast a horoscope when Andropov became General Secretary in 1982.

None of this made Vronsky rich, and his last years were marked by hardship. Nevertheless he was never idle and produced a number of books including an encyclopedia of astrology. In 1990 a remarkable interview with him was recorded in his Moscow flat, conducted by Christian Borup with Farida Assadulina as interpreter.[23] In the conversation he revealed himself to be a charming, sprightly man and a fascinating raconteur.

He lived until 1998, long enough to see his books widely read and astrology firmly established in Russia with centers like the St. Petersburg Astrological Academy.

PARAPSYCHOLOGISTS, HIPPIES, AND PATRIOTS

In 1937 something happened to cause a U-turn in the official attitude toward research in the field of the paranormal. Perhaps the authorities realized that the research could be a two-edged sword and that the mysterious energies that were being investigated could be turned against the regime. Whatever the reason, virtually all the programs in this field were suddenly shut down and remained in deep freeze for about twenty years. Then in the late 1950s research in this area was resumed, and in the early 1960s it received a new impetus when the Russian Minister of Defense learned about US experiments in the military use of telepathy.[24]

One famous case of the paranormal in the 1960s involved a woman called Nina Kulagina, who discovered she had the power of psychokinesis—the ability to move objects around without touching them, using mental energy. She could cause a ping-pong ball to float in the air or a watch or a matchbox to slide across a table. These sessions were a great physical strain for her, causing sweating, headaches, and a high pulse rate. She was tested many times to see if there was trickery involved, but none was ever found.

As Birgit Menzel writes in an article on occult and esoteric movements in Russia:

According to Marxist-Leninist ideology the humanities were defined as part of the sciences, and their borders were much less strictly defined than in the West so that—paradoxically—phenomena excluded from the Western scientific paradigm were studied and supported within the Soviet academic system. . . . Medicine, physics, and parapsychology mingled and opened new fields of research. All this, together with an unprecedented optimism on conquering nature and the cosmos under conditions of the Cold War, led to a highly paradoxical relationship between politics, science, religion, and the occult.[25]

A psychic who straddled the Soviet and post-Soviet eras was Yevgenia Yuvashevna Davidashvili (1949–2015), who operated under the name of Djuna. Unlike the homely Nina Kulagina, Djuna was a glamorous woman of strong charisma. Born into a family of Assyrian descent in the Krasnodarsk region next to the Black Sea, she became famous as a healer, astrologer, and clairvoyant. During the Soviet era she treated many prominent people including Leonid Brezhnev and the film director Andrey Tarkovsky and took part in officially approved experiments into paranormal phenomena. In postcommunist Russia she became even more of a celebrity, but in 2001 was shattered by the death of her son and remained a recluse until her own death in 2015.[26]

The era of Leonid Brezhnev as leader of the Soviet Union (1964–1982) brought renewed restrictions on the alternative spiritual milieu. Facing the danger of incarceration or enforced treatment in a psychiatric hospital, its members once again turned inward, pursuing their paths alone or in secret or semisecret groups. Typical of this era was the treatment of the writer Alexander Solzhenitsyn (1918–2008). Under Khrushchev he had been able to publish his novel *One Day in the Life of Ivan Denisovich* (1962), which caused a sensation in the Soviet Union by exposing the horrors of the Stalinist Gulag system. His next three books were *Cancer Ward* (1968), *August 1914* (1971), and

The Gulag Archipelago (1973), all of which he had to publish abroad because of the Brezhnev freeze. The authorities were outraged by these works, and in 1974 he lost his Soviet citizenship and was expelled from the country. Via Germany and Switzerland he moved with his family to the United States and settled in Vermont, where he lived until 1994 when he was able to return to Russia.

Paradoxically the Brezhnev era saw the emergence of a hippie movement in Russia. Over in the west, especially in the United States, the movement was in full swing by the late 1960s with its flower power, love-ins, communes, gurus, pop festivals, and antiwar demonstrations. The laid-back American hippies, with their long hair and loose-fitting clothes, soon found their imitators in Russia and eastern Europe, albeit in much smaller numbers. In the Soviet atmosphere of Orwellian conformism, being a hippie was an earnest and often dangerous business and required courage and commitment. Followers called themselves the *Sistema* (System), a curious name for a countercultural movement.

In an article on Russian hippiedom and the Tolstoy movement, Irina Gordeeva writes:

> The driving force behind this phenomenon was a protest against Soviet reality. In many respects, it was a generational, aesthetic, and anti-authoritarian protest that manifested itself in alienation and—often—in the self-destructive practices of "negative freedom" (drug addiction, alcoholism, suicidal tendencies, and contacts with criminals). Unfortunately, the cost of such behavior was high, and included sojourns in mental hospitals, early deaths, ruined family lives, etc.[27]

Over time these hippies underwent a transformation. Rejecting the Marxist orthodoxy of their upbringing, they became nihilists and *enfants terribles,* but at the same time they were driven by a passionate search for deeper meaning and more lasting values. Many of them found their way to the Orthodox Church and some became ordained. Others turned to alternative religious milieux such as the Tolstoy movement. In the process of their search they became phenomenal autodidacts. One veteran of that era, Andrei Madison, related to Irina Gordeeva that over the 1970s and '80s his reading included Tolstoy, Lao Tse, Confucius, Krishnamurti, Vivekananda, Wilfredo Pareto, Theodor Adorno, Nikolai Berdyaev, Sergei Bulgakov, Vasily Rozanov, Konstantin Leontiev, Mikhail Bakunin, Abby Hoffman, Jerry Rubin, Novalis, Jean Paul, Alexander Solzhenitsyn, Friedrich Nietzsche, Oswald Spengler, Henry Thoreau, and Ken Kesey.[28]

One of the more radical groups of this era was the Iuzhinsky Circle in Moscow, named after the address of their initial venue, the small apartment of the poet and novelist Yuri Mamleev, author of a novel entitled *The Sublimes,* a morbid story of violence and depravity, which has somehow become a cult work. The members of the circle eagerly devoured anything they could get hold of on occult and esoteric subjects. In 1978 the building was demolished, and the circle moved elsewhere. Mamleev had left the country in 1974, only to return after the collapse of communism. After his departure the circle was continued by the poet Yevgeny Golovin, the Islamist Geydar Dzhemal and the Gurdjieffian Vladimir Stepanov. The group continued to pursue occult and esoteric themes, but now leaned toward conservative thinkers like the Italian Julius Evola.

They also flirted with the symbolism and vocabulary of the Third Reich and the SS, even to the extent of adopting German-sounding pseudonyms and titles. Their aim was to shock the establishment, and flaunting the trappings of Russia's deadly enemy in the Second World War was an effective way of doing so. They were like rebellious adolescents using words forbidden by their parents. It was a phase that most of them grew out of in due course.

In addition they practiced various "extreme experiences" designed to raise the participants above everyday consciousness. These included orgies and the drinking of much alcohol.[29] One of the members in the early 1980s was Alexander Dugin, now famous as a conservative philosopher and an influential figure in Putin's Russia, to whom I shall return later.

Meanwhile the plight of the Orthodox Church continued to worsen, as both Khrushchev and Brezhnev pursued an antireligious policy, leading to further wholesale closures of churches. Those denied the ability to attend Christian worship found various forms of ersatz religion. One obvious example was the cult of Lenin. Visiting his tomb in Red Square in 1992 was like visiting the shrine of a saint. I was required to remove my hat at the entrance before processing through the dim inner sanctum, where Lenin's embalmed, spotlit body lay, watched over by uniformed guards standing at attention. Then there is the cult surrounding the memory of the Second World War, the "Great Patriotic War," as it is called in Russia.

An interesting insight into these cults and into the bleak religious scene in the early 1970s is provided by Colin Thubron in his book *Among the Russians,* describing a journey by car through Russia and neighboring countries. At one point Thubron encountered a dissident called Nikolai who told him: "The old women take to God, the men take to drink . . . Unfortunately it's easier to find a bottle of vodka than a church in Moscow."[30] He went on to say: "In my own lifetime I've seen an enormous growth of nationalistic ritual. These cults were very big during the war; then they faded, but now they're returning. They're like an attempt to replace Christian ceremonial. War memorials, you know, are our national altars."[31]

Describing these memorials, Thubron writes:

The countryside bristles with memorials, of which many are quite new—tanks and field-guns elevated on concrete plinths, mounds and circles of glory, eternal flames, sculptured heroes, obelisks, symbols, epitaphs. In every city callow-looking cadets of Komsomol stand guard in twenty-minute shifts at the monuments of a war which even their fathers are too young to remember . . . These are the points of sanctity which married couples visit after their weddings. Shivering with cold, the thin-clad bride lays her bouquet at the shrine; the pair poses for a ritual photograph, lingers awhile as if something else might happen, then drifts away.[32]

Part of the iconography of these memorials is a colossal Amazon-like figure, proudly brandishing a sword—the personification of *rodina*, the motherland. Interestingly, the Russians have two words for the native country, the other being *otechestvo*, the fatherland. But it is the *rodina* that really stirs their hearts. Not being able to eliminate her, the communists tried to enlist her for their cause. Nationalism was a genie that was released temporarily, put back, and then released again when the regime realized that the genie could not be bottled up. By the mid-1960s, among those clamoring for change the nationalists were

Fig. 3.2. A postage stamp from 1971 commemorating the Battle of Stalingrad and depicting the statue of Mat' Rodina (Mother Homeland) in Volgograd
WIKIMEDIA COMMONS

increasingly at odds with the faction who favored internationalism and reform along western liberal lines. The Brezhnev regime, while coming down heavily on the liberal reformers, decided to make concessions to the nationalists in the hope of containing them.

The first such concession was when the Kremlin in 1965 approved the creation of a new organization called the All-Russian Society for the Preservation of Historic and Cultural Monuments (*vserossiskoe obshchestvo ochrani pamyatnikov istorii i kulturi* or VOOPIK). According to Charles Clover it went beyond its declared purpose and acted as a geopolitical think tank and pressure group, a sort of safety valve devised by the regime to keep the nationalist boiler from exploding.[33] Today VOOPIK still exists and has a website. A message from the honorary president, Galina Malanicheva, states: "In saving churches, estates, documents, we preserve something more than just walls, decoration, monuments of material culture, we preserve the Russian soul."[34]

This underlines how in Russia the issue of preserving cultural heritage is both a political and a spiritual issue. After all, it has been painfully brought home to the Russians how precarious and fragile that heritage is. They saw the dynamiting of beautiful churches like the Cathedral of Christ the Savior in Moscow (since rebuilt), the desecration of the St. Petersburg Buddhist temple, the vandalization of country houses and landscape gardens. These acts were politically motivated, and the effort to prevent their repetition is therefore also political—but it is also spiritual in a way that is more obvious than in other countries. Supporters of the British National Trust, for example, do not talk about "saving the British soul" when they campaign for the preservation of old buildings—although here they might learn something from the Russians.

By the early 1970s the nationalist faction was firmly entrenched in upper echelons of the communist establishment, to the chagrin of the orthodox Marxists, and the ideological division between the two sides was becoming ever clearer. Clover relates how in 1972 a champion of the traditional communist faction and bureaucrat of the Central Committee, Alexander Yakovlev, published an attack on the nationalists in the newspaper *Literaturnaya Gazeta* (Literary Gazette). Yakovlev put his finger on a fundamental question: Is the world composed of individual peoples, each with its special characteristics and its own destiny, as the nationalists maintained? Or is humanity one homogeneous mass progressing through history according to the laws discovered by Marx and Engels? Yakovlev of course took the latter position. The nationalists were outraged by the article, and in the ensuing row Yakovlev lost his position with the Central Committee and was subjected to a relatively benign exile as ambassador to Canada.[35] Later he became a key supporter of Gorbachev's reforms.

The dispute raised by Yakovlev might seem highly abstract, but in fact it had very concrete implications, depending on which side one took. Only a year earlier the samizdat journal *Veche* had published an article lamenting an ugly high-rise development in typical Soviet style that cut through the charming old Arbat district of Moscow.[36] To the Marxists this development was simply a case of progress taking precedence over nostalgia. To its opponents, it was another blow struck at the soul of old Russia.

 **FOUR**

A House of Rumor

A thorough-fare of news: where some devise
Things never heard, some mingle truth with lies;
The troubled air with empty sounds they beat,
Intent to hear, and eager to repeat.
Error sits brooding there, with added train
Of vain credulity, and joys as vain:
Suspicion, with sedition join'd, are near,
And rumours rais'd, and murmurs mix'd,
        and panique fear.

THE HOUSE OF FAME (GODDESS OF RUMOR)
IN OVID'S *METAMORPHOSES*, BOOK 12

As Charles Clover writes, "Russia has always had the dubious distinction of being the conspiracy capital of the world."[1]

This was especially true in the tense period from perestroika through the chaotic aftermath of the collapse of communism, when the country became like the House of Fame, or Rumor, in Ovid's *Metamorphoses,* or like a hall of distorting mirrors, a place of disinformation, confusion, plots and counter-plots, false flags—a topsy-turvy place where often left was right and up was down. The atmosphere was highly conducive to conspiracy theories and to real conspiracies.

At times of uncertainty, turmoil, and hardship it is tempting to believe that events are being steered by a hidden hand with its own agenda, often seen as having an occult or esoteric dimension. And at the same time such an era breeds actual conspiracies. When public institutions are in turmoil, taking part in a secret or semisecret plot can bring a sense of empowerment.

One of the more sinister phenomena to emerge at this period was the Pamyat movement (from the Russian word for "memory"), both a conspiracy and a purveyor of conspiracy theories, which appeared toward the end of the 1970s. Pamyat was not so much a single organization as a cluster of several different groups, using the Pamyat label and generally marked by a militaristic, nationalistic image and an anti-Semitic and anti-Masonic outlook. They included: the Worldwide Anti-Zionist and Anti-Masonic Front "Pamyat"; the National Patriotic Front "Pamyat"; and the Historic-Patriotic Union "Pamyat." In addition there were many other organizations broadly sharing the aims and outlook of the Pamyat groups.[2]

The Pamyat movement included some distinctly unsavory characters such as Konstantin Smirnov-Ostashvili, who in 1990 led an attack on a meeting at the Central House of Writers in Moscow, at which the journalist and author Anatoli Kurchatkin was beaten up. After the attack Smirnov-Ostashvili was sentenced to two years in a labor camp, where he was found hanged shortly before he was due to be released. Whether it was suicide or murder remains unclear. What also remains unclear is who was really behind the Pamyat. Charles Clover quotes an interview in 1997 with Gorbachev's right-hand man, Alexander Yakovlev, who was convinced that the KGB created the Pamyat to take some steam out of the dissident movement but then lost control over their creation and thus gave birth to Russian fascism.[3]

The Pamyat phenomenon had largely petered out by around 2010, but at least one branch of it is still active at the time of writing, namely the National Patriotic Front "Pamyat," which describes itself as "an Orthodox monarchical national movement of loyal citizens of the Russian State, united by a single spiritual discipline based on Orthodox identity, with the aim of serving the Lord God, the sacred purity of the Russian throne and our historically based national interests."[4] While the Pamyat may no longer be the force that it once was, this mixture of Orthodoxy, monarchism, nationalism, and traditionalism is one that evidently still appeals to many Russians.

It is a mixture that has led to strange bedfellows, as in August 1991, when nationalists and traditionalists made common cause with the revanchists in the military, who attempted to seize power while President Gorbachev was under house arrest and incommunicado at his dacha for three days. But was it really house arrest? Some maintain that he was cannily waiting on the sidelines to see which way the coup would go, and that if the plotters had won, he would simply have returned to the Kremlin and resumed his presidential duties, which is what he did when the coup failed.

One senior army officer who would probably have been in sympathy with the plotters was Major General Konstantin Petrov, who at the time was working at the army space program base at Krasnoznamensk in Moscow province but a safe distance from the capital. Subsequently Petrov entered politics, founded a highly conservative political party, and became a proponent of an extravagant conspiracy theory, targeting a secret world mafia that he called the "Global Predictor." The party managed to win 1.17 per cent of the votes but failed to gain any seats and was eventually deregistered by the Ministry of Justice. Petrov's activities became an embarrassment for the army, which dismissed him, but he continued his campaign undeterred. He could be seen preaching his message through internet podcast videos, a squat, elderly, bald-headed man, still wearing his general's uniform. But at the same time he had a very different persona as a neo-pagan priest, known to his followers as Magus Meragor. In this role he featured in neo-pagan rituals, dressed in a robe and brandishing a long staff like some Russian

Gandalf. In 2009, shortly after founding a new political party, Petrov died of cancer and was buried with military honors. The movement he started still continues on a small scale.[5]

WAR OF THE CONTINENTS

Many questions remain from the failed coup of 1991, such as why the conspirators were dealt with so leniently. The leaders were put on trial but soon acquitted, and most of those involved were able to quickly resume their normal lives. One of them was a prominent journalist, writer, and publisher called Alexander Prokhanov, who had close ties to the military and had spent some time covering the war in Afghanistan. In 1990 he had founded a new journal called *Den* (*Day*) as a conservative, nationalist rival to the liberal *Literaturnaya Gazeta* (*Literary Gazette*). One of its star writers was Alexander Dugin, who caused a sensation with his February 1991 article "The Great War of the Continents," the precursor to his later best-selling book *The Foundations of Geopolitics* (1997).[6] In the article he acknowledged his debt to three pioneers in the study of geopolitics, namely the Swede Rudolf Kjellén (1864–1922), who originally coined the term, the British geographer Sir Halford Mackinder (1861–1947), and the German Karl Haushofer (1869–1946).

What Dugin presented was the mother of all conspiracy theories. The Cold War, he said, was not simply a conflict between the communist and the capitalist worlds but something much deeper and more esoteric. He posited a "planetary 'conspiracy' of two opposing 'occult' forces, whose secret opposition and invisible struggle have determined the logic of world history." These forces, he explained, "are characterized primarily not by national conditions and not by belonging to a secret organization of the Masonic or para-Masonic type, but by a radical difference in their geopolitical orientations."[7] He revealed that the world is divided between two opposing factions in the contest for territorial mastery, namely the "land" faction and the "sea" faction. Entire peoples, nations, and regions are profoundly marked by one modality or the other in regard to their historical consciousness, their foreign and domestic policies, their psychology, and their worldview. The maritime powers, he says, are essentially mercantile, capitalistic societies in which economics takes precedence over politics. In the land powers it is the other way round. Looking back over history, he points to the Punic War as a struggle between a sea power (Carthage) and a land power (Rome), and he goes on to categorize England and the United States of America as sea powers, and the Russian, Austro-Hungarian, and German empires as land powers. He also uses the term "Atlanteanism" and "Eurasianism" to refer to the two sides.

Based on this analysis, he asserts, we can perceive an "Atlantean" strategy on the part of the "New Carthage," that is, England and the United States. This involves a campaign of espionage and political lobbying, and a network of "secret and occult organizations . . . lodges and semi-closed clubs . . . penetrating all continental 'Eurasian' powers."[8] Thus, Dugin writes, one can speak of a historical conspiracy of Atlanteans, pursuing the same political goals over the centuries. This is epic stuff—*Star Wars* with the Atlanteans in the role of the Evil Empire, and here again we see the Russians' propensity to cast themselves in a great drama of mythical dimensions.

Dugin went on to write further articles for *Den*, but in 1993 the newspaper was shut down in the wake of the dramatic events of that year when the Russian President Yeltsin's troops stormed the White House in Moscow, seat of the recalcitrant Parliament. Prokhanov, who had sided with Parliament, went into hiding in a forest for a few months— unnecessarily, as it turned out, as he was not on any wanted list. Shortly afterward he started a similar newspaper called *Zavtra* (*Tomorrow*), which is still going today. In 2011 *Den* was reincarnated as Den-TV, an internet broadcasting channel with a strong conservative and patriotic agenda, as is clear from the mission statement on its website:

Over the past twenty "liberal" years, when the country was destroyed, the potential for development lost and the public consciousness flooded with chimeras, we patriots were able to develop a number of productive ideas for the future. The "Russian idea," which has undergone intensive discussion, will become a blueprint for the country's future revival. The parameters of this idea are clear and comprehensible. Russia should be huge, combining great spaces and numerous people . . . The Russian nation, taking on the main role of management and construction, will openly interact with other peoples and build a single imperial project.[9]

Prokhanov was among the audience at the premiere of a startling play called *Krot* (*The Mole*), which opened at the Theatre on the Boards, Moscow, in October 2019. The play is an allegory of perestroika, which the author and director Sergei Kurginyan regards as a disaster. The "Mole" is a train driver on the Moscow Metro system, but he is also the "mole of history," the force that burrows beneath the surface of events yet can cause tumultuous changes. Speaking about the play to a group of theatergoers, Kurginyan spoke of sinister forces that he saw at work behind perestroika, and the influence of "dark esotericism" on the political elite. He talked of "the colossal betrayal committed by the Soviet creative intelligentsia, which en masse cursed and betrayed what it had previously praised."[10]

Speaking about the play afterward, Prokhanov said:

The Mole tells about how the Kingdom of Heaven left the earth, how it left the Soviet Union. And the removal of the Kingdom of Heaven from the earth, from the Soviet Union, was accompanied by a great mystery of decay and finality . . . there were tears, dramas, curses, different versions of what was happening, heroes of the past were resurrected and heroes of the present died.[11]

FIVE

The New Millennium

When communism collapsed in 1991 it must have seemed to many Russians that the new millennium had arrived nine years ahead of schedule—but what kind of millennium was it to be? Suddenly, instead of the state-imposed Marxist paradigm, there were a thousand different paradigms to choose from, and spiritually hungry people, after the starvation diet of the Soviet years, were faced with an embarrassment of riches. In 1990 Russia passed a law guaranteeing freedom of religion, but this led to new tensions. The Orthodox Church, an immediate beneficiary of the new order, soon became alarmed by the plethora of alternative spiritual movements and New Age cults that were emerging, and this disquiet was shared by secular and anticult factions. Consequently in 1997 a new law on freedom of religion came into force, introducing additional restrictions such as that religious bodies could only be founded by Russian citizens, that they must have a clearly defined religious purpose and must have existed for at least fifteen years in any given region unless affiliated with an already recognized organization. Furthermore the law gave the state the right to dissolve a religious organization under certain circumstances.[1]

Between the various movements themselves there were and are fundamental differences of belief and purpose. Their clientele also varies greatly, ranging from the New Age groupie to the deeply committed seeker. While a serious commitment was indispensable to members of the spiritual counterculture in Soviet times, given the constant danger of harassment and arrest, after perestroika that danger was removed, and dabblers also entered the field. What remained, however, from earlier times was a marked eclecticism—readers and practitioners were still hungry for whatever they could get hold of.

Signs of a thaw in the policy of censorship had begun as early as 1988 with the appearance of newspaper articles dealing in a balanced tone with various aspects of alternative science such as UFOs, yoga, parapsychology, and the like. Somewhat surprisingly, the way was led by *Komsomolskaya Pravda,* and other newspapers followed. Soon there were specialist journals in the esoteric domain, such as *Anomaliia* (Anomaly), *Orakul* (Oracle), *Tainaia Vlast* (Secret Power), *Era Volodeia* (Age of Aquarius), and *Anomalnye Novosti* (Paranormal News). Commensurately, there was a growth in books on similar topics as well as mass media coverage. Star performers began to enter the field, such as the healer Anatoly Kashpirovsky, who performed miracle cures before vast audiences, and the astrologer couple Pavel and Tamara Globa (since divorced), who had a regular television program.[2] Popular singers also joined the esoteric bandwagon, for example Katya Lel, who became an outspoken esotericist, talking about her UFO experiences and conducting interviews with kindred spirits like the conspirologist David Icke and the rock musician turned human rights activist Sacha Stone. Russia's New Age movement had arrived.

Characteristic of the present-day New Age scene in Russia are the esoteric bookshops that have opened in many cities. A typical example is the White Clouds bookshop and cultural center, located in Pokrovka Street in the Basmanny district of Moscow, an area of older buildings that largely survived Soviet redevelopment and now has a slightly frayed but inviting charm. Apart from the language factor, the shop could be one of its kind anywhere in the West. Here you can find not only a wide selection of esoteric and New Age books but also crystals, essential oils, incense, statuettes of Buddha, and much more. There is also a café and a space for lectures and workshops. The lecture program is also much like what one might find in the West. It includes talks on yoga, astrology, numerology, the tarot, alternative healing, and various forms of self-improvement such as how to develop self-confidence or how to improve one's effectiveness and earning power. The lecturers who have spoken at the shop include Nikolai Zhuravlev, who has written books on the tarot, magic, and the runes, Alexander Kolesnikov, a prolific author on astrology, and Helena Stoll, who has spoken on "Vedic numerology."

The same eclectic range is also found in the publications for sale. As one would expect, there are Russian translations of esoteric books by authors familiar in the West such as A. E. Waite, Helena Blavatsky, Paul Brunton, and G. I. Gurdjieff. Authors from the east are also much in evidence, including the Dalai Lama, Sai Baba, and Osho (alias Baghwan Rajneesh)—the last-named has a huge number of titles for sale, reflecting the strong following that Osho's teachings have in Russia and the former Soviet bloc countries. Also for sale are the works of Nikolai and Helena Roerich dealing with Shambhala and their doctrine of agni yoga, as well as those of another home-grown guru, Lev Klykov, author of titles such as *The Human Being in a World of Love, The Human Spirit,* and *A Message to Humanity.* Klykov (born 1934) stares out from the covers looking like the classic rustic sage with his flowing white hair and beard, haggard face, and somewhat melancholy eyes. The teaching he propounds is called Unified Knowledge (*yedino znanie*). Its message is essentially that the present world, with its destructive culture, is dying, and God is creating a new one in which we can take our place with the right spiritual preparedness. The millenarian notion that we are passing from one world or age to another has, as we have seen, a long tradition in Russia. Hence it is not surprising that the term *perekhod* (transition) is much used by Russian New Agers, commensurate with the popularity of notions such as the Age of Aquarius or Crowley's Age of Horus.

A St. Petersburg counterpart to the White Clouds is the Roza Mira bookshop in Sadovaya Street in the heart of the city. The name of the shop refers to Daniil Andreev's visionary work *Roza Mira* (*Rose of the World*), a cult New Age classic in Russia, of which more will be said in a later chapter.

RUSSIA AND THE AEON OF HORUS

Another name that is increasingly heard in Russian esoteric circles is that of the British magician Aleister Crowley (1875–1947).[3] All of Crowley's major works have been published in Russian, including his classic *Magick in Theory and Practice* and his channeled gospel *The Book of the Law*. His religion of Thelema, based on his Rabelaisian doctrine of "Do what thou wilt shall be the whole of the law" has had a foothold in Russia since 2000 when his magical order, the Ordo Templi Orientis (Order of Templars of the Orient, OTO), established its first so-called Caliphate (leadership) on Russian soil.

Crowley himself visited Russia in 1897, when he went to St. Petersburg to study the Russian language, as he was at that time considering a diplomatic career. He went again to Russia in 1913, this time to Moscow, as impresario of a violin sextet called the Ragged Ragtime Girls. He was stunned by the beauty of the city, which he vividly describes in his *Confessions:*

> In Moscow, in the summer months, day fades into night, night brightens into day with imperceptible subtlety. There is a spiritual clarity in the air itself which is indescribable. From time to time the bells reinforce the silence with an unearthly music which never jars or tires. The hours stream by so intoxicatingly that the idea of time itself disappears from consciousness.[4]

While in Moscow Crowley paid little attention to recruiting new followers, but the city and the Dionysian spirit of Russia prompted him to write two of his most inspired works: the poem "Hymn to Pan" and the Gnostic Mass, the central ceremony of the OTO and its related organization, the Gnostic Catholic Church (Ecclesia Gnostica Catholica). This was the gift that Russia gave him and that he posthumously reciprocated when his movement came to Russia almost a century later.

In my introduction I quoted Nietzsche's pronouncement that "the strength to will . . . is strongest in Russia," and Crowley would no doubt have seen this as confirmation that Russia was ready for his doctrine of "Do what thou wilt shall be the whole of the law." To some extent the ground had already been prepared by the influence in Russia of thinkers like Arthur Schopenhauer (1788–1860), who perceived the history of the world as being driven by a relentless, amoral, insatiable force of will. Crowley's view was, however, less pessimistic than Schopenhauer's. His injunction to "Do what thou wilt" meant that you should always act according to the will of your authentic, innermost self, which is the same as acting according to the divine will within you. This is a noble ideal but in fact impossible to apply on the level of a nation or community. By giving supremacy to the individual will it leaves out the importance of shared values, customs, and inherited traditions. However, after the soulless dogmas of Marxism, Crowley's Thelema can seem an attractive option for someone thirsty for something vital and life-affirming.

Another key part of Crowley's teaching is his threefold notion of history, taken from Egyptian mythology. First came the age of Isis, the Great Mother, an age of goddess worship, when womanhood was writ large. Then, in about 500 BCE came the age of Osiris, the husband of Isis, which was an age of manhood, fatherhood and the patriarchal religions of Judaism, Christianity, and Islam. This era, it is claimed, came to an end in 1904 when Crowley channeled the *Book of the Law*, marking the beginning of the aeon of Horus, the child, an aeon of life-affirming joy and freedom from the constraints of traditional religion.[5]

Here we are on the familiar territory of the threefold, millenarian pattern going back to the book of Revelation and deeply engrained in the Russian religious mind. Present-day Thelemites have no difficulty in perceiving Russian history since the beginning of the twentieth century in the light of Crowley's doctrine of the eons. For example, on the website of an organization called Omnisophia is the following statement:

> The arrival of the Aeon of Horus will take some centuries, but it is impossible not to be aware of it. This is not something that approaches in soft slippers, without knocking, unnoticed by anyone. Its beginning was marked by world wars and revolutions. The old world began to crumble to pieces right before our eyes, violent and bloody. Yesterday's believers today have destroyed the churches of the god of the Aeon of Osiris, and new religions blossom before our eyes. The world is returning to magic and the conjuring of spirits. New spiritual paths are being sought.[6]

At the time of writing the OTO has branches in Moscow, St. Petersburg, Kaliningrad, Pskov, Tomsk, Voronezh, and Nizhny Novgorod. Stanislav Panin, in a scholarly thesis on Thelema in Russia, writing in 2010, says that the OTO is numerically not very strong, with a core membership that can be counted in the tens rather than hundreds. Relations between groups are often marked by tension, conflict, rivalries, and secessions.[7] Nevertheless the OTO and similar organizations as well as unaffiliated people interested in Crowley's ideas are making a significant contribution to modern Russian culture through publishing, lectures, and not least through the internet.

NEW AGERS AND TRADITIONALISTS

Common to most of the -isms and -ologies described so far is an optimistic attitude that says: we are entering a new and more spiritually enlightened age, whether we call it the Aeon of Horus, the Age of Aquarius, or by some other name. To that extent it overlaps with the millenarian tradition that is so pervasive in Russia. However there is a very different type of millenarian thinking, characteristic of the movement known as traditionalism, which says that we are not at the beginning of a glorious New Age but rather still in a process of decline from some more perfect state far in the past. And, whereas the New Age mentality tends to believe in a plurality of spiritual beliefs and the right of each individual to choose their own path, the traditionalists hold that there is one true religious tradition that at some point became fragmented and that only by reconnecting with that single authentic source or one of its offshoots is there any hope for humanity. The generally acknowledged founder of traditionalism was the French philosopher René Guénon (1886–1951), who became a Muslim and emigrated to Egypt. Other representatives of traditionalism include the Italian conservative thinker Julius Evola (1898–1974), the Swiss philosopher Frithjof Schuon (1907–1998) and the Anglo-Sri Lankan art historian and philosopher Ananda Coomaraswamy (1877–1947).

In Russia the traditionalist movement has some fervent devotees, the best known of whom is the already mentioned philosopher Alexander Dugin. Born in 1962 in Moscow into a family of the Soviet elite, Dugin has followed an often-contradictory ideological path. As a young man in the days before perestroika he was a member of the Iuzhinskii circle of rebellious intellectuals and served a term of imprisonment as a dissident. Subsequently he has been alternately—and sometimes simultaneously—a member of the ultra-nationalist Pamyat movement, a national Bolshevist, a Stalinist, a monarchist, a member of the Old Believers sect of Orthodox Christianity, and an apologist for Slavic paganism. His intellectual career has also been varied, involving a curtailed course at the Moscow Aviation Institute, a period of study by correspondence, a doctorate in sociology from the University of Rostock on the Don, and a period as a professor at Moscow State University from which he was dismissed because of his controversial views. Over the years he has acquired exceptionally wide knowledge, as reflected in his books on philosophy, geopolitics, sociology, and more.

Fig. 5.1. Alexander Dugin, prominent writer and political philosopher
WIKIMEDIA COMMONS

Dugin is widely regarded, especially in the West, as an *enfant terrible,* a kind of fascist evil genius at the heart of Putin's Russia, but I believe one can understand him better if one sees him as standing in the tradition of the Russian starets, the independent holy man and prophet, a type we have already encountered in Rasputin and others. The starets may employ a degree of provocation and controversy while at the same time conveying a serious message. To be successful in the role he must also have a high degree of charisma, which Dugin undoubtedly has. Here are some quotes from a speech he gave in 2018 on the subject of tradition:

We are told that tradition is in the past. This is a major misconception. . . . The word tradition means that which is handed on. We are talking about what is handed on from the past to the present. Tradition is a positive understanding of what is eternal . . . not old and not past, but here and now. And people transmit this from generation to generation, from age to age. . . . Each generation decides whether to pass something on or not. . . . Tradition passes on only what is really important, really significant. . . . Tradition safeguards the transmission of the eternal. . . . It unites the beginning with the end . . . past, present, and future in a great circle. . . . It is a celebration of the eternal. . . . It is very important in our age to retain tradition. For the modern age tradition is in the past. There is no conception of eternity.[8]

Dugin's form of traditionalism is what underlies his main geopolitical agenda, namely Eurasianism, a movement that has penetrated deeply into many domains of Russian life from academe to foreign policy. Eurasianism has to be seen in the context of the multinational nature of Russia with its multiplicity of different peoples and more than two hundred languages. The issue of nationality was one that bedeviled the communist regime from the start. According to orthodox Marxist doctrine what drives history forward is the class struggle. It was believed that, once the proletariat of the world had made common cause, things like loyalty to one's nation and pride in one's regional traditions would become obsolete, and villagers in Siberia, Georgia, Kazakhstan, and Ukraine would be singing the communist hymn, the *Internationale,* instead of local patriotic songs.

However, as the existence of so many different nationalities within the Soviet Union was a reality that could not be eliminated overnight, the party stalwarts took the view that the nationalities should be tolerated for a time, but that sooner or later all national sentiments would fade away in the bright sunlight of international communism. They were proved wrong. Neither local nor national patriotism went away.

When the Second World War called for a huge national mobilization, Stalin realized that the Russian people could not be roused to the necessary effort and self-sacrifice unless one appealed to their patriotism and their cherished traditions. The slogans of Marxism would not do the trick. He therefore performed several abrupt U-turns. He summoned the remnant of the Orthodox hierarchy and announced a new policy of reconciliation, promising that churches would be reopened and new ones built. He replaced the *Internationale* as the country's hymn with the *Soviet State Anthem* (of which the words were changed but the melody kept after 1991). In his speeches and broadcasts he addressed the public as "Brothers and Sisters" rather than "Comrades and Citizens." And suddenly posters appeared everywhere showing the image of a heroic-looking woman, with one arm dramatically raised, and the slogan, "Mother Homeland calls!"

After the war the nationality problem remained, and a split began to appear in the ruling Soviet establishment between those who adhered to the Marxist doctrine of internationalism and those who had a sense of national pride as Russians. The latter became increasingly vociferous in the decades following Stalin's death in 1953 and especially after the fall of communism in 1991, but the dilemma they faced was how to uphold Russian nationalism and at the same time reach out to the many other nationalities within Russia and around its borders. It was here that the doctrine of Eurasianism came to the rescue and offered an ingenious solution for having it both ways.

Eurasianism started as a linguistic theory and became transferred to geopolitics. Its history is searchingly described in Charles Clover's book *Black Wind, White Snow*. The original linguistic theory was developed after the Russian Revolution by members of the expatriate Russian community in various European capitals—Prague, Berlin, Vienna, Paris, and Sofia—during the 1920s and '30s. The leading figures in its development were Prince Nikolai Trubetskoy, Roman Jakobson, and Pyotr Savitsky—the first two being linguists and philologists and the latter a geographer.

The essence of the theory they developed was that languages have an internal dynamic, a kind of built-in genetic program that determines how they develop and how they interact with other languages. This dynamic cannot be explained in terms of the historical factors that the Marxists would point to. Moreover, certain languages possess a kind of chemical affinity with each other and have a tendency to form into groups.

Trubetskoy and his friends soon extended this theory to the wider realm of culture and nationality. As Clover writes, they "sought to argue that cultures and civilizations have natural boundaries that delineate the extent of the unconscious architecture of a unique cultural geometry. They are characterized by an entire substratum of unconscious relationships between language sounds, music scales, folk dress, art and even architecture."[9]

One of these boundaries was traced from the Kola peninsula in the far north of Russia down to Romania and the Black Sea. The Eurasianists pointed out many fascinating differences between the two sides of this line. "On one side is the Orthodox world, on the other side the Catholic. On one side many Russian songs are composed on the pentatonic scale, which is . . . barely to be found on the other side of the line."[10]

There were also structural features common to the languages on one side but not on the other. Thus the Eurasianists argued that there was in effect a separate continent, the continent of Eurasia, stretching to the borders of China and comprising not only the Russians but also the neighboring Finno-Ugric, Turkic, and Mongol groups, and all the peoples of the steppes.

Although the original Eurasian group eventually fell apart, the torch of Eurasianism was later taken up by a remarkable and charismatic figure named Lev Gumilyov (1912–1992), a historian, ethnologist, and compelling writer and speaker, who took the Eurasian movement to a new level. He was the son of two celebrated poets, Nikolai Gumilyov and Anna Akhmatova, both of whom fell afoul of the communist regime—the former was shot in 1921. Early in his life Gumilyov decided to devote himself to the study of history and became particularly fascinated by the various waves of nomadic tribes that had periodically swept over Russia. Victimized by the communist authorities on account of his parental background, Gumilyov served two terms in the Gulag, yet managed to pursue his studies in the camps and to write his first book using prison food sacks as paper. The book was a study of the Xiongnu tribe of steppe nomads. With the thaw under Khrushchev he was able to pursue an academic career, becoming famous as a spellbinding lecturer. Despite intermittent bans by the censors, his books became immensely popular, and by the time of his death in 1992 he was a national celebrity.

In his magnum opus, *Ethnogenesis and the Biosphere of the Earth* (1976), Gumilyov argued that nations are living organisms with a life cycle. Each nation has something akin to a unique soul, which he called an "ethnos." An ethnos comes into being when a community or national group becomes seized with enthusiasm for some common goal. This state of enthusiasm he called "passionarity" (*passiarnost*). As long as it remains strong the nation thrives, but eventually it subsides, and the lifespan of the nation comes to an end. This passionarity, he said, was caused by cosmic rays entering the earth's biosphere. At the same time he embraced the notion of Eurasia, which he saw as a unique zone in which the various peoples shared an affinity based on natural and geographical conditions.

In the post-Soviet era, Eurasianism provides a worldview that conservative thinkers like Alexander Dugin can identify with. Dugin in turn has added his own perspective to the Eurasian movement. As Mark Sedgwick writes in a paper on Dugin, he has "modified the definition of Eurasia in line with the work of two non-Russian interwar intellectuals, the British geographer Sir Halford Mackinder and the German geopolitical theorist Karl Haushofer, which pitted a 'Eurasian heartland' consisting of Germany and Russia against an Atlantic world comprising maritime nations predisposed toward free trade and democratic liberalism."[11]

Dugin's traditionalism is, as already mentioned, an essential plank of his Eurasianist position, as it offers an alternative to communism as a way of creating common ground between the various peoples and nations making up the Eurasian bloc. As Sedgwick points out: "On the basis of a shared perennial truth, Dugin can easily include Muslims and Jews in his Eurasian Movement (as he does), and propose an Orthodox alliance with Muslim nations, whether former Soviet republics or neighboring states such as Iran and Turkey."[12]

As might be expected, Dugin is a supporter of the principle of monarchy, but not necessarily in a dynastic form. In an article on this subject he writes about the problem of finding an appropriate form of monarchy for Russia and suggests that there could be a kind of non-hereditary monarchy:

Uppermost would be someone who embodies the will of the people. This is not so much a dynastic arrangement as a vertical organization of society in which the monarch is not the servant of the people, but the people are the servants of the monarch. But who wants to be the servant of another person? We are willing to be slaves of God, to obey one who does not act on his own behalf, but in the name of a higher power. Hence the idea of the sacred nature of the monarchy. Without the sacred, it is despotism, tyranny.[13]

This notion of sacredness is a central feature of Russian monarchism. Whereas the constitutional monarchies of western Europe are eager to present themselves as modern and democratically minded, playing down the notion of the monarch's divine right, the Russian supporters of monarchy see it as a sacred institution. The murder of the Tsar and his family in 1918 bestowed on them a nimbus of holy martyrdom, which led to their canonization in 2000 along with various of the servants who died with them. There are now icons in the traditional style showing the haloed figures of Tsar Nicholas, Tsarina Alexandra, and their five children, and gatherings of monarchists in Russian cities are often accompanied by hymn singing and liturgy.

The level of support in Russia for a return of the monarchy is difficult to quantify. One poll showed 8 percent of the Russian population in favor of restoring the monarchy, while 19 percent said it would depend on who would wear the crown, and another 66 percent were categorically opposed to the return of the monarchy. Other estimates put the level of support for restoration as high as 25 percent.[14]

To bring about a return of the monarchy would be a complicated task, not least because of the different claimants to the throne. What appears at first glance to be a straightforward hierarchy of succession turns out to be cat's cradle with numerous candidates and counter-candidates, black sheep and white, a history of marriages that may or may not have been morganatic, and children who may or may not have been legitimate. One of the strongest claimants is the Grand Duchess Maria Vladimirovna, great-great-granddaughter of the Emperor Alexander II and mother of Prince George Mikhailovich, who would arguably be next in line. But there are various counterclaimants from other branches of the Romanov family, whose blood ties extend into several of the royal houses of Europe, including the British. There has even been talk of finding a descendant of the Rurik dynasty as a candidate, should no one from the Romanov family be suitable.[15]

Talk of a return to the Rurik dynasty opens up the question of whether the roots of the Russian people are Viking or Slavic or both— or perhaps something else entirely. Paradoxically, the Russian New Age involves much burrowing into the past in search of a sense of meaning and identity. Typical of this tendency is the movement celebrating the legacy of the Scythians. The original Scythians were a largely nomadic people who, from their original homeland in what is now Ukraine, built a vast empire stretching from the Baltic to central Asia and from the Arctic coast to the Persian frontier, reaching the height of their power around the fourth century BCE. The memory of Scythians continues to exert a certain mystique among certain groups such as the New Scythians, led by Pavel Zarifullin (born 1977) with a center in Moscow, called the Gumilyov Center in acknowledgment of the man they regard as their guiding light. The group glorifies the Scythian vigor, nobility, and grandeur that came from their nomadic heritage. In his book *The New Scythians,* Zarifullin writes:

> Endless opportunities are opening up for the "Scythians," as they are the avant-garde of the impending mobilization. Like the Cossacks and Hussars of Denis Davydov, who were the "roaming center" and the salt of the "Scythian War" with Napoleon's army. Let's remember that the Scythians are "discovered" in the most active and revolutionary moments in history. Like red cranes, the Scythian Era pecks at our cold windows with its diamond beak.[16]

The desire to probe the distant past has produced a rich crop of eccentric theories, such as those of Prof. Valeriy Chudinov (born 1942). Having graduated in both physics and philology, he took a doctorate in philosophy of science and obtained a professorship, then began to produce controversial theories in the area of Russian history and paleography. Chudinov believes that there was an ancient Slavic Vedic civilization, which was older than all other known civilizations and used what was essentially the Russian language along with a script that resembled but ante-dated Cyrillic. He concludes that Russian is one of the oldest languages on earth, and that Russian writing has existed for at least two million years. He claims to have discovered inscriptions in this lettering on rocks and on the surface of the Earth, the moon, and Mars, as seen from space. He also produces curious etymological theories to prove that Russian is the primal language of Europe (e.g. that the syllable "rus" as in "Etruscan" is derived from the root "rus" as in *russki* (Russian)." Predictably, Chudinov is also an advocate of the Hyperborean theory, which we have already encountered.

As George Orwell wrote in 1984: "Who controls the past controls the future."

The eagerness of the Russians to rediscover a past that they can celebrate has led both to serious research on the part of archaeologists and historians as well as to some highly outlandish theories. The pre-Christian past is a particularly rich field for both the former and the latter, as we shall see.

 SIX

The Strange Case of the
Book of Veles

Habent sua fata libelli [books have their fates].

TERENTIANUS MAURUS

(ROMAN GRAMMARIAN, SECOND CENTURY CE)

"We implore Veles to lift Suri's horses into the sky, so that Surya may rise above us to rotate the eternal golden wheels."[1] Thus reads a passage from the *Book of Veles,* a mysterious text said to have been discovered in 1919 by a White Russian officer, Col. Feodor Arturovich Izenbek, and purporting to be a history of the Slavic people and their struggles and wanderings over a period of about fourteen centuries from about the seventh century BCE. Since the book was published in the San Francisco-based Russian émigré journal *Firebird (Zhar-ptitsa)* in the late 1950s, it has been hailed by some as a supreme literary treasure, the Russian equivalent of the Norse sagas, and by others as a blatant forgery. Whatever the truth of the matter, the book has become immensely popular in Russia and Ukraine as well as in the Russian diaspora and has found hundreds of thousands of readers eager to celebrate the glory of their Slavic forebears. Before looking at the arguments for and against the authenticity of the book, let me recount what we know of its history, which in itself is a story worthy of a thriller. The events surrounding its discovery have been dramatically recounted by Izenbek's friend and associate Yuri Mirolyubov—if the latter's account is to be believed. Mirolyubov's story goes as follows.[2]

In 1919, during the Russian Civil War between the revolutionary (Red) and antirevolutionary (White) forces, a White artillery unit, led by Colonel Izenbek and campaigning in eastern Ukraine near the city of Kharkiv, came to an imposing country mansion with a vast columned portico. Finding the house deserted and evidently recently vandalized and looted, Colonel Izenbek searched the premises, including what remained of the plundered library, and found a set of forty-two wooden tablets, each measuring thirty-eight by twenty-two centimeters with a thickness of about half a centimeter. They were inscribed with a text written in a curious script—part runic, part Gothic, part old Slavonic—the letters joined at the top by lines that ran across each slab.

Izenbek was a cultured man who had studied art in Paris and then become an archaeologist and taken part in excavations in Central Asia. Unable to read the text on the tablets but realizing they might contain important information, he asked his orderly Koshelev to put them into a bag for transportation. The unit then retreated before an approaching Red Army troop, led by one J. V. Stalin, and in the chaos of the retreat Izenbek and Koshelev became separated. Izenbek made his way to the port of Theodosius in Crimea and boarded a ship. As the vessel was pulling out, he looked back at the quay and saw someone hurrying through the crowd. It was Koshelev, carrying the bag containing the tablets. The faithful orderly threw the bag across the widening strip of water, and it landed safely on the ship.

Izenbek made his way to Belgrade and remained there for several years, pursuing a career as an artist. In 1923 he tried unsuccessfully to sell the tablets to the Belgrade library and museum. In 1925 he settled in Brussels, where he continued his artistic career. Evidently he was an inwardly tormented character who suffered from a narcotics addiction and presented a withdrawn, uncommunicative personality. His paintings are a curious mixture of the conventional and the wildly surrealistic and bizarre. In Brussels he frequented the Russian Club and there he came into contact with another Russian émigré named Yuri Petrovich Mirolyubov, with whom he struck up a friendship.

Mirolyubov, like Izenbek, had a colorful background. He was born in 1892 in the Bakhmut region of Ukraine. His father was a priest; his mother from a distinguished Cossack family. In childhood he encountered an old Cossack tradition from southern Russia, which he believed to contain remnants of the Vedic thought of the ancient Indo-Europeans. His education was unusually eclectic. At his gymnasium he studied Latin, Greek, and Church Slavonic, then went on to study medicine for a time at the universities of Warsaw and Kiev. In the First World War he served voluntarily at the front as an ensign (roughly equivalent to second lieutenant), then fought in the Russian Civil War on the White side. After the defeat of the White Army in 1920 he began a period of travel that took him to Egypt, Africa, India, and Turkey. Returning to Europe, he settled for a while in Prague, where he studied chemical engineering and took a doctorate and at the same time attended lectures in Slavonic studies. In 1924 he settled in Belgium where, at the Russian Club in Brussels, he met and befriended the strange, reserved painter Izenbek.

At Izenbek's studio he saw the wooden tablets, and Izenbek rather hesitantly allowed him to transcribe them. This was a time-consuming process, as he had to work in the studio and only at certain times. The transcription itself was difficult, as the lines of letters had no gaps or punctuation. Hence the task stretched over some fifteen years, but at last Mirolyubov produced a transcription and a translation using old Slavonic lettering, an earlier variation of Cyrillic, as it most closely resembled the original.

The Second World War came and in 1941 the German army occupied Belgium. In the same year Izenbek died and the tablets disappeared. All that remained were Mirolyubov's transcriptions and translations as well as photographs of some of the boards. In 1948 Mirolyubov wrote to the Russian émigré journal *Firebird* in San Francisco, describing the tablets. The editor, N. S. Chirkov, received the letter but lost the envelope with the return address and so was unable to reply. However, word about the contents of the letter eventually reached the ears of Alexander Kurenkov, a Russian assyriologist living in Palo Alto. Intrigued, he published an article in the journal in 1953, drawing attention to the potential importance of the tablets. Mirolyubov saw the article and entered into correspondence with Kurenkov, who then set to work producing a modern Russian version of the text, which he published in *Firebird* over a series of issues between March 1957 and May 1959, by which time Mirolyubov had emigrated to California.

THE BOOK AS A MISSING LINK

The publication of the *Book of Veles,* as it came to be called, was for many Russians a sensational revelation. For those of a Slavophile turn of mind it provided a vital missing link in the hitherto scanty record of the early Slavs. Here at last was not only evidence of a pre-Cyrillic Slavic script, but also a heroic chronicle of the Slavs and their pre-Christian gods. It was a patriotic Russian's dream. However, it was not long before scholars within and outside Russia began to investigate it critically, and most concluded that the book was a forgery. This has remained the majority consensus until today, although some scholars have defended it, and the controversy still continues. So is the book genuine? Let us look at the content to see if it throws any light on this question. I am relying here on the version provided by Alexander Asov in an extensively annotated and commented edition.[3]

The text begins with some verses in praise of the "Great Three" (i.e., the three supreme gods of the Slavic pantheon: Svarog, Perun, and Sviatovit). There follows a long list of other gods, and throughout the text many deities are mentioned, both Slavic and Hindu. An interesting reference to Hinduism comes later in the book in the passage quoted at the beginning of this chapter: "We implore Veles to lift Suri's horses into the sky, so that Surya may rise above us to rotate the eternal golden wheels."

Surya is the Hindu sun god, counterpart of Apollo in the Greek pantheon, and he rides in a golden chariot pulled by seven horses, representing the seven meters of Vedic poetry.[4] But why would a Slavic god be called upon to raise the Indian sun god into the sky? Perhaps this is part of an attempt to present the Slavs as the true carriers of Vedic wisdom.

Turning to the main narrative, the first chapter begins with the passage: "The progenitors were led out by Yar to the borderlands of Russia for, if they had remained, they would have suffered the Great Cold."[5] This could tie in with the theory promulgated by the Indian writer Bâl Gangâdar Tilak (1856–1920), namely that the Aryans originally lived in the far north until they were driven out by the advent of the ice age. But the reference to Russia is curious, as Russia would not yet have existed at the time of such an exodus from the north. The state of Kievan Rus was only founded in the late ninth century CE. Of course the scribe could have been writing after that date, but there are other anomalies and inconsistencies that crop up as one reads through the text.

The people who form the subject of the epic are variously described as Slavs, Aryans, and Russians, and the deities they worship vary accordingly. For example in the first chapter there is the passage: "Glory to the name of Indra! We the Aryans went out from the Aryan lands to the Indian region." This again appears anachronistic, as, according to etymologists, the term Aryan was only used from about the 1830s to describe an ethno-linguistic group.

As an example of the inconsistencies in the text, early on there is a reference to "father" Yarun, who had three sons, Kiy, Shcheck, and Khoriv, who became the progenitors of all the Slavic people.[6] Yet later the "father" is called Ariy and the three sons are called Kiy, Pashek, and Gorovato.[7] Such inconsistencies would in fact tend to support the authenticity of the text, since a forger would surely try to ensure consistency.

As regards the linguistic evidence, most of the experts have declared the book to be a forgery on the grounds that many features of the vocabulary, spelling, and grammar are incompatible with the early Slavic language in which the text purports to be written. They estimate that it was composed in the 1940s or '50s or, less likely, in the early nineteenth century. The two main candidates for the role of forger are Mirolyubov himself and the bibliophile and collector Alexander Sulakadzev (1771–1829), who is known to have forged a number of documents. However, there are a few scholars who have braved academic ostracism by asserting the authenticity of the book. One is the biochemist Anatole Klyosov, who has thrown much light on the early history of the Slavs through his research using DNA analysis.[8] Another is the Ukrainian scholar Valentin Taranets who, after carrying out a detailed historical and linguistic analysis of the text, came to the conclusion that it was genuine and had been written in the thirteenth century.[9]

If the book is a forgery the question arises: who was behind it and for what reason? If Mirolyubov was the forger that would mean that he had deliberately written a text that was difficult to make sense of, then pretended that he had struggled for many years to produce an imperfect translation. It would also mean that he had created the boards himself and invented the whole story of their discovery by Izenbek and the episode of the orderly throwing them on to the ship in a bag. Conceivably it was a co-conspiracy with Izenbek, but to what end? And surely they would have produced a more plausible and consistent narrative. Sulakadzev seems a more likely candidate, but, as an experienced forger he would surely also have taken care to produce a convincing and consistent text. Furthermore, there are signs (variations in the shapes of letters, for instance) that more than one person was involved in the writing. It may not be a simple question of either/or—forgery or not. Possibly parts of it are genuinely ancient and have been embellished and added to.

It may be instructive to compare the *Book of Veles* with the Ossian forgery, the collection of poems allegedly written by an ancient Gaelic bard but in fact largely written by the Scots folklorist James Macpherson (1736–1796), although some of the poems were taken from genuine Gaelic fragments. Both the Ossian poems and the *Book of Veles* can be seen in the context of the romanticizing of the folk and the nation, which came to the fore in the late eighteenth century and continued to burgeon throughout the nineteenth. The Russians, like many European peoples, were caught up in this trend, and the *Book of Veles* would have spoken to their yearning to celebrate their ancient heritage, just as the Ossian poems spoke to a similar yearning among the Scots. The early nineteenth century would therefore seem a likely date for the composition or compilation of the *Book of Veles*. But the question then arises of why it was kept hidden away for so long in a country house in Ukraine. Every theory about the book raises more questions than it answers, and perhaps that is what its creators intended.

A mystery can be a powerful force in history, as witness the Rosicrucian manifestos of the early seventeenth century, which sent out ripples that are still being felt today, and the same can be said of the *Book of Veles*. It leads us on to the subject of the survival and revival of Paganism in Russia, which we shall look at next.

 SEVEN

Survival of the Old Gods

The old pagan gods have never disappeared from Russia. Even during the bleak Bolshevik years they were there in vernacular customs and traditions, in folk songs and tales, among surviving pagan communities, and in many aspects of the Orthodox Church itself, for Russian paganism and Orthodoxy are intertwined and have coexisted to the present day in a sometimes peaceful but often conflictual relationship. Many members of the Orthodox hierarchy have openly voiced their dismay in various fora about the resurgence of paganism. For example, in March 2016 a conference on combating neo-paganism was held at the Magnitogorsk State Technical University, at which the bishop of the diocese, speaking at the opening of the conference, said that modern paganism posed a greater threat to the Church than atheism. At the same time certain nationalistic voices have claimed an ancient Aryan and Vedic origin for the true Orthodox tradition.[1] Today many Russians keep a foot in both camps, practicing what is often referred to as "dual belief" (*dvoyeverie*). This dual belief is more than just a *modus vivendi*. It is rooted in a quality of the Russian soul that goes beyond the categories of pagan and Christian. It is perhaps best expressed by word "epiphany" (manifestation of the divine). It was this quality that the poet Rainer Maria Rilke experienced when looking at Russian icons.[2]

Rilke was aware that in Russia this quality of epiphany could be found not just in icons but in myriad things in the world. This comes across in a medieval epic called *The Song of Igor's Campaign,* about a battle between Christian knights and a Turkish army, which Rilke translated into German. Despite its ostensibly Christian theme, it is full of pagan motifs. The Christian leader Igor and his brother are described as descendants of Dazhbog, the sun god, and the sun itself appears as a deity, issuing warnings through, for example, going into an eclipse. Other gods mentioned include Veles, roughly the Russian counterpart to Pan, and Stribog, the wind god. Animals also influence events and give warnings. In fact the whole of nature is animate and ensouled. The sun, the winds, night, rivers, trees, the earth, the Russian land itself—all are living beings that interact with the world of humans. The overall message, while given some Christian window dressing, is profoundly pagan. Igor's final defeat is due to his ignoring the warnings of the pagan powers. A shamanistic element also comes across in the poem. A seer and bard called Boyan is described as having the power of shape-shifting, and Prince Igor and his companion Olvur have a similar power, being able to change into animals such as a duck, wolf, or falcon—a capacity typical of the shaman.[3]

What else do we know about the pre-Christian traditions of the region that is now Russia and the surrounding territories? Pavel Zarifullin writes in his book *The New Scythians:*

> The Great Russian nation is seemingly homogeneous, but in fact resembles a complex giant pie. This pie has a Proto-Iranian (Sarmato-Scythian) piece, as well as Turkic and Finno-Ugric pieces. There is a piece that is Orthodox-Byzantine. And there is an inherently Slavic piece, handed down from their tribal ancestors: the Vyatichi and the Ilmen Slovenes: an ontology of a God-seeking and God-bearing people.[4]

Russia is indeed a pie with many ingredients and, if you add the Sami of the far northwest and the Mongol peoples of Siberia, such as the Yakut and the Buryat, the pie becomes even bigger. But let us begin with the Slavs and their mythology.

The Slavs, from their original home somewhere between the Black Sea and the Baltic, began to spread out from around the sixth century CE and eventually settled over a massive swathe of territory, stretching from eastern Germany to the Bering Strait. Written information about them and their religious beliefs is scarce. All we have are some fragments provided by Greek and Roman historians and the chronicles of Orthodox monks, which are often inaccurate. But from these and from the folklore that has been handed down over the centuries, we can piece together some idea of the old beliefs and customs of the Slavs. We shall then be better able to understand their present-day revival within the modern neo-pagan movement.

The supreme creator god, whose name is Rod, is infinitely mysterious and ineffable. From him flows the entire manifest world. The word *rod* conveys generating and bringing into being and also, by association, family and kin. It appears as the root in many Russian words such as *rodina* (the motherland), *roditeli* (parents), *rodstvenniki* (relatives), *narod* (the folk, the people of a nation), *rodnik* (spring or well), and *priroda* (nature). Thus the pagan worldview of the ancient Slavs is embedded in the Russian language (which is the subject of a later chapter).

After Rod, the two next important deities are Byelobog (the White God) and Chernobog (the Black God), named after the words for white and black respectively and representing two sides of a sharp dualism: light and dark, good and evil, creation and destruction. This worldview may possibly have been influenced by the Persian Zoroastrian religion, but it also has parallels in other mythologies. Chernobog, who has similarities to Set, the Egyptian god of destruction, has been taken up in the domain of computer games. One of them, produced by Titan Forge Games, is entitled *Chernobog, Lord of Darkness*.[5] I have not found any equivalent game for Byelobog—the devil has the best tunes, as the saying goes.

Another important deity is the god of the sky, Svarog, whose name is cognate with the Sanskrit word *svar*, meaning bright or clear. He has some similarities to Jupiter and to the Nordic god Thor. Svarog has two sons. One is the Sun, Dazhbog, and the other is Fire, Ogon (cognate with the Sanskrit word for fire, *agni*). The fire element was an object of reverence for the ancient Slavs. Hence in Slavic households, when the fire was lit, the young ones were forbidden to swear or shout.[6] The motif of fire also appears in the mythological figure of the Firebird, a magical creature whose plumage is perpetually aflame. The theme of the Firebird was immortalized by the Diaghilev ballet of that name, with original choreography by Michel Fokine and music by Igor Stravinsky.

Fig. 7.1. The Firebird, a ubiquitous motif in Russian mythology and folklore (See also color plate 6)
WIKIMEDIA COMMONS

Even more important than the sky god is the earth goddess, Mat Sira Zemlya (literally "Mother-Moist-Earth"), often identified with Mokosh, goddess of fertility and childbirth and spinner of the web of life and death. Reverence for Mat Sira Zemlya lies deep in the Russian soul, as does reverence for the earth itself. Indeed she *is* the earth itself, a sentient being who can protect and advise human beings and predict the future. In certain parts of Russia, if you wished to consult the earth you would dig a hole in the ground, put your ear to it, and listen to whatever sounds came forth. In legal disputes the earth was often called upon as a witness. If you swore an oath with a clod of earth on your head, then the oath was considered binding and trustworthy.[7]

ORTHODOXY AND THE OLD GODS

When Orthodoxy came to Russia in the tenth century many of the old deities and mythological figures were transformed into Christian saints. One of the most popular was and is Paraskeva, usually called Paraskeva-Piatnitsa (Paraskeva-Friday) from the Greek word παρασκευη, meaning Friday, on account of the fact that Friday is her sacred day. If you look up Paraskeva in an Orthodox list of saints today you will find a historical saint of that name, but you will be unlikely to find any mention of the apocryphal Saint Paraskeva, based on an ancient Slavic goddess, who has been merged with the historical figure to disguise the pagan associations.

Paraskeva is a complex figure with aspects of other deities such as the great earth goddess Mokosh or Mother Moist Earth. Paraskeva is, among other things, goddess of the earth, of animals and the hunt, patroness of marriage, and bringer of children. At the same time she is associated with death and the underworld. For centuries she was worshipped in a thoroughly pagan manner, to the extent that her cult was condemned in 1589 by the Patriarch of Constantinople. It was reported that on twelve Fridays during the year men and women would strip naked and dance around in wild abandon. In the late sixteenth century the Stoglav Council, established by Ivan the Terrible, condemned her along with two other saints of pagan origin—Sreda (the Russian word for Wednesday) and Nedelia (meaning week). Together they were regarded as being the three goddesses of fate, similar to the Norns in Nordic mythology, and therefore incompatible with Christian teaching, which would reject any agent of fate apart from God. Paraskeva's cult was so entrenched that at one time in Red Square, Moscow, there was a chapel to her, open to women only, who would go there on Fridays to worship her.[8]

The cult proved very difficult for the Church to dislodge, and only after many centuries did it begin to wane. Today, in her old form, she is honored again by pagans, who tend to bracket her with Mokosh. In pagan art she is typically depicted as a radiant, full-blooded goddess, surrounded by the fruits of the earth. In a sense she has begun to free herself from the Christian appropriation and return to her old self.

A similar appropriation took place with Perun, the pagan god of thunder and war and the equivalent of Thor in the Nordic tradition. Perun was amalgamated with the prophet Elijah who, like Perun, could summon rain or lightning. Another Slavic pagan deity, Volos or Veles, god of cattle and the equivalent of the Greek god Pan, was transformed into Saint Blasius, similarly known as the protector of cattle.[9] He also is one of the deities venerated by Russian neo-pagans.

Perhaps the most striking instance of a pagan element being reborn in Christian form is in the case of the Virgin Mary, who occupies a unique position in Russian Orthodoxy. She is the greatest of the saints and the only human being to be deified and to have already crossed the threshold into the eternal kingdom rather than having to wait for the return of Christ.[10] The intense devotion of the Orthodox toward her is shown by an event that took place in 2011, involving a belt of the Virgin that had been brought from Mount Athos in Greece to be shown to worshippers in various Russian cities. In Moscow tens of thousands of people lined up in subzero temperatures to venerate the relic. My correspondent Dana reports that a neighbor of hers went there to pray for a marriage, as many other women did, and actually met her future husband in the enormous queue.[11] This deep veneration has undoubtedly built on the worship of the ancient pagan omnipresent goddess, known to the Slavic peoples under countless different names. She is Mother Earth, Mokosh, Paraskeva, and, half disguised as a patriotic symbol, she is the Rodina, Mother Russia.

A particularly striking way in which pagan practices coexist with Christian ones is in certain religious festivals. An example is the midsummer festival of Ivan Kupala. It is held June 23–24 in the Julian (traditional Russian) calendar (i.e., July 6–7 in the Gregorian or modern calendar) and therefore has slipped back a couple of weeks from the actual midsummer date. Kupala is the ancient Slavic god of summer, fertility, harvest, and the bounty of nature. After the coming of Christianity, the festival was merged with that of Saint John the Baptist, and Kupala became Ivan (John) Kupala, but the celebrations are carried out in an unashamedly pagan manner. People dress in traditional folk costumes, and the women wear enormous headdresses of flowers and leaves. There is much singing, dancing, and leaping over a bonfire.

Apart from the deities already mentioned there are various minor ones. Originally there was a multiplicity of these. There were domestic spirits like the *bannik* who lived in the bathhouse, the *dvorovoi* whose domain was the yard, and the *ovinnik* who inhabited the barn. Then there were the spirits of the natural world such as the *leshy,* a forest divinity, the *vodyanoi,* a water sprite, and the *polevik,* a spirit of the fields. Some of these have survived in folk tradition and custom. One that is still popular is the spirit of the home called the *domovoi,* from the Russian word *dom,* meaning house. The *domovoi* is typically portrayed as a small, hairy, monkey-like humanoid, sometimes with the features of a cat or other domestic animal. He is basically a friendly spirit, who protects the house and the family, but he must be treated with respect and consideration, such as by leaving out small items of food for him. Also, he expects the family to keep a tidy and well-ordered household, otherwise he will resort to mischievous behavior. When a family moves house, they customarily take the *domovoi* with them. Belief in the *domovoi* is still widespread, and in markets selling items of folk craft, you can buy statuettes of him.

INHERITORS OF THE ANCIENT RELIGION

Today paganism in Russia, in addition to its survival in folk traditions and practices such as those mentioned above, exists in: (a) a few communities that have retained a native paganism to this day, and (b) the modern neo-pagan movement. A remarkable case in the former category is that of the Mari, a Finno-Ugric people, who have their own republic, Mari El, within the Russian Federation, lying adjacent to the north bank of the Volga about five hundred kilometers eastward from Moscow to the republic's western border.* It occupies four hundred square kilometers with a population of some seven hundred thousand, of which about 43 percent are indigenous Mari, while some 49 percent are Russian. The two official languages are Mari and Russian.

Over the centuries the ancient pagan religion of the Mari has struggled to survive against Christian proselytizing and later against the antireligious persecution of the Stalinist era, when some four thousand culturally prominent Maris, including many priests of the old pagan religion, were murdered. Consequently from the 1950s to the 1980s practice of the old religion was minimal, but with the coming of perestroika and the collapse of communism, there came a new impetus to promote Mari language and culture including pre-Christian customs and practices. Although the majority of the Mari are officially Orthodox Christians, their ancestral paganism is alive

---

*For an account of the pagan traditions of the Mari, see Ulrike Kahrs, "Die weißen, reinen Mari," 150–51.

and well, albeit still not safe from attack. As with all the indigenous people of the regions bordering the Arctic Circle, they have a shamanistic culture.

In the Mari pantheon the supreme deity is Oš Kugu Jumo (roughly translated as "Great White God"). Under him there are four groups of deities. In the first group are the gods representing great, overarching concepts, such as Tünja Jumo (God of the Universe), Oš Keče Jumo (God of the Sun and of Light), and Mer Kugu Jumo (Benefactor of Humankind). The second group comprises nature deities like the thunder god Küdyrčö Jumo and Üžara Jumo (God of the Sunrise). The third group encompasses deities of the elements and suchlike, including Mlande Jumo (God of the Earth) and Tul Jumo (Fire God). In the fourth group are deities with a more seasonal or marginal significance, such as Saska Jumo (God of the Fruits) and Tütyra Jumo (God of the Mist). In addition to these main deities there are numerous lesser spirits, benevolent and malevolent. There is also the underworld where the dead reside. Thus, in keeping with the classic shamanistic pattern, the Mari cosmos is divided into three realms: the upper realm of the gods, the middle world of human beings and spirits, and the lower domain of the departed.

The community is continually in contact with the gods and supernatural entities, celebrating them, asking for their help and advice, and offering them gifts. The appropriate rituals are performed in sacred groves, of which there are two kinds: an unenclosed group of deciduous trees, exclusively devoted to the gods of the upper realm, and a grove of conifers, enclosed by a fence and devoted to an evil spirit called Keremet. In the middle of each sacred grove stands a special tree or several such, before which a sacrificial altar has been set up. The priests who officiate and offer up the sacrifices enjoy a high standing in the community. In a sacred grove it is forbidden to curse, whistle, laugh loudly, lie, boast, or leave litter. Furthermore no one is allowed to fell the trees. Sadly, in 1929 the Soviet government passed a law forbidding all religious gatherings outside officially approved places of worship such as churches, mosques, and synagogues, and in the enforcement of this law many groves were destroyed.

The Mari year is a perpetual round of seasonal celebrations. For example, around the beginning of June is Agavajrem (Plough Festival), which marks the beginning of work in the fields. The residents of the village process with the priest to the sacred grove and place offerings of food on a table. Various deities such as the Thunder God and the Wind Mother are invoked by the priest, who asks them to bless the sowing and the harvest with good weather conditions. A portion of the food is set apart for the gods and put into a fire as a sacrifice. Homemade beer is also poured into the fire. More beer is then sprinkled by the priest in all four compass directions. All present then enjoy a feast with the remaining food. The ceremonial stage ends with a ritual of purification in which each person leaps three times over the embers of the fire. There follows a series of games and competitive sports. Finally the group processes around the grove then bows deeply and departs back into the everyday world.

Another seasonal event is the festival in honor of the dead, which takes place in the spring. Death and the afterworld play an important role in the worldview of the Mari. They believe that human beings have two souls, a "breath soul" and a "free soul." The breath soul is inseparable from the body and only leaves it at death. The free soul can leave and return to the body at any time, such as when the person is asleep or unconscious. It is therefore similar to the theosophical concept of the astral body. Before the free soul goes to the Underworld it lingers for a certain time in the everyday world and can appear to the living, often in the form of a sparrow. The departed continue to live in the Underworld and are able to contact the living and influence their lives. In keeping with these beliefs the Mari have elaborate rites surrounding everything to do with death and the dead. They also attach great importance to honoring departed national heroes such as the tribal leader Čumbylat, who stoutly defended the Mari territory in the eleventh and twelfth centuries.

Ulrike Kahrs, an ethnologist specializing in Finno-Ugric culture who has made a special study of the Mari, reported in an article published in 2006 that they face many problems in their efforts to preserve and revive their ancient religion and folk traditions. They are only very sparsely represented in the administration, which is dominated by Russians. They also face discrimination in their efforts to assert their identity as a people. Another problem reported by Dr. Kahrs is the erosion of the collective memory of genuine customs and traditions, due partly to the fact that the cultural revival is to a large extent in the hands of the urban population, that is to say those most affected by the Russian influence. Nevertheless it is a remarkable achievement that their ancient religion has been able to survive at all despite centuries of Christian missionizing and decades of Soviet oppression. Dr. Kahrs reports that, in a 2001 census among the Mari, 52.5 percent of the sample professed the Russian Orthodox faith, 25.6 percent had a foot in both pagan and Christian camps, and 5.3 percent (i.e., over 15,500 people) were exclusively pagan.[12]

If the Mari have had to struggle to maintain their ancient native religion, the same is true of other indigenous peoples with a shamanic culture, such as the Sami, whom we have already encountered in connection with the Barchenko expedition. The Sami, or Lapp, people extend over northern Norway, Sweden, Finland, and Russia. Out of a total estimated population of between fifty thousand and one hundred thousand, only about two thousand live in Russia.[13] After centuries of being subjected to aggressive Christian missionizing, the Sami have been reviving their shamanism, partly with the help of the American ethnologist, the late Prof. Michael Harner. It is to be hoped that this process will continue.

The biggest concentration of shamanism within Russia is among the Mongol tribes of Siberia such as the Buryat, Tungus, and Yakut. There is some dispute about the origin of the term "shaman," but it probably originates from the Tungus word *šaman* or *xaman,* meaning roughly "agitated," "excited," or "raised."[14] It was picked up by German writers from the late seventeenth century and subsequently came to be applied generally to a system of belief and practice found preeminently in Siberia and Central Asia but also in other regions of the world. Both men and women can be shamans, and the gender balance varies according to region and country. In some places, such as Korea, female shamans are in the majority.

Some experts would say that shamanism is not a religion but a modality that exists within or alongside a variety of religions, as in Siberia, which encompasses Russian Orthodoxy, Buddhism, Islam, and other creeds. However, it is often described and treated as a religion in its own right. What we can say is that the shaman generally has a different role from the priest. Whereas the priest leads worship, makes sacrificial offerings, and conducts weddings, funerals, and the like, the shaman is a kind of spiritual troubleshooter who knows how to communicate with the spirits and induce states of ecstasy in which the soul can leave the body and travel between the upper world of the gods and spirits, the middle world of human beings, and the underworld of the dead. He or she is called for as a healer of body or mind, a soothsayer, a magician, and a psychopomp, one who conducts the souls of the deceased to the underworld. Totem animals play an important role in shamanism, both in the initiation process and as guides and helpers in the shaman's work. Typical accoutrements of the shaman include a drum or tambourine, a rattle, a costume festooned with feathers, ribbons, or other symbolic decorations, and a copper mirror that the shaman uses to see a dead person's soul or for other clairvoyant purposes. When a trance state is called for it is typically induced by drumming, chanting, intense body movements, and often the consumption of psychedelic substances or alcohol.

Shamanism has sometimes been called the world's oldest religion. At any rate, certain legends told about its origins suggest something of great antiquity. According to Buryat legend there was once a golden age when human beings lived happily and healthily. This came to an end when evil spirits appeared on the earth and spread disease and death. To combat these afflictions the gods sent a shaman in the form of an eagle, but humans did not understand its language, and the eagle went back to the gods and requested them either to give him the gift of speech or to send a Buryat shaman to humankind. The gods sent the eagle back into the world with instructions to give the gift of shamanizing to the first person he encountered, who turned out to be a woman asleep under a tree. The eagle mated with the woman, and in due course she gave birth to a son who became the first shaman. In another version it was the woman herself who became a shaman.[15]

This story has striking parallels in the Bible, with the golden age and the advent of the evil spirits corresponding to the Garden of Eden and the fall in the Old Testament. The parallels with the New Testament and the account of the birth of Jesus are even more remarkable. In the Gospel narrative the Holy Spirit in the form of a dove descends and impregnates the Virgin Mary, who gives birth to the Savior. In the Buryat legend the dove becomes an eagle, the Virgin Mary becomes the woman under the tree, and the divine son to whom Mary gives birth becomes the first shaman. Of course it is possible that the Buryat borrowed and adapted the story from Christianity, but Eliade records, quoting *The Primordial Ocean* by W. J. Perry, that a similar legend is found among the Pondo people of South Africa.[16] It seems likely that all three accounts stem from an ancient motif, whether transmitted or part of the collective mind of humanity.

A vivid description of a shamanic ceremony is given in a report written by the Russian explorer Nikolai Iadrintsev in 1880 after witnessing an Altai shaman in action:

I remember that night when I had to stop at that place. That mysterious beautiful night with thousands of bright stars spread over the awesome mountains full of savage beauty and poetic charm. I saw the shaman in a fantastic costume decorated with rattles and snake-like plaits. Feathers were sticking from his helmet, and in his hands he held a mysterious drum. At first, the shaman circled around the fire. Then he jumped out of the shelter of bark into the open air. My ears can still hear his magnificent howling, his call for spirits, and the wild mountain echo that responded to his invocations.[17]

After the communists came to power in Russia, they at first generally avoided persecution of the shamans, preferring to concentrate their attacks on Christianity. Soviet ethnographers even went to Siberia to study shamanic cultures. Indigenous shamanism, freed from the powerful opposition of the Church, temporarily flourished, and many practitioners and followers, who had been baptized, returned to shamanism. All this changed in the 1930s when the shamans were declared to be class enemies, and a period of militant collectivization ensued, accompanied by violent repression by the secret police and the murder of many shamans. The situation eased in the 1960s, and Soviet ethnographers resumed their studies of shamanism. When communism collapsed in the early 1990s shamans were again able to practice freely.[18] However, sometimes shamans attract unwelcome attention, as the case of the Yakut shaman Alexander Gabyshev, who in 2019 announced that God told him that President Putin was not human but a demon and must be driven out. To this end he embarked on a two-thousand-mile trek from Yakutia to Moscow but was halted when he reached Buryatia and was placed in a psychiatric clinic.[19]

Such cases have not prevented a strong revival of shamanism, and many new candidates are hearing a call from the ancestors and coming forward for ordination as shamans. The vitality of this revival is typified by the Tengeri shamanic center in the Buryat capital of Ulan-Ude, which trains and initiates shamans and also functions as a place where people can go to consult a shaman about their personal problems or attend a shamanic ceremony. The center, with its vigorous promotional activities and advertised events, is thriving and attracting participants from far and wide, including many non-Buryats and even people from abroad. At the same time, those Buryats with ties to the old rural shamanism are often critical of the center's approach.[20]

While shamanism is once again flourishing, the traditional cultures in which it is embedded are under threat. The autonomous Republic of Tuva is a striking example of this problem. The Stalin regime forced the Mongol tribes of Tuva to abandon their nomadic way of life, thus striking at the very soul of their community. Since the collapse of communism they have been faced with new threats posed by capitalism and the free market. Unemployment has soared, alcoholism, drug addiction, and criminality are rife, life expectancy is low, and many young Tuvans are leaving their homeland, seduced by life in the big cities further west. In the struggle to defend the Tuvan culture and traditions, the shamans are playing a vital role. They are keeping alive ancient customs, preserving the unique musical tradition of Tuva, and using their healing skills to treat alcoholics and drug addicts. One prominent shaman has said that salvation for the Tuvans lies in a renewal of pride in their nation and a turning back to their ancestral ways.*

Tuva's problems reflect a wider challenge facing Russia as a whole as well as other nations and cultures that are in danger of being submerged in the synthetic culture of the global shopping mall that is spreading everywhere. Communities with a strong spiritual tradition and sense of pride in their culture are better able to resist this threat. So the success or failure of places like Tuva in hanging on to their authenticity will have far-reaching consequences. In that struggle the shamans are playing a vital role.

---

*See the documentary film *The Shamans of Tuva,* made in 2011 for SBS television, Australia; viewable on YouTube.

I would argue that the influence of shamanism in Russia is also present in less obvious ways that possibly date from the period between the thirteenth and fifteenth centuries when the country was ruled by the Mongols, who had a shamanic culture. There are, for example, certain shamanic features in the tradition of the yurodiviy, the holy fool or fool for Christ, that is a man or woman who adopts a highly ascetic, unconventional, and unworldly way of life devoted to preaching, wandering, and setting an example of holiness. Typically the holy fool would deliberately adopt the behavior of an insane person and would practice various forms of self-mortification such as travelling around naked or in chains and subsisting on a meager diet, and some of them would deliberately flout conventional standards of morality. Sometimes these holy fools had to endure mockery, but more often they would be treated with great respect and accorded a freedom to speak unwelcome truths, even to monarchs. Before becoming a holy fool or a shaman, the person concerned had to feel a powerful calling, such as by experiencing a severe illness and a miraculous cure. While the two types of individual, the holy fool and the shaman, are very different in their worldviews and religious beliefs, both are characterized by ecstasy-inducing practices. Russian history, literature, and hagiography are full of examples of the holy fool and the related tradition of the starets. As we have seen, Rasputin had something of both types about him and something of the shaman as well.

One well-known example of a fool for Christ was Saint Xenia of St. Petersburg.* Born in the early part of the eighteenth century, she married an army officer and court chorister Col. Andrei Petrov, with whom she lived happily until his sudden death while drinking at a party. The twenty-six-year-old widow, utterly grief-stricken, gave away her house and possessions and disappeared from St. Petersburg for eight years, during which time it is believed that she sought advice on the spiritual life from certain Orthodox contemplatives. On her return

---

*Website of the St. Xenia Orthodox Church, Methuen, Massachusetts, USA.

to St. Petersburg she embarked on the life of a fool for Christ, wearing her husband's uniform and calling herself Andrei, ministering to the poor, performing good works, and praying at night alone in the fields. When the uniform wore out she dressed in rags. At first she was often ridiculed and insulted, but gradually she began to acquire fame as a holy woman with a special radiance, gifts of prophecy and healing, and a way of making people feel blessed by her presence.

A characteristic incident was when she told a woman called Paraskeva Antonova that God had given her a son and she should go immediately to the Smolensky Cemetery in St. Petersburg. Puzzled, Paraskeva set off for the cemetery and on the way saw that a crowd had gathered where a pregnant woman had been knocked down by a coach, given birth on the spot, and then died. Paraskeva took pity on the child, a boy, carried him home, and in due course adopted him when no father or other relatives could be traced.[21]

Xenia died at the age of seventy-one and was canonized by the Orthodox Church outside Russia in 1978 and within Russia in 1988. She is buried, fittingly, in the Smolensky Cemetery, her grave marked by an ornate chapel. There are many churches named after her in various countries.

Of course other countries have their saints who are renowned for great feats of asceticism and self-sacrifice, but there is something quintessentially Russian about people like Xenia, with their combination of deeply felt religiosity, humility, intense passion, and steely, unbreakable stoicism. It is partly these qualities that enabled the nation to endure the nightmare of Stalinism and the Second World War.

 EIGHT

The New Paganism
A Spiritual Counterrevolution

To misquote Karl Marx's *Communist Manifesto:* a specter is haunting Russia, the specter of paganism. One can see it at work in a thousand places all over the country at the times of the seasonal pagan festivals, such as the equinoxes and solstices, when followers gather, preferably in the open air, to sing, dance and leap over bonfires in an atmosphere of joyful exuberance, typically watched over by huge figures of Slavic gods, carved out of tree trunks.

While such pagan events have only been celebrated on a large scale since the end of the communist era, they are in fact a manifestation of a process that has been going on for much longer, a process that is part of the ceaseless task of self-interrogation and deliberation about the true spiritual identity of the Russians.

As the philosopher Nikolai Berdyaev has observed: "Two contradictory principles lay at the foundation of the structure of the Russian soul, the one a natural, Dionysian, elemental paganism and the other ascetic monastic Orthodoxy."[1] As I have already pointed out when speaking about the survival of the old gods, pagan customs and beliefs are deeply rooted in Russian folk tradition and often exist side by side with Orthodox practice. Therefore the distinction between paganism and neo-paganism is not always clear-cut. However, I shall generally opt for the latter term when referring to the revived form of paganism.

We can trace the revival back to the romantic movement of the late eighteenth and early nineteenth centuries, which included a new and romanticized celebration of national identity. In the Slavic realm this pagan nationalism emerged initially not so much in Russia as in Poland and Ukraine. An early champion of paganism was the Polish archaeologist and folklorist Zoryan Dolenga-Khodakovsky (real name: Adam Charnotsky, 1784–1825). In 1818 he published a work in Polish entitled *On the Slavs before Christianity,* in which he declared himself a pagan and asserted that the adoption of Christianity was a mistake.[2] Another Pole, Bronislav Trentovsky, followed up in 1848 with his book *Slavic Faith, or Ethics Governing the Universe,* in which he argued that the Slavic gods are different manifestations of the God worshipped by the Christians. By the 1920s enthusiasm for the pre-Christian Slavic religion was giving birth to organized groups, such as the Holy Circle of Sviatovit's Followers, founded in 1921 by the Pole Vladislav Kolodzei.

In Russia itself such organized pagan groups came later, but meanwhile a pagan undercurrent made itself felt in the arts. In literature there were poets like Sergei Gorodetsky, who began as a symbolist and whose early collections of poems, *Yar* and *Perun,* celebrated the ancient Slavic gods. Later he abandoned symbolism and turned to realism. In the performing arts there was the path-breaking ballet *Rite of Spring,* produced by Sergei Diaghilev's company and subtitled *Pictures of Pagan Russia in Two Parts.* It premiered in Paris in 1913 with music by Igor Stravinsky, choreography by Vaslav Nijinsky and scenery by the artist Nikolai Roerich, whom we have already encountered in chapter 1. In the ballet a young girl dances herself to death as part of a pagan spring ritual. Stravinsky's highly original music, with its jarring tones and complicated rhythms, was matched by Nijinsky's minimalist choreography and awkward-seeming movements. It was all too revolutionary for the Paris audience, and the premiere sparked a riot. It was as though the spirit of pagan Russia had been unleashed in full force.

That spirit is also evident elsewhere in the art of Roerich, many of whose paintings show the world of Slavic paganism. One, for example, entitled *The Idols*, painted in 1901, depicts a bleak stretch of countryside by a river. In the foreground are five huge tree trunks, carved and painted with vaguely humanoid figures and surrounded by a circle of standing stones, interspersed with horses' skulls. The picture has an eerie feeling, accentuated by the fact that the circle is deserted. A pagan spirit also pervades Roerich's famous set design for the ballet *The Rite of Spring*, which has been revived many times since the original performance in 1913. Roerich designed some new sets for a Massine revival in the 1940s, one of which shows a group

Fig. 8.1. *The Idols*, a painting by Nikolai Roerich reflecting the world of Slavic paganism (See also color plate 7)

WIKIMEDIA COMMONS

of white-robed women performing a circle dance on top of a hillock overlooking a lake, while to one side a small orchestra is playing.

After the revolution the Slavic pagan spirit became subdued for a time, although in the Stalinist period some research into the ancient Slavic religion was carried out with the approval of Stalin, apparently in the search for some pre-Christian national ethos. Under Stalin's successors there came signs of an appreciable reawakening of Slavic pagan consciousness in Russia. There was a distinct lunatic fringe to this movement, consisting of such figures as Valerii Emelianov (1929–1999), a crazed prophet with extreme anti-Judaic and anti-Masonic views, who in the 1980s spent six years in a Leningrad mental hospital being treated for schizophrenia after being convicted of killing his wife and chopping her up with an axe. In 1989, three years after his release, he formed a pagan community in Moscow, and in 1991 he cofounded an organization called the Slavic Council. After several more sojourns in mental hospitals he died in 1999.[3]

A near contemporary of Emelianov and also a proponent of the neo-pagan movement was the artist and writer Igor Ivanovich Sinyavin (1937–2000). From the predominantly abstract and "modern" style of his paintings and the fact that he spent a number of years in the United States, one might have expected him to have had a left-liberal, democratic outlook, but in fact he became a radical traditionalist and fervent Russian nationalist, as is clear from his book *The Path to Truth* (*Stezya Pravdy*), published in 1996, in which he wrote:

> Russia was and remains a state under continuous siege . . . And therefore it should be more like a monastery or an army than a booth at a bazaar. There is only one way out of today's chaos and plunder: an even more centralized system, more strictly totalitarian, more ideocratic, more unified than under Stalin. . . . We follow the path of our ancient ancestors. . . . They possessed higher knowledge, higher Wisdom. They were the embodiment of that Wisdom. This ancient

Wisdom was destroyed, distorted, slandered by a false and alien religion hostile to the Russian spirit . . . you are either a Russian or a Christian . . . "world" religions, especially Christianity, impose perversion of natural morality, denial of life, destruction of social foundations and national culture. Paganism is life, world religions are death . . . the preachers of these religions should be treated like provocateurs, terrorists, and dangerous criminals.[4]

Characteristically, he spells the word for wisdom or special knowledge, *Vyedenie* (in Cyrillic *Ведение*), with a capital to emphasize that he is referring to the belief that the Russians are the inheritors of the same wisdom tradition contained in the Hindu scriptures, the *Vedas*.

While the domestic neo-pagan movement was in its early stages, there was meanwhile an increasing interchange between neo-pagans in the Russian diaspora and those in the homeland. The *Book of Veles,* with its alleged account of the early Slavs and their gods, having first been published in San Francisco, was fed back to Russia, where it found many enthusiastic readers. At the same time a number of Russian scholars were writing about the ancient Slavs and their religious traditions. There was, for example, Boris Ribakov (1908–2001), author of *The Paganism of the Ancient Slavs* (*Yazichestvo drevnich slavyan*), first published in 1981, which begins with a grandiose claim: "Slavic paganism is a part of a huge universal complex of primal beliefs and rituals, coming from many millennia ago and serving as the basis of all later world religions."[5] Being a product of Soviet-era academe, Ribakov is careful to say at the outset that he is writing from a Marxist-Leninist perspective, but, reading between the lines, it is clear that he feels a personal connection with the cultures he is writing about. The book, which is richly illustrated with photographs and drawings, gives a detailed picture of a great many aspects of Slav culture, ranging from the decorative patterns on clothes and furniture to shamanic ritual practices. His many other books include

The Paganism of Ancient Russia (Yazichestvo drevnei Rossii), published in 1987.

Ribakov lived to the age of ninety-three, long enough to see the mushrooming of Slavic neo-paganism after about 1990, bringing with it a spate of new books, mostly of the popular, mass-market kind. One of the most prolific authors of the present phase is Alexander Asov (born in 1964), a champion of the *Book of Veles,* of which he has produced several editions with detailed commentaries (see chapter 6). With over forty books to his name, encompassing both fiction and nonfiction, Asov is nothing if not prolific. The titles include: *Myths and Legends of the Ancient Slavs; Slavic Astrology; Atlantis and Ancient Russia; Russia, Sacred Ancestral Home of the Slavs; Secrets of the Russian Magi; Atlanteans, Aryans, Slavs: History and Faith; Gods of the Slavs and the Birth of Rus; Runes, Signs and Mysteries of the Slavs; Calendar of the Russian Magi; Stars of the Ancient Slavs; The Holy Russian Vedas;* and *Slavic Runes.*

In his book *The Great Secrets of Rus* Asov writes: "After the collapse of the Soviet Union, we were essentially left without ideological and moral support and therefore we are again trying to turn to the experience of the past centuries. We wish to return to our roots. A 'spiritual counterrevolution' is underway in the country."[6] He clearly perceives Russia's spiritual roots as lying in a pre-Christian precursor civilization, which he links with Atlantis, Hyperborea, and the Vedic civilization of India.

Asov's works, whose accuracy has often been challenged, are nevertheless a colorful and intriguing bricolage of mythology, folklore, alternative prehistory, and much else. He frequently alludes to motifs from legend, such as the figure of the Gamayun, a fabled bird of paradise with colorful plumage. In Asov's work the Gamayun becomes a carrier of the ancient Vedic wisdom. In his children's book *The Feather of Gamayun* he writes:

It is known that the feather of the Gamayun bird will lead you to the Magic Land. Where is this wonderful country? It is both far and near. The way to it can be found only far from big cities and highways—for example, in the mysterious forests beyond the Volga near Lake Svetloyar. There, as every novice wizard knows, there is a gate of fire leading to the invisible city of Kitezh. Following the feather of the wondrous bird, you can go through that gate and see not a few miraculous things beyond them. There, in Kitezh, myths and fairy tales come to life, dreams come true, and gods and wizards, as well as dragons, mermaids, pitchforks, and elves, are found at every step and do not surprise anyone.[7]

This is the perennial Russian dream of the never-never land that we have already encountered. Kitezh is the name of a legendary town that was said to have stood on the shores of Lake Svetloyar in central Russia. The story goes that in the thirteenth century the city was attacked by a Mongol army but disappeared into the lake before the Mongols could capture it. Legend further says that sometimes the sound of church bells and singing voices can faintly be heard coming from below the surface of the lake, but that only the pure in heart can find their way to Kitezh. The legend is the subject of an opera written in 1907 by Nikolai Rimsky-Korsakov entitled *The Legend of the Invisible City of Kitezh and the Maiden Fevroniya.*

The theme of magical birds appears in this story, as in many Russian legends. A well-known example is the Firebird, somewhat similar to the Gamayun and often depicted in works of decorative art and as a heraldic motif. The Firebird has brightly flaming plumage and can bestow great good fortune as well as doom. This motif is the subject of the ballet *The Firebird Suite,* choreographed by Michel Fokine with music by Igor Stravinsky and first performed at the Paris Opera in 1910. The bird is often the object of an arduous quest, sometimes ending with the hero taking possession of one of its magic feathers. It can therefore be seen as a kind of Russian equivalent to the Holy Grail.

A FAST-GROWING RELIGION

While such motifs from Russian mythology have helped to nourish the neo-pagan movement, so has modern fantasy fiction. One of the best-known exponents of this genre is Yuri Nikitin, whose works include a cycle of novels, *Three from the Forest* (*Dvoye iz lyesa*), which moves from a Tolkienesque world set in Slavic antiquity up to the present day. In a similar fantasy vein are the works of Maria Semyonova, such as her sword-and-sorcery epic *Wolfhound* (*Volkodav*), which has sold over 80,000 copies and been made into a 2006 blockbuster film on a budget of ten million dollars, one of the highest in the history of the Russian cinema.

The works of writers like these as well as the promotional opportunities offered by the internet have greatly helped to facilitate the spectacular growth of neo-paganism in Russia since the 1990s. The movement is commonly called *Rodnoverie* (native faith), usually anglicized to Rodnover. Alternative names include *slavianskoye neo-yazichestvo* (Slavic neo-paganism), *slavianskaya vera* (Slavic faith), and a variety of others. The first Rodnover organization to be officially registered in Russia was the Moscow Slavic Pagan Community, established in February 1994 with the approval of the Ministry of Justice and still active at the time of writing. From the start the Moscow group endeavored to establish as genuine a connection as possible with the ancient Slavic religion, using the work of scholars such as Ribakov as well as evidence from folklore and personal experience of vernacular traditions. The website of the group states: "The main task of the Moscow Slavic Pagan Community at present is to study the bioenergetic and interactive aspects of the various magical systems of the peoples of Russia. An attempt has been made to explore the entire magical arsenal left by our ancestors. Two groups from the community have worked to this end."[8]

In addition to celebrating the seasonal festivals with dancing, feasting, and ritual, the Moscow group, like others of its kind, is keen to honor the heroic past of the Slavic people with such activities as wrestling matches and battle enactments. For the latter purpose they collaborate with a group called Arkona, which specializes in mock battles involving rival teams in heavy armor. Such enactments are not exclusive to Russia—in England, for example, there is a group called the Sealed Knot, which regularly meets to reenact Civil War battles. Many of the

Fig. 8.2. Beloyar, a priest of the pagan religion Rodnoverie, conducting a ceremony in which a boy receives a man's belt as a rite of passage

Rodnover groups also conduct weddings and memorial ceremonies and organize concerts, craft fairs, and much else.

Numerous Rodnover groups have appeared since the 1990s, and some of them have formed umbrella organizations. The first to emerge was the Union of Slavic Communities of the Slavic Native Faith (USC SNF), established in 1997. Its aims include preserving and fostering Slavic religious traditions and practices, working to create a coherent set of tenets, supporting the member communities with financial, legal, or other assistance, and cooperating with foreign communities and related pagan organizations in various countries of the world. In 2015 the USC SNF opened its own place of worship, the Temple of Fire of Svarozhich (*Chram ognya Svarozhicha*) in the Kaluga district near Moscow—in Slavic mythology Svarozhich is the son of the Slavic sky god Svarog. The Temple is a sturdy building of logs with a central fireplace for the sacred fire.

The USC SNF was followed in 1999 by the Circle of Veles, which currently has about ten member groups from various parts of Russia. Another umbrella organization, the Circle of Pagan Tradition, founded in 2002, has a very large membership with several dozen regional groups from Russia as well as a number in Scandinavia and Ukraine. Like many other Rodnover organizations it has links to the European Congress of Ethnic Religions, based in Vilnius, Lithuania.

In terms of their political stance, the Russian Rodnover groups cover a very wide spectrum. There are of course groups within Rodnover, as there are among the Christian community, that adopt a radically chauvinist and Slavic supremacist position, but others take exactly the opposite stance. The Circle of Pagan Tradition, for example, is emphatically non-chauvinistic in outlook. A statement on its website rejects national or religious intolerance and condemns the abuse of pagan symbols by chauvinistic elements, but at the same time affirms that each culture has a value in itself.[9] The Circle of Veles has a similar position, as affirmed in an interview with Veleslav, leader of Rodolubye (meaning roughly "love of the kin"), one of the Circle's constituent groups. Veleslav stated:

> Paganism, for all its all-embracing nature, has a very concrete and vital human aspect. For every pagan, indeed for every human being, the notions of kinship and kindred exist, and one should not renounce them. This does not mean that others are inferior. But, if you grew up in this particular forest, this piece of nature, then the birch tree will evoke in you a very different feeling from what a palm tree evokes. This does not mean that palm trees are worse, simply that you begin your journey from a given set of circumstances, and you will perceive your own spiritual sky through the medium of the Russian language. . . . If I lived in Africa I think I would regard palms in the same way that I now regard birches.[10]

The numerical strength of the Rodnover movement is difficult to determine, but one can get some indication by the number of people who follow the various Russian neo-pagan groups on the internet. Just on one Russian platform I counted thirteen such groups with a total membership of well over 670,000. Admittedly some people will be members of more than one group, and not all will be active in Rodnover, but still the number is striking.

SACRED SITES

One also has to take into account the thousands of people who flock to sites of archaeological or legendary significance to celebrate the solar festivals and other pagan events. The mystique attached to these sites is particularly striking in the case of Arkaim in the southern Urals, which is often called the "Russian Stonehenge." The region in which it is located is rich in archaeological sites, some going back to two thousand years or more BCE. The archaeologists had long categorized these sites as belonging to a rather primitive bronze age culture, but in the 1960s and '70s excavations began to turn up remains of settlements that were puzzling to the experts, as they indicated a higher level of culture than would fit with what had previously been found in the region. Aerial reconnaissance revealed outlines of a particularly intriguing settlement in the vicinity of Arkaim at the confluence of two rivers, and in 1987 a team of archaeologists, led by Gennady B. Zdanovich (1938–2020), was sent to investigate it. The problem was that the Ministry of Water Resources had earmarked the spot for a reservoir to supply water for local agriculture. Technical plans were complete, dams were under construction, pipelines had been laid, and the flooding of the area was imminent. Realizing the great historical importance of the site, Zdanovich began a campaign to save it from being submerged. He had the support of influential authorities including members of the Institute of Archaeologists of the USSR Academy of Sciences and, after a three-year battle that had the makings of a dramatic film script, the dam project was canceled by order of the Russian Council of Ministers. A crucial role in the cancellation was played by local residents and farmers, who realized the importance of the site and evidently gave more weight to its value than to their need for water.[11]

There was a particularly compelling reason why the site was considered so important, namely that it was thought to hold important clues regarding the early history of the Indo-Europeans (or Aryans, as they are often referred to in Russia). The Indo-Europeans are believed to have originated somewhere in Europe or Central Asia or possibly in the far north and then to have migrated in various directions, one branch settling in India, others going west and south. Their legacy is seen today in most of the European languages and their many commonalities with Sanskrit. Similarly, the mythologies and religions of Europe and India also reveal striking similarities, leading some people to believe in an ancient Indo-European wisdom tradition, handed down over the centuries. This belief, as we have seen, has a strong following in Russia, and many Russians see themselves as the most direct descendants and inheritors of the Indo-European civilization.

Consequently there is much speculation in Russia about where the original Aryan or Indo-European homeland was located. One popular theory places it in the Arctic region, in the fabled place known to the ancient Greeks as Hyperborea, a theory supported by the works of the Indian writer Bâl Gangâdar Tilak, as mentioned earlier. Another body of opinion locates it in southern Russia. Hence the excitement over the discovery of Arkaim.

The excavation of the site revealed it to be a fortified town, surrounded by two rings of defensive walls and ditches with a ring of adjacent dwellings of wood and adobe behind each wall—the prehistoric equivalent of terraced housing. The population was estimated to have been 1,500–2,000, a sizeable settlement in those days. The site also had bronze foundries, a temple, and what had probably been an observatory. Finds included pottery, weapons, and jewelry. With a rectangular courtyard in the center, the layout of the site resembled one of the mandalas of Hinduism and Buddhism, a further possible indication of an Indo-European connection. When the archaeologists surveyed the surrounding region they found that Arkaim was only one of over twenty similar settlements, forming what Zdanovich called a "country of cities" stretching along the eastern slopes of the southern Urals for 400 kilometers north to south and 100–150 kilometers east to west.[12]

Within a very short period Arkaim and its surroundings had acquired a powerful mystique as the long-sought original home of the Aryans. It was invested with an aura of holiness and became a magnet for a multiplicity of different spiritual, religious, and nationalist groups. Neo-pagans began to descend on the site en masse, especially at the times of the solar festivals such as the midsummer Ivan Kupala celebration, communing with the earth energies and spiraling their way through a labyrinth that they had laid out in stones nearby. Arkaim also attracts followers of the Roerich movement, members of the Hare Krishna sect, and Russian Zoroastrians, who claim that Zoroaster himself was born in the Urals. The reputation of the site as an observatory has attracted the attention of astrologers such as the couple Pavel and Tamara Globa. The latter has declared Arkaim to be an enormous horoscope predicting the future return of the Aryans to their homeland.[13] While the Arkaim enthusiasts are of many different persuasions they tend to share a mystically colored patriotism. At a time when the collapse of the Soviet Union is still a relatively recent memory, Russian patriots can derive a renewed pride in the thought that they are the heirs to the ancient Aryan civilization with its Vedic wisdom and its ancestral home in the Urals.

A few hundred miles southwest from Arkaim, near the coast of the Black Sea, lies another remarkable collection of prehistoric remains, namely the dolmens of the North Caucasus. Thought to date from

Fig. 8.3. Prehistoric dolmen in the Krasnodar region of the North Caucasus
<small>Photograph courtesy of Yuri Smirnov</small>

between the second and fourth millennium BCE, these structures are made of stone blocks or slabs, very precisely dressed and fitted together, with an opening, usually a round hole, at one side. They number about three thousand and their origin remains a mystery. Since the late 1990s they have attracted thousands of pilgrims, drawn to the area in the belief that the megaliths are linked with the ancient Vedic wisdom and that they exert powerful energies. Many have reported profound spiritual experiences while meditating at these sites.

The North Caucasus area is also the location for a series of festivals, some continuing the ancient pagan seasonal events, others of more recent origin. One of the most popular is the Festival of Positive Creation, held in clearings near the village of Vozrozhdenie close to the east coast of the Black Sea, which attracts over a thousand visitors each year. This is a festival of music and dance but much more. It includes seminars, master classes, and round tables on topics including ecology, health, relationships, and resource-saving technologies.[14]

Fig. 8.4. A circle dance during the Festival of Positive Creation near the village of Vozrozhdenie in the North Caucasus

Photograph courtesy of Yuri Smirnov

A similar mystique to that of the North Caucasus has become attached to the area of the Kola peninsula and the White Sea in the far northwest of Russia, which is believed by some archaeologists and researchers to have been the original land that the ancient Greeks called Hyperborea (Land Beyond the North Wind). Increasing numbers of tourists are going there to visit the prehistoric sites—pyramids, labyrinths, and stone pavings—and to commune with the "Vedic" wisdom of the Hyperboreans. The town of Kovdor, close to the Finnish border, is even being promoted by the local tourist board as the "capital of Hyperborea."

Thus Russia's mystical quest is, for many Russians as well as for people of other nations, a process of reconnection with the relics of ancient civilizations that are believed to have once inhabited Russian territory.

 **NINE**

Saints, Doctors, and Cunning Folk

According to a report in *The Times* of London of November 26, 2018, by Moscow correspondent Marc Bennetts, Russia has more faith healers than doctors. The article quotes the Russian Academy of Sciences as saying that are about 800,000 occultists and faith healers in the country but only 640,000 doctors. The report goes on to say that 67 percent of women and 25 percent of men have at some time sought help from a psychic or sorcerer.[1]

It should be noted, however, that faith healing is not the exclusive domain of occultists and sorcerers. There is a long tradition of faith healing within the Orthodox Church. We have already encountered Rasputin, who had well-attested healing powers despite his unruly and far from saintly personality. A total contrast to Rasputin was Saint Matrona of Moscow (1881–1952), one of the most famous Orthodox healers and clairvoyants of the past two centuries.* Her extraordinary life was all the more extraordinary in that she resolutely continued her mission through the horrific years of the communist rule.

The child of very poor parents, Dmitry and Natalia Nikonov,

---

*For information on her life I have relied on the account posted on the website of the Matrona Museum in her native district (only available in Russian).

she was born blind, and from the start there were signs that she was marked for a special destiny. When she was baptized a cloud of sweet-smelling vapor rose from the font, causing the astonished priest to say that she would be a *pravedinyets* (an especially pious and holy person). As a very young child she woke up one night and somehow made her way to the corner where the icons were kept. Her mother found her there talking to the icons. From about the age of seven she began to display healing gifts, and sick people began to flock to the house to be treated by her. At seventeen she lost the use of her legs and remained unable to walk for the rest of her life. She predicted the revolution with all of its horrors, which she said was a contagion brought on by demons that had possessed the country.

In 1925 she had to leave home because the large numbers of people coming to her for healing were becoming an embarrass-ment to her two communist brothers. She moved to Moscow, where she lived with various well-wishers. Constantly in danger of arrest, she clairvoyantly anticipated when the secret police were about to arrive, and always moved on just in time. All the time she went on healing anyone who came to her. She died in 1952 and was canonized in 1999.

FOLK MEDICINE

Matrona was a very devout Orthodox believer and had no time for folk healers and cunning men and women, believing that they worked with demons. In this regard many Orthodox Christians take a more flexible view and see nothing wrong in consulting a folk healer. I myself had some experience of folk medicine in Russia at a time when I was suffering from a rash on the lower part of both legs. I was advised to consult a local folk healer or *znachar,* to use the Russian word, which literally means "one who knows." In England this type of healer is called a "cunning man" or "cunning woman," the word "cunning" in its original meaning also implying knowledge or skill. The znachar, like the cunning man, is a combination of healer, herbalist, and sometimes magician. Nearly every Russian village has one, or at least used to. Very often the znachar is an elderly woman. In this case, however, it was a young man. He showed me a znachar's encyclopedia that he possessed—a fascinating compendium of folk remedies, herbal lore, spells, and talismanic symbols, all mixed up with Christian references rather in the manner of Voodoo or Santeria. To treat my skin problem he used a plant called *konsky shchavel* (horse sorrel), which grew abundantly in the area where he lived. A poultice of the leaves was taped to my legs and left overnight, bringing an immediate improvement the next day.

These folk healers possess an immense wealth of knowledge and skill for health maintenance and treatment, built up over many centuries, and they still provide a much-valued resource that exists side by side with the regular health care system. In almost any bookshop in Russia you will find a section full of titles like *Russian Folk-Household Medicine, Natural Ways of Curing Heart Conditions, Healing through Vinegar,* or the *Encyclopedia of Herbal Remedies.* There is also a commensurate number of popular journals full of dietary advice, instructions for making herbal preparations, and tips about traditional treatments for every conceivable ailment. Then there are the healers with a mass following, such as Anatoly Kashpirovsky (born 1969), who came to prominence in 1989 after a televised operation in which he claimed to have enabled a woman to undergo abdominal surgery without anesthetic and without experiencing pain. The woman, Lesya Yershova, later said that she had in fact suffered acute pain during the operation, but this did nothing to diminish Kashpirovsky's following. In the early 1990s he appeared frequently on television and traveled around the country performing spectacular feats of healing in packed stadiums. In 1993 he was elected to the Russian Parliament, the Duma, and for some years curtailed his healing performances. But following the outbreak of the coronavirus pandemic in the spring of 2020, he returned to the limelight and at the time of writing operates a YouTube channel.*

One might have expected that the Communist regime would have disapproved of folk medicine, but in fact this was only partly the case. The late Paul M. Kourennoff, in his book *Russian Folk Medicine,* writes that the orthodox medical profession in Russia traditionally maintained an attitude of tolerance and respect toward folk medicine practitioners, and that this attitude survived the revolution. With the pharmaceutical industry nationalized and subsidized by the state and with private medical practice nonexistent, the doctors and drug manufacturers had no vested interest in opposing their folk-healer counterparts. Doctors would even sometimes advise a patient to go to a folk medicine practitioner.[2] Furthermore, the Soviet scientific establishment diligently researched the effectiveness of traditional remedies. In 1919 a laboratory was set up in Petrograd (as it was then called) to investigate the healing properties of plants and herbs, and later a national research institute was established, with regional laboratories, to carry out similar experimental work. Interest in herbalism received a boost during the Second World War when drugs were scarce and medical services overstretched.[3]

In post-Soviet Russia the situation in the health sector has become a great deal more complex. There have been measures to regularize the practice of complementary and alternative medicine (CAM), to use the modern term, by introducing required qualifications and registration for practitioners, although the village cunning folk still continue to practice unofficially as they have always done. In addition, various systems of treatment such as acupuncture, homeopathy, Reiki, and Ayurveda are penetrating Russia along with other global influences.

---

*For information on Kashpirovsky, see the article, "As COVID-19 Hits Russia, A Self-Styled Psychic Healer And Soviet-Era Icon Returns" on the RadioFreeEurope/RadioLiberty website as well as the Wikipedia entry on him. See also his YouTube channel.

At the same time there is a new flourishing of local medical traditions and practices. Russia, with its vast territory and multiplicity of cultures and ethnic groups, has a commensurately wide variety of approaches to matters of health. To a large extent these involve commonsense rules for staying healthy—a good diet or periodic fasting, for example—but some of the treatments appear bizarre unless one knows their scientific basis. For example, in Siberia and other parts of Russia, a traditional remedy for arthritis involves digging up an anthill—ants, earth, and all—putting the contents into a bag, boiling it for half an hour, then immersing it in a hot bath for the patient to lie in. The scientific explanation for the efficacy of this technique is that ants' bodies contain formic acid, which has been found to relieve arthritis. In addition the effect of the remedy is enhanced by a substance secreted by the ants during the construction of their anthills.[4]

Much of the folk medical knowledge in Russia stems from the period of the Tatar-Mongol occupation of Russia, the so-called Tatar Yoke (1237–1480). An example is the drink called *kumys*, consisting of fermented mare's milk. A favorite beverage of the Mongol horsemen, it was said to have contributed to their legendary strength and stamina. The best kumys came from the small Mongol horses, especially those that fed on the pastures of the southwestern steppes around the lower reaches of the Volga, which evidently had special qualities. The region had numerous curative centers where kumys was drunk in large quantities, and it was there that sick Mongol warriors were sent to recover. As Paul Kourennoff writes: "It is no exaggeration to say that, historically, Western civilization was almost destroyed by mare's milk!"[5] The heyday of the Mongol warriors and their horse breeding passed, but the making of kumys continued, and it is still made today in both Russia and Mongolia, although for commercial production it now tends to be made from cow's milk, fortified to make its chemical composition closer to mare's milk.

The resurgence of shamanism, especially among the various

Mongol peoples of Russia, has brought with it a corresponding revival of shamanic healing practices. One of these involves the therapeutic use of sound. Chanting, incantation, and the rhythmic beating of the shaman's drum can affect the nervous system and bring about organic changes. I have already mentioned the case of Rasputin's treatment of the Tsarevich through his voice alone, a technique that he could have learned from shamanic healers.

Shamanic healing traditions are now attracting increasing attention from mainstream doctors such as Olga Kharitidi, who has achieved fame with a series of books drawing on her experiences with Siberian shamanism. In the first book, *Entering the Circle,* she tells how this came about. While working in a psychiatric clinic in Novosibirsk she was persuaded by a friend to visit a female shaman living in a remote Siberian village, who taught her certain shamanic techniques for dealing with mental illness. Such illness, in the shamanic view, has two possible causes: (a) if the soul or part of it has become lost; or (b) if the person has been overwhelmed by an alien power. Returning to her clinic she treated a woman suffering from acute schizophrenia who was believed to be incurable. Using the approach she had learned from the shaman she was able to cure the woman to the point where she could return home and resume a normal life.

Subsequently she received further insights from a physicist friend called Dmitri, who had an experimental laboratory and was researching the theories of the astrophysicist Nikolai Alexandrovich Kozyrev (1908–1983), who had postulated, among other things, the reversibility of time under certain conditions. Seated in a kind of tubular device known as a "Kozyrev mirror" in Dmitri's laboratory, she received a revelation that humanity, like a chrysalis about to turn into a butterfly, is on the verge of a new evolutionary stage in which we would intersect with other civilizations in hitherto invisible dimensions of reality. There are, she was told, places where channels open up between these dimensions.

Plate 1. The Maria Ascension Church in Astrakhan, showing the screen known as the iconostasis, concealing the inner sanctum from the congregation

Plate 2. A 1930s cartoon by Olaf Gulbransson, caricaturing the German historian Oswald Spengler. The woman in the background riding a bear symbolizes Spengler's prediction that a new culture will come out of Russia.

Plate 3. Andrei Biely, writer and esotericist, as portrayed by Leon Bakst. Biely's extraordinary novel *Petersburg* captures the feverish atmosphere of pre-revolutionary Russia.

Plate 4. The Buddhist temple in St. Petersburg, built just before the revolution

Plate 5. Mural of the fabled land of Byelovodye on an
apartment block in Omsk

Plate 6. The Firebird, a ubiquitous motif in Russian mythology and folklore

Plate 7. *The Idols,* a painting by Nikolai Roerich reflecting
the world of Slavic paganism

Plate 8. Anastasia as portrayed by Kumar Alzhanov

Plate 9. *Old Slavic Pagan Ceremony,*
a painting by Alexander Uglanov
COURTESY OF THE ARTIST

Plate 10. A Kozyrev mirror, developed by research scientists in Akademgorodok, Siberia. Here the mirror is being tested for its consciousness-expanding properties.

Altai is such a place, and Belovodye is another name for the same phenomenon. Dr. Kharitidi subsequently emigrated to the United States where she has continued her writing career. Her work evinces some of the egregores and stock themes that we have encountered earlier, such as the new millennium and the never-never land, and it has helped to draw attention to the rich shamanic tradition that the Mongols have brought to Russia.

After the end of the Tatar Yoke in the fifteenth century there was little Mongol migration into Russia until the second half of the seventeenth century, when various Mongol tribes moved into Siberia. On top of their ancient shamanic culture, they started in the early eighteenth century to absorb Tibetan Buddhism along with its highly developed system of medicine. By 1850 there were forty-five monasteries, several of which also functioned as medical colleges. This synergy between religion and medicine continued until 1929 when the Stalin regime outlawed the practice and teaching of medicine in religious institutions, dealing a blow to Tibetan medicine in the region, from which it only began to recover in the 1960s.[6]

Today there are basically two regions of the former Soviet Union where Tibetan Buddhism is practiced: (a) the cluster of autonomous regions to the north of the Mongolian border, including the Tuva, Yakut, and Buryat Republics; (b) the Kalmyk Republic, situated at the western side of Russia north of the Caspian Sea. These are multiconfessional regions where there are adherents of many faiths: shamanism, Orthodoxy, Islam, and others, alongside Tibetan Buddhism.

Tibetan medicine has roots going back more than two thousand years and draws on the medical traditions of India, China, Persia, and other cultures. It involves an integration of mind, body, and spirit and is geared to the individual patient rather than the ailment per se. When assessing a case, the Tibetan doctor will determine which of the four "humors" the patient corresponds to, the humors being wind (or air), fire, earth, and water—that is to say essentially the four elements of the European classical tradition. Each is characterized by a particular body type and a predisposition to certain ailments. In applying treatment the doctor may prescribe, in addition to herbal medicines, certain meditations and rituals.

Following perestroika there was a rush to the znachars, shamans, Mongol healers, and the like, whose practices were often a bricolage of traditional knowledge combined with New Age methods of treatment imported from abroad. In the new atmosphere of freedom numerous associations, alternative health centers, and training courses sprang up. Soon the authorities felt compelled to introduce some order into the alternative health sector, and laws were passed at national and regional levels specifying various categories of treatment and introducing required qualifications for practitioners. A distinction was made, for example, between (a) the vernacular folk healers or znachars, who practiced herbal medicine, bone-setting, naturopathy, and the like, and (b) practitioners of an established medical tradition, such as Tibetan medicine, who had undergone an appropriate training.

Regulations and categories vary from one region to another. In Buryatia, for example, where there are several organizations of shamans, the regulation of their activities comes under a law relating to religious institutions, which permits the practice of traditional medicine and the creation of corresponding medical organizations such as the Federal Centre for Oriental Medicine, founded in the 1990s.

A good example of how folk medicine and orthodox medicine can work together can be seen in Tuva, where folk healing is also predominantly connected with shamanism. Legislation since perestroika has regularized the practice of shamanic healing and defined the areas in which it can operate. One of the most active shamanic centers in Tuva is the Ai-Churek Center in the Tuvan capital Kyzyl, which is named after its director, Ai-Churek Oyun. In addition to various forms of healing, the center offers seminars and classes on singing, fortune-telling, traditional shamanic rituals, and ways of attracting happiness, wealth, and longevity. Kyzil also has a more official Centre for Traditional Medicine.[7]

Efforts to create a synergy between orthodox and alternative forms of medicine have a precedent in the work of Albert Schweitzer, the great Alsatian physician, philosopher, and theologian who in 1913 founded a hospital in the jungle of Gabon. There his practice was carried on in close collaboration with local healers, who achieved good results with, for example, patients with psychological problems. Patients with serious conditions requiring surgery or complex drug therapy were treated by a doctor.[8]

Russia is thus engaged in a concerted attempt to integrate different forms of medicine—orthodox, folk, and traditional—and, depending on how well it succeeds, there will be much that can be learned from its example.

 TEN

The Woman Clothed with the Sun
Russian Spirituality and the Erotic

"The Russians have not been given to moderation and they have readily gone to extremes." Thus wrote the philosopher Nikolai Berdyaev in his book *The Russian Idea,* and nowhere is his statement more true than in the realm of love and eros.[1] To understand the interconnection between this realm and Russia's spiritual quest, we must make a brief excursion into the sexual history of Russia.

Let us begin by going back to the time before the conversion to Christianity when the vast rural population were pagans, worshipping the old Slavic gods, living according to the rhythms of nature, and observing a continual round of seasonal festivals. For them sexuality was simply part of the natural order and was woven into certain customs concerned with agriculture and the promotion of fertility. Many of these customs survived Christianization. For example, as late as the nineteenth century, if you ventured into a rural community you might see a trouserless peasant ploughing a field or a scantily dressed woman running around a vegetable patch or a naked couple making love on the soft earth of spring—actions all intended to bring fertility to the land.[2]

With the conversion of the kingdom of Rus to Orthodoxy in the

154

tenth century came an attitude to sexuality that was very different from the down-to-earth approach of the pagan Slavs. Initially the influence of Christianity did not go far beyond the confines of the cities, and the rural masses continued their pagan ways as before, but gradually the Church extended its reach and by the fifteenth century it had established a sexual code that brought all kinds of rules and prohibitions to the intimate sphere. While elsewhere in Europe, most of all in Italy, the Renaissance was in full bloom with its newfound celebration of the human body and its sensual images of pagan gods and goddesses, no equivalent took place in Russia. Essentially the Church of that era regarded sex as a regrettable necessity for procreation. It was permitted only within marriage, only in the missionary position, and only on certain days. All kinds of penances, such as fasting, were imposed for infringement of these rules.

However, the Church's rules were one thing, and what people actually practiced was quite another. The German traveler Adam Olearius, who went to Russia in the 1630s with a trade delegation from the Duke of Holstein, paints a very unflattering picture of Russian mores in his account of the journey. At their entertainments, he writes, "all their discourse is of the abominations which they themselves have done, or seen committed by others . . . they are wholly given up to licentiousness, even to sins against Nature, not only with Men, but also with Beasts." He also recounts the goings-on at an annual religious festival that attracted many pilgrims to the capital, as recounted to him by the interpreter of the Grand Duke of Muscovy:

> "He who is allow'd to keep a tippling house, gets a permission from the Metropolitan to pitch several Tents, for the accommodation of the Pilgrims of both Sexes." The interpreter's account goes on to relate that "some of them instead of minding their devotions spend the day in drinking. . . . A woman got so drunk there, that coming

out of the tent she fell down; and fell asleep, naked as she was, in the street, in the day time. Which gave occasion to a *Muscovite*, who was also drunk, to lye down by her, and, having made use of her, to fall also asleep in the sight of so many people."[3]

THE TWO APHRODITES

There was at that time, even among the upper strata, little or no refined culture of eros such as had existed in medieval western Europe. In Russia there was no equivalent of the troubadours and the tradition of courtly love, nor of the kind of idealized love that Dante had for Beatrice. In the absence of such moderating influences, the Russian tendency toward extremes, which Berdyaev refers to, made itself felt in the domain of sexuality as elsewhere.

With the advent of Peter the Great and his westernizing reforms from the end of the seventeenth century, things began to change in the erotic sphere as in many others. Church restrictions on sexuality were eased, there was a new culture of gallantry, and it became fashionable for married people of the upper classes to have love affairs on the side. At the same time, sex remained a topic that was generally not talked about openly in polite society.

Up to the eighteenth century Russian literature is very reticent about the erotic domain. In the nineteenth century this situation changed, as though a Pandora's box had suddenly been opened. Many of the great Russian writers of that era, from Tolstoy to Dostoyevsky, addressed the theme of erotic love in their works. But here again we see that Russian tendency toward extremes: high and low, the spiritual and the physical, sainthood and depravity. Often these contrasts are evident in one and the same writer. Take, for example, Dostoyevsky's novel *Zapiski iz podpolya*, usually translated as *Notes from Underground* (actually the title carries a double meaning, as *iz podpolya* also means "from below the floor," in other words, from

where the vermin live and grime gathers). The anonymous narrator is a misanthropic, self-hating former civil servant, and the whole
narrative is an exercise in despair, gloom, and squalor. It features an
encounter with a prostitute, in whom the reader senses a spark of
goodness, but whom the narrator callously abuses and tosses aside. By
contrast, in Dostoyevsky's more famous novel *Crime and Punishment,*
the central figure Raskolnikov, after committing a murder and serving a sentence in a Siberian penal colony, is redeemed by Sonya, the
woman who loves him. Sonya herself embodies a contrast. She is
deeply religious but has for a time chosen to work as a prostitute to
support her family.

While in nineteenth-century Russia there was no shortage of literary works dealing with love, this was not the case in the domain
of philosophy, where writing on the subject was scarce. However, in
the Silver Age of the prerevolutionary period many philosophers and
writers suddenly turned their attention to this domain. This was the
period when in the west Freud's theories about human sexuality were
starting to attract attention, but in Russia Freudianism did not achieve
the same popularity. In the introduction to a collection of twentieth-
century writings on eros in Russia, Vyacheslav Shestakov writes:

> In contrast to western philosophers, the Russian thinkers of the
> early 20th century developed a humanistic understanding of love
> and, turning their attention to the question of sex, linked human
> sexual energy not only to procreation but to the spiritual culture
> of humanity—to religion, artistic creativity and the search for new
> moral values. The philosophy of love revealed itself as being at the
> same time a matter of ethics, aesthetics, psychology and the under-
> standing of the divine. [4]

One of the most significant writers on the subject of love was
the philosopher Vladimir Solovyov (1853–1900). Among his most

thought-provoking works is his treatise *The Meaning of Love*—and here he means both emotional and physical love.[5] Whereas so many philosophers and religious thinkers have attempted to drive a wedge between the two, Solovyov is intent on bringing them together, his ultimate ideal being a kind of primal androgyny in which there would be no need for sex. Rejecting the common view that sexuality exists merely for the purpose of procreation, Solovyov points out that many organisms reproduce in nonsexual ways, therefore nature did not need to invent sex if reproduction was the only purpose. He goes on to argue that the higher you go in the scale of living organisms, the less prolific they become in terms of reproduction but the stronger the sexual attraction becomes. At the lower end of the scale, the female fish produces millions of embryos, which are fertilized by the male outside of the female's body, a method that does not indicate a great power of attraction. Going up the scale, birds have a weaker power of reproduction but a stronger mutual attraction. And at the top of the scale human beings are the least prolific reproducers but have the strongest feelings of attraction to one another. Therefore sexual love must have a higher purpose. Male and female, Solovyov argues, are earthly reflections of two aspects of God, which yet form a perfect unity, toward which we strive through union with another human being. This ideal unity, he writes, is something "towards which our world is aspiring, and which constitutes the end of the cosmic and historical process."[6]

True love, for Solovyov, is both ascending and descending like the two Aphrodites that Plato writes about in the *Symposium*— Aphrodite Urania (the heavenly Aphrodite) and Aphrodite Pandemos (the earthly Aphrodite). These two Aphrodites were celebrated in Renaissance Italy in the paintings of Botticelli, and they inspired the refined philosophy of love developed by the Florentine Platonists of that period. The notion of the two Aphrodites overlaps in Solovyov's worldview with his veneration of the figure of Sophia, the personification of the principle of wisdom. Although identified in traditional Christianity with Christ as the Logos, Sophia came to be widely portrayed as a woman, especially in the Orthodox Church, where the wisdom tradition has an especially important place, as evidenced by the fact that the most magnificent cathedral of the Orthodox world was that of Saint Sophia in Constantinople.

Solovyov, during the course of his life, experienced three visions of the Sophia, whom he conceived as having both a heavenly and an earthly manifestation. In his poem of 1898, *Das Ewig-Weibliche* (the "Eternal Feminine," a much-quoted phrase from Goethe's *Faust*) he wrote:

> *Know this: The Eternal Feminine*
> *Is now coming to earth in an imperishable body.*
> *In the unfading light of the new Goddess*
> *Heaven has merged with the depths of the ocean.*[7]*

Solovyov's concept of the Sophia as a manifestation of the Eternal Feminine influenced a number of writers of the Silver age, especially the Symbolist poets Andrei Biely (1880–1934) and Alexander Blok (1880–1921), both of whom went so far as to believe that Blok's future wife, Lyubov, was the incarnation of Sophia. However, Lyubov disliked having this role thrust upon her, as did a number of other women in the Symbolist milieu.[8] For Biely the Divine Feminine was not only Sophia but the "Radiant Virgin, Maiden of the Rainbow Gates, World Soul, Moon Virgin, Astarte." Furthermore "The apocalyptic aspect was becoming predominant, with Sophia as the Woman Clothed in the Sun becoming identified with Mother Russia."[9] On another level, Sophia, the divine Wisdom, was also the Holy Spirit and the ruler of the third age in Joachim of Fiore's prophetic scheme

---

*My translation.

of three ages or realms, ruled successively by the Father, the Son, and the Holy Spirit—the first marked by divine power and authority, the second by faith and the message of the Gospels, and the third by love, joy, and freedom

The ideal of androgyny that we find in Solovyov and Fyodorov expressed itself in the lives of many intellectuals in the form of celibate marriage, as in the case of Berdyaev. Another example is the poet Zinaida Gippius (1869–1945), a forceful and flamboyant woman who liked to challenge gender stereotypes by sometimes dressing as a man. Both she and her husband, the writer and critic Dimitry Merezhkovsky, were prominent members of the literary milieu in St. Petersburg, where they ran a salon. Impelled by the revolution to leave Russia, they ended up in Paris where they were active in Russian expatriate circles.

Zinaida Gippius had a deeply felt Christian religiosity of a rather

Fig. 10.1. Zinaida Gippius, a poet, feminist, and advocate of sexual freedom
WIKIMEDIA COMMONS

mystical kind, in which esoteric numerology, especially the number three, played a key role. The Russian media producer and researcher Tatiana Klevantseva writes that for Gippius:

> Ethics were threefold: personal, sexual, and social, and the sexual act could be represented by an isosceles triangle, of which the horizontal line stood for the "earthly" union of man in the left corner, and woman in the right, while "an invisible vertical line" that ascended "from the middle of the base" to the apex symbolized their "spiritual journey" to Christ. (Without this imaginary line to Christ, the apex, men and women would be no more than beasts.)[10]

Klevantseva also writes of Gippius that she had a vision of spiritual transformation, central to which "was her concept of holy erotic love, whereby all erotic love, homosexual, heterosexual or other, was to be sanctified and thus permissible in the future utopian society. Her experiments with gender indeterminism have been the focus of increased academic attention in recent years."[11] While Zinaida Gippius had many sexual adventures with both men and women, her marriage to Merezhkovsky remained celibate.

Both Zinaida and her husband believed in the Joachite notion of three successive ages and were convinced that the age of the Holy Spirit was already dawning. In this third age all present antitheses would be resolved—"sex and asceticism, individualism and society, slavery and freedom, atheism and religiosity. . . . Earth and Heaven, the flesh and the spirit"—and a new era of peace, harmony, and love would ensue.[12]

In the early 1900s Merezhkovsky and Zinaida, along with other prominent writers and philosophers of the Silver Age, formed a group called the God-Seekers, which aimed to promote a new religious consciousness. For a time they met regularly with members of the Orthodox Church, but in 1903 the lay procurator of the Holy

Synod, Konstantin Pobedonostsev, an ultra-conservative statesman and advisor to the Tsar, stepped in and banned the Orthodox representatives from taking part.[13] Had the Church joined forces with the God-Seekers and similar groups, Russia might have embarked on a new spiritual era, but this moment of great opportunity was lost, and a few years later all sides went down in the maelstrom of the revolution.

ELEVEN

The Pursuit of the Rural Ideal

While many people in Russia, especially the young, are leaving the rural areas and moving to the cities, others are going in the opposite direction and seeking to live off the land—either as family units or in communities of like-minded spirits. They are prepared to brave the rigors and dangers of such a life for a variety of reasons: the desire for a healthier and more environmentally friendly existence for themselves and their children, the pursuit of the honest peasant life close to the black earth, and in many cases the vision inherent in some spiritual teaching. In Russia, there are now several hundred settlements of such people—eco-villages, family homesteads, agricultural communes, and communities of settlers sharing a particular religious belief or world-view. Some of these settlements are commercial ventures, such as the Veda Village in St. Petersburg, a complex of seven low-rise apartment blocks, built between 2016 and 2021 and laid out according to the principles of feng-shui (Chinese geomancy) and the Indian system called *vastu*, which involves harmonizing the components of a house with the five elements of Vedic tradition (earth, water, air, fire, and space or ether) and their corresponding compass directions.

There is a long tradition of ideal communities in Russia, going back to the Old Believers and including the movement inspired by the writer

Count Lev Tolstoy (1828–1910). After a tempestuous youth Tolstoy worked his way toward a mode of life and set of values derived from a deeply felt religiosity, which gave supremacy to the individual conscience as the voice of God and rejected the Orthodox Church, which excommunicated him. He proclaimed a form of anarchism, opposed the state and all its institutions, and advocated nonviolence, abstinence from alcohol, vegetarianism, and a life of chastity. He came to practice what he preached by living a simple, spartan life on his estate at Yasnaya Polyana, working in the fields together with the local peasants, and founding a school for their children. In his old age, with his flowing white beard and his peasant's tunic, boots, and baggy trousers, he looked every inch like a rustic sage from one of his own novels.

Tolstoy set out his philosophy of life in works such as *Confession, What I Believe* (1884), *What Then Must We Do?* (1886), and *The Kingdom of God Is Within You* (1893). Even in his lifetime people inspired by his ideas began to form groups and colonies, not only in Russia but in other countries including Britain and the United States. Among other things, his influence helped to spread the vegetarian and pacifist movements. Those influenced by him included Mahatma Gandhi, Martin Luther King, and the philosopher Ludwig Wittgenstein.

For most of the communist era, while Tolstoy continued to be celebrated as the great Russian novelist and champion of the people, his views on how to live a virtuous life were rejected. His deep religiosity, anarchism, and pacifism did not fit the communist agenda. Nevertheless, in the 1970s a younger generation began independently to rediscover Tolstoy's ideas and to disseminate them by word of mouth and through samizdat literature. In an article on this Tolstoyan revival, Irina Gordeeva writes:

At some point, many representatives of the Soviet underground faced the need to replace their marginalization, the burden of "nega-

tive freedom," denial, rejection, escapism, and destructive practices with a system of ideas that offered a more positive vision of
the world. The Soviet cultural underground, and the association
of Soviet hippies in particular, were clearly explorative in nature;
all members were on a mission, searching for their proper place in
society, a religion, and an ideology just like their Western coevals.
Within the space of the underground, the period of juvenile nihil-
ism shifted into a period of acquiring new values.[1]

For many of these young people, attracted by the Christian message
but alienated from the Orthodox Church, Tolstoy's ideas gave them a
belief system that they could hold on to. Today those ideas are more
honored abroad than in Russia. Tolstoy the anarchist, pacifist, and religious thinker still has his devotees there, but they are not generally
found among the Russian establishment. While there are Tolstoyan
communities in many parts of the world, in Russia itself they are few
and far between and do not form a significant part of the New Age
landscape.

THE GOSPEL OF ANASTASIA

The same cannot be said of another visionary movement, namely the
Ringing Cedars of Russia, otherwise known as the Anastasia movement, one of the most remarkable phenomena to come out of modern Russia and one that has found considerable resonance in other
countries. The extraordinary story of how the movement came into
being involves a former entrepreneur called Vladimir Megre (born
1950).* He relates that in 1994 he took a flotilla of three small ships
on a 3,500-mile voyage down the river Ob from Novosibirsk in central

---

*See the *Ringing Cedars of Russia* series of eleven books, published in Russian from
1996. There are many foreign editions including English versions of first eight volumes
by various translators. See also the movement's website of the same name.

Russia to the far northern town of Salekhard, about two hundred kilo-meters from where the river flows into the Arctic Ocean.* The purpose of the trip was to trade with the inhabitants of the settlements along the river.

On the return journey the expedition stopped at a small village, and Megre went down the gangway to take a walk. As he stepped ashore he saw two old men standing there. The younger of the two asked him if he could provide a team of men to go into the taiga (the Siberian pine forest) to cut down a "ringing" cedar tree. The man then proceeded to tell Megre about the special properties of these trees. He explained that God created the cedars as reservoirs of cosmic energy, which they accumulate and transmit to human beings and all living things on earth. But occasionally a cedar would store the energy and delay giving it out until five hundred years had passed. Then it would start to emit a ringing sound as a signal that it was time for the tree to be harvested and its wood distributed so that people could benefit from the accumulated energy. A small piece of such wood, worn as a pendant, would ensure health and longevity and generally have great vitalizing properties.

After telling the two men that he unfortunately could not meet their request, he went back on board the ship and the expedition proceeded. The following year he made a further expedition down the river in a single ship. He stopped at the place where he had met the old men, disembarked in a small boat, and had the ship proceed. Mooring the boat on the riverbank he saw a lone woman standing there, wearing a quilted jacket, a long skirt, and a headscarf that made her age difficult to determine. When he told her about the two old men that he had met there, she replied, using his name and the famil-iar pronoun *ty,* that it was her grandfather and great-grandfather that he had talked to. She then invited him to go with her to the taiga

---

*The account is contained in Vladimir Nikolaevich Megre, *Anastasia,* expanded edition (Moscow: AST publishing, 2020)

Fig. 11.1. Anastasia as portrayed by Kumar Alzhanov (see also color plate 8)

COURTESY OF THE ARTIST

twenty-five kilometers away, where she would show him the ringing cedar, and he agreed.

He spent three days with her in a bear's cave where she lived, during which time she shared with him her teachings on gardening, child-rearing, healing, plant lore, sexuality, religion, and much more, and asked him to pass on what he had learned. Afterward he abandoned his business career, went to Moscow, and wrote a book about what she had taught him, appropriately called *Anastasia,* which became a bestseller. He went on write to nine more books about the teachings of Anastasia, with whom he claims to be in regular contact, although she never shows herself to the public. He also speaks of their having a son and a daughter together.

Predictably the books have been met with both euphoria and skepticism—often they are described as novels. But the fact is that they have sold millions of copies in many different languages and have sparked a worldwide movement. Followers form what are called "kin's domains," that is smallholdings of one hectare (2.5 acres) with natural conditions enabling a family to live there with maximum self-sufficiency. These smallholdings are grouped into settlements comprising a number of kin's domains. In Russia and Ukraine there are currently over four hundred such settlements, encompassing many thousands of families. Kin's domains have also been founded in other countries, including the United States, Canada, Poland, Germany, and Australia. Various politicians, including President Putin, have expressed approval of the movement.

The aims of the movement include persuading governments to pass a law giving one hectare to any family wishing to live on the land. The property would be free of tax and could be passed on to descendants but could not be sold. The Russian government has already begun to implement such a policy, offering one-hectare plots of land free of charge in the vast, underinhabited eastern region and more recently in the northwestern area bordering the Arctic Ocean.

Similar initiatives are also in operation at the local level, such as in the Belgorod oblast, adjacent to the Ukrainian border. The long-term vision of the movement is that the kin's domains will be a blueprint for a more harmonious and ecologically responsible world, in which the participants will become "cocreators" with nature. The way of life practiced in the settlements includes the cultivation of local traditions and crafts and a round of festivals and ceremonies, part pagan, part New Age, with music, song, and dances.

Various people involved in the Anastasia movement have described to me how, on reading the books for the first time, they experienced an inner light going on and an opening of the heart. One of them is Dr. Svetlana Light (an adopted surname), a Russian gynecologist who emigrated to Australia and acquired a house with a hectare of land on the Sunshine Coast of Queensland. Following the Anastasia principles and using permaculture, she created a natural fence consisting of native plants, turned the swimming pool into a fishpond, and set about planting trees that could flourish in the subtropical climate, such as lychee, mango, pecan, and macadamia nut trees. She believes that Anastasia is a real being, sharing knowledge given out by the universe.

Particularly striking is the case of Yuri Smirnov, a Russian who lived for several years in Australia and New Zealand but returned to Russia in 2008 and settled in the Krasnodar region of the North Caucasus, east of the Black Sea. The stages of his spiritual journey included Orthodox Christianity, theosophy, agni yoga, and other paths. Then he happened to read the Anastasia books by Vladimir Megre and experienced a revelation. Every word resonated with him, and he decided to spread Anastasia's teaching and ideas around the world.

He proceeded to set up a magazine and website called Space of Love in English and Russian. (The former has ceased publication; the latter is still accessible on the internet but no longer actively maintained.) Subsequently he has concentrated on running a series of "Vedic tours" of the prehistoric dolmens of the North Caucasus. He is also the founder of the Eco-Minded Club, an organization for helping people in eco-villages and organic smallholdings to sell their produce and craftwork to eco-minded city dwellers.

Fig. 11.2. Yuri Smirnov, proponent of the Anastasia teachings and leader
of tours to sacred sites of ancient Russia
COURTESY OF YURI SMIRNOV

According to Anastasia these dolmens offer a way of contacting the spirit of the ancient Vedic civilization that once flourished in the Russian territories. In the second of the Ringing Cedars books by Vladimir Megre, Anastasia explained that elderly people close to death would enter one of these chambers and remain there until they passed away in a state of eternal meditation. Their spirits remained connected with the dolmens, so that in later times people could visit the sites and draw wisdom, strength, and mystical insight from them. All utopian visions encounter stumbling blocks when it comes to their practical realization, and the Ringing Cedars project is no exception. One source of difficulty is the fact that the participants in a settlement have different reasons for acquiring their plot. Some wish to build a house and move in right away on a full-time basis. Others want a long period of preparation or to use the place as a part-time retreat while continuing to live in the city. This can lead to disagreements over, for example, spending money on amenities for the whole settlement. And there is of course sometimes the kind of friction between neighbors that occurs in any community. Nevertheless, the achievements of the Ringing Cedars movement since its foundation in the late 1990s have been impressive.

The question arises: What are we to make of Megre's whole narrative? Is it fact or fiction? Remembering the phenomenon of the egregore, the collective thought-form on an invisible plane, I suggest that Anastasia is a manifestation of a very powerful Russian egregore that we have encountered before in the Woman Clothed with the Sun, Mother Russia, the cults of Sophia and the Virgin Mary, Paraskeva, and Mokosh. We find her also as a nature goddess figure in the paintings of the modern pagan school of artists. She is one of a number of egregores that have influenced the Russian mind, another being the old, gray-bearded sage, exemplified by Tolstoy. But the relative insignificance of the Tolstoy movement in comparison to the Anastasia phenomenon shows that the latter is based on a much more potent egregore. Megre appears to have undergone a shift of consciousness during which he made contact with this egregore, possibly personified by a real woman. He then became a channel through which he wrote his books and created the Ringing Cedars movement. There is also another familiar egregore involved. The mysterious cedar forest in a remote part of Siberia, where Anastasia lives concealed from the everyday world, is a kind of never-never land with echoes of Byelovodye and Shambhala. None of this, however, invalidates the Ringing Cedars movement, which has achieved remarkable things in its pursuit of the rural ideal and continues to attract followers beyond the borders of Russia.

TWELVE

The Arts and the Spiritual in Russia from the Revolution to the Present

In Russia, more so than in the west, the creative artist—whether writer, painter, or film maker—has traditionally enjoyed something of the status of a guru, with a mission to explore deep ethical, philosophical, religious, or social questions and exert a thought-provoking and uplifting influence. All the great Russian writers, from Pushkin to Solzhenitsyn, have taken on this role and been regarded in this way by the reading public. This situation continued after the revolution, which merely changed the set of issues that could be addressed, insisting that socialist realism be the governing orthodoxy. Mystical and esoteric themes were of course officially rejected, but people often found ways of circumventing these restrictions, finding loopholes, stretching what was officially permitted or, if necessary, pursuing their activities underground, such as through samizdat (self-published) literature. Thus, even as the communist establishment preached the prosaic doctrine of socialist realism, one could still find "Charm'd magic casements / Opening on the foam of perilous seas, in faery lands forlorn."[1] Escaping into those realms offered a form of "inner emigration," to use a phrase often heard in the Soviet bloc. One strategy for doing this without attracting unwelcome attention from the authorities was to adopt the position of an ethnographer visiting a region to study the curious habits of the natives.

IMAGINING THE FUTURE

One of the loopholes that existed even in officially approved literature was the genre of science fiction, or science fantasy as it is called in Russia, which continued to flourish in the Soviet period in parallel with real developments in the scientific world. The vision of Russia leading a never-ending onward march of science was part of the communist rhetoric, and the space program was the flagship endeavor. As a striking example of how fantasy can drive reality, the seeds of Russian rocket engineering, the launching of Sputnik 1 in 1957 and the orbital voyage of Yuri Gagarin in 1961 lay in the dreams of the group now known as the "Cosmists," notably Nikolai Fyodorov (1828–1903) and Konstantin Tsiolkovsky (1857–1935). The former cherished the age-old dream of immortality but went even further and argued that we could resurrect our ancestors by reanimating the dust from their bodies, thus obviating the need for sexual reproduction. He also advocated detaching the planet Earth from the sun and using it as a spaceship to explore the universe. His ideas, especially on social issues, impressed Dostoyevsky and Solovyov among others, but it was left to his disciple Tsiolkovsky to combine vision with practicality. In his youth Tsiolkovsky was fired up by the stories of Jules Verne, especially his space travel novel *De la Terre à la Lune* (*From the Earth to the Moon*), first published in 1865. Tsiolkovsky became a brilliant mathematician and physicist, and his calculations and experiments in aerodynamics helped to lay the foundations for the Soviet space program. We shall return to the subject of the Cosmists in a later chapter.

These achievements spurred on science fiction writers like Alexander Bogdanov (1873–1928), who was also a pioneering physician, a philosopher, and a revolutionary who played a leading role in the communist movement both before and after the revolution, even though he quarreled with Lenin over doctrinal issues. As a science fiction writer he is best known for his novel *Red Star* (first published in 1908), describing a civilization on the planet Mars that corresponds to his idea of a communist utopia. The society is characterized by the submergence of the individual in the collective. Everybody dresses in the same standard clothes, and outward differences between men and women are minimized, so that the narrator finds it difficult to tell the difference. There is little or nothing in the work that could be considered spiritual. By contrast, there were other science fiction writers who found that they could explore occult and mystical themes by presenting them as part of a reality not yet explained by science. An example of this approach is found in the work of Ivan Yefremov (1908–1972), a paleontologist and pioneer of the study of fossils who also had a successful career as a science fiction writer. His remarkable novel *The Razor's Edge* (1963), for instance, explores profound metaphysical and spiritual issues. The Prologue sets the tone: "In human existence there are invisible coincidences, long established links between circumstances, delicate threads connecting this or that fortuity, and these make up a tightly welded chain that exerts a pull on human lives . . ."[2]

Running through the novel is the theme of beauty, and the title comes from a debate on the subject that takes place in an art gallery between the main character, the doctor Ivan Girin, and various other visitors. Some fundamental questions are discussed about the nature of beauty. Does it only exist in the eye of the beholder? Is it created by the artist? Or does it exist in the world as an objective reality? Girin takes the view that it does indeed have an objective existence: "It is not difficult, knowing the materialist dialectic, to see that beauty is the true middle line in the struggle of opposites for unity, the mean between the two sides of every phenomenon, which the ancient Greeks called *ariston,* the best. . . . I imagine this mean as being something extremely thin like a razor blade . . . so sharp as to be almost invisible."[3]

In a parallel story line in the book, a group of Italians, led by an artist called Cesare, go to South Africa in search of diamonds. They hire a yacht and set about diving off the coast. Instead of diamonds they find a mysterious jeweled crown, reputed to have belonged to Alexander the Great, which is found to have a mysterious effect on the memory of the wearer. Unfortunately the crown is accidentally dropped back into the water when an actress and former beauty queen puts it on and stumbles.

A further story line follows an Indian sculptor called Dayaram Ramamurti, who is intent on portraying his idea of perfect beauty. At one point he declares: "For eleven years I have been not only looking for the ideal of beauty, but also trying to grasp why it is beautiful. What is it that everyone understands as the exciting beauty of a woman? I have to give it to people. Only beauty can support us in life, comfort us in fatigue and failures and alleviate the cruelty of knowledge and victory."[4]

Eventually he finds his way to a guru called Vitarkananda, who explains to him that beauty is connected with reverence for the feminine, which humanity has forgotten since the end of matriarchy. He reminds Dayaram of the supreme importance of the task of raising a child to adulthood, and tells him:

> In this task, beauty is one of the main forces, if only people can learn
> to understand it correctly and value it, and also apply it. That is why
> I want to help you in every way—you will first fight against those
> who discredit and belittle beauty, and then you will create it for
> everyone and for the future.[5]

The final part of the book weaves the three story lines together and features a deep conversation between Girin, Vitarkananda, and some other Indians, in which they discuss a possible marriage between Soviet science and the ancient wisdom of India with its concepts of karma and the *gunas,* the three basic forces in the universe—all of which would not have belonged in normally accepted discourse under communism. Girin speaks about the Vedic religion as being greatly superior to Christianity. In the former, he says, the holy men retired for their meditations to the cool, majestic heights of the Himalayas, whereas "the founders of the Christian church . . . went to the deserts . . . Here, scorched by merciless heat . . . they were subjected to dreadful hallucinations. The brain, inflamed by the raging sun, intensifying the suppressed desires of the flesh, gave rise to the whole insane concept of a malicious, punitive god, hell, woman as the source of evil, horrifying images of the Last Judgment and the end of the world, and the terrible intrigues of Satan."[6]

The theme of womanhood is another important one in the novel, which contains many passages idealizing women and condemning their mistreatment.

In some ways Yefremov's work is recognizably of the Soviet era. Whether out of conviction or necessity he periodically praises the communist system. But he is also typically Russian in his willingness to grapple with themes such as that of beauty in a way that few novelists in the west would do.

Other science fiction novels of the same era venture even further into realms where the marvels of the future and of outer space become virtually indistinguishable from magic. One example is *Humans Like Gods* (*Lyudi kak bogi*) by Sergei Snegov, a massive three-volume work, published over the period 1966–1977. The narrative features fire-breathing dragons, angels, humanoids, planets with invisible inhabitants, a technique for travelling faster than light, and other such wonders.

In a similar vein, mixing a space-age narrative with mythical and magical themes, are the works of the Ukrainian writer Oles (Alexander) Berdnyk. His novel *The Heroic Deed of Vaivasvata* (*Podvig Vaivasvaty*) appeared in 1965 in Ukrainian, was rapidly translated into

Russian, and became extremely popular in both countries. It deals with the theme of Atlantis, which is presented as an evil power led by dark magicians and which is at war with the idyllic and highly advanced civilization on the island of Shvet-Dvip, inhabited by immortals from the planet Shakra. As the Slavist scholar Leonid Heller writes:

> It is . . . obvious that this story ostensibly paints an esoteric picture of the world, drawing on Theosophical and Hindu sources . . . Berdnyk's subjects, which recur in his other writings, are clearly esoteric: immortality, the interrelatedness of all elements in the world, a link between micro- and macrocosm, the striving for the reunification of all things into One, the Cosmic Magnet, and alien gods . . . Shvet Dvip is the island of the Light or the White Island mentioned in the Mahabharata and also described by Blavatsky. It is sometimes identified with the Tibetan Shambhala.[7]

From science fantasy it is not a very large step to magical realism, another genre that has taken root in Russia. Unlike pure fantasy, which describes imaginary worlds, magical realism makes the strange and mysterious intrude into the everyday world in startling ways. The genre is associated particularly with the names of two Latin American writers, the Argentinian Jorge Luis Borges (1899–1986) and the Colombian Gabriel García Márquez (1927–2014), both of whom are published in Russian translation. Their works fell on fertile ground in Russia, which already had its own tradition of magical realism in, for example, the work of Mikhail Bulgakov (1891–1940) with his extraordinary novel *The Master and Margarita*.

Written between 1928 and 1940 at the height of the Stalin dictatorship, the novel was not published until 1966–67, when it appeared in abridged form in two installments in the magazine *Moscow*. Given its defiant content, it was a miracle that it got past the censors at all, even with the cuts they demanded. Deservedly, it became a cult novel overnight. Readers were astounded and entranced by its combination of myth, fantasy, the supernatural, everyday reality, and deep reflection on moral and religious issues. The Master of the title is an author, clearly based on Bulgakov himself, while Margarita is his lover, muse, and soul mate and echoes the theme of the woman clothed with the sun. We learn that the Master has written a novel about the trial and execution of Jesus Christ, a story that alternates with the main narrative, set in the Moscow of Bulgakov's time.

The novel opens with a conversation in a Moscow park between the Devil, appearing incognito (later he uses the name Voland), and two Russians: Berlioz, editor of a literary magazine and head of a writers' club, and a poet who writes under the name Homeless. The Russians are talking about Jesus and parroting the party line that he never existed. The Devil steps into the conversation and insists that he did exist. Later various companions of the Devil appear, including a giant black cat called Behemoth and a tall man in a checked suit, wearing a pince-nez. Voland and his friends engage in all sorts of antics, including a performance at a variety theatre, where they cause an uproar by producing banknotes and expensive clothes and items of jewelry out of thin air, causing the audience to scramble for them. They also organize an extravagant ball featuring jazz-playing monkeys, a swimming pool filled with champagne, reanimated corpses, and a motley assembly of guests including "kings, dukes, knights, suicides, poisoners, gallows-birds, procuresses, jailers, card-sharpers, hangmen, informers, traitors, madmen, detectives, and seducers."[8] One thing that strikes the reader is that the world of Stalinist Russia appears like a mad, surrealistic charade, whereas the scenes in Jerusalem at the time of Christ are starkly real. This is Bulgakov's way of turning the atheist worldview on its head and saying: what you describe as illusion is in fact the truth, and the real illusion is your materialist pipe dream.

A near contemporary of Bulgakov but a writer in a very different genre was Daniil Andreev (1906–1959), author of the treatise

The Rose of the World, partly a sort of Plato's *Republic* extended to the entire globe, partly a work of Apocalyptic vision. Writing it was a heroic feat, especially as it was largely composed in a Soviet prison. After serving in the Second World War as a medical orderly, Andreev was arrested in Moscow along with his wife, Alla, and charged with anti-Soviet propaganda and taking part in a plot to kill Stalin. Both were sentenced to twenty-five years in prison, reduced to ten during the Khrushchev thaw. In prison Andreev experienced mystical visions and was able to communicate with the spirits of great Russians of the past such as Mikhail Lermontov, Fyodor Dostoyevsky, and Alexander Blok. Out of these visions and communications arose what became *The Rose of the World.* Andreev completed the work after his release in 1957 and before his early death from a heart condition in 1959.

The Rose of the title symbolizes the happier and more harmonious global order that Andreev envisaged. In the work he struggles to resolve a familiar dilemma—namely, how to achieve a global consensus and at the same time preserve a plurality of cultures and belief systems. In his vision there would be a global federation of states, overseen by an incorruptible and respected body which he calls the League for the Transformation of the State. The religions of the world would be the petals of an eclectic pan-religion, which would allow for many different conceptions of the divine and would encompass both monotheism and polytheism.

The book starts off like a straight political-philosophical manifesto with proposals relating to government, science, culture, religion, and social relations, but as it goes on it reads more and more like a combination of science fantasy and a new version of the book of *Revelation.* Andreev has invented or channeled strange-sounding terms, which he elucidates in a glossary at the end of the book. The term *bramfatura,* for example, he explains as a system of interconnected layers of different material, which every celestial body possesses. In most cases what unites the layers is the struggle between the godly and demonic forces. Some *bramfaturas* have fallen completely under the sway of the latter force, others have freed themselves from it. The *bramfatura* of our own planet is called the *shadanakar* and consists of over 240 layers of nonspatial and nontemporal material. Then there are the *zatomises,* the highest strata of the metacultures or celestial countries of humanity (by the term "celestial country" he appears to mean a sort of higher soul of a country existing on a superior level). The *zatomises* are the abode of the *synclites,* enlightened human souls rather like the Ascended Masters of Theosophy. Thus Heavenly Russia is the *zatomis* of the Russian metaculture and the abode of its *synclite.*[9]

One of the central arguments of the book concerns the feminine principle, the Sophia or Wisdom, whom Andreev sees as one person of the Trinity, taking the place of the Holy Ghost. The latter, in his view, is identical with God the Father. Therefore the Trinity consists of (a) God the Father and the Holy Ghost, (b) God the Son, and (c) the Sophia.

Andreev believes that a new age, the age of the Rose of the World, is imminent, in which the feminine principle will be writ large. He writes:

> No one except the Lord God knows where and when the fire of the Rose of the World will begin to shine forth. The country, Russia, is only a prediction; tragic events are still possible that will jeopardize this mystical development and force it to be transferred to another country . . . disastrous cataclysms can happen, causing the date to be postponed for many years. . . . But whether here in this country or in another, whether a decade earlier or later . . . the Rose of the World will appear. . . .[10]

Here again is the egregore or archetype that we have encountered repeatedly in Russian history, literature, mythology, and religion: Sophia, the Divine Wisdom, the woman clothed with the sun, the earth goddess Mat-Sira-Zemlya, the figure of Anastasia in the Ringing Cedars movement, and Mother Russia herself.

Andreev's teaching has a dedicated following in Russia today, as a search on the internet will reveal.

VISIONARY ARTISTS AND ARCHITECTS

When we turn from literature to the visual arts we find a similar interconnection with esoteric, occult, mystical, and neo-pagan ideas. This was already noticeable in the early part of the twentieth century, which was a heyday of artistic "-isms"—suprematism, intuitivism, cosmism. The "-isms" came and went as artists struggled to find a sense of orientation in the tumultuous world around them. Some, like Nikolai Roerich, looked to the east and the wisdom of India. Another who did so was Kazimir Malevich (1879–1935), generally hailed as a pioneer of the avant-garde with works such as his *Black Square,* consisting simply of a black rectangle against a white background. What is less well known is that Malevich was profoundly influenced by Indian thought and the Vedic notion that the innermost self is identical with the supreme realm of the divine.

Vedic philosophy, mingled with the cosmist ideas of Nikolai Fedorov, fed into an artistic movement called Amaravella (a Sanskrit word meaning roughly "bearing light" or "radiating energy"), which emerged in the 1920s and was led by Pyotr Fateyev (1891–1971). The works of this group attempted to fuse a cosmic consciousness with the visions of the individual artist. Predictably, as they failed to conform to socialist realism, they were suppressed in the early 1930s.

As with literature, there were artists who managed to defy the Soviet cultural establishment. One striking example was Konstantin Vasiliev (1942–1976). He was born in the small town of Maikop, near the northeast side of the Black Sea, during the German occupation, an experience that evidently did not make him anti-German but rather may have instilled in him the fascination for things Teutonic that he later evinced in his art. Vasiliev began painting as a child and was selected for a privileged art education in Moscow and Kazan. After experimenting with surrealism and abstract expressionism and undergoing a psychological crisis in his midtwenties, he began to paint heroic and mythological themes, drawing on his fascination for the writings of Friedrich Nietzsche, the operas of Richard Wagner, and the world of Teutonic, Scandinavian, and Slavic mythology. His paintings are marked by a bold, highly arresting style and great technical virtuosity, and they strongly evoke the egregore of the hero. While many of his works celebrate Russia's heroic struggle in the Second World War, his favored style has more than a touch of the rather intimidating monumentalism associated with the art of the Third Reich. "The artist," wrote Vasiliev, "experiences delight in the proportionality of the parts, pleasure in true proportions, dissatisfaction in disproportions . . . The man of science expresses the laws of nature in numbers, the artist contemplates them, making them the object of his creativity. Here is natural order. Here is beauty."[11]

The cultural authorities must have been perplexed by Vasiliev. He conformed to the favored realistic style, and he celebrated the Russian military victories in the war, but what were these Valkyries, these Nordic and Slavic gods, these dragon-slaying heroes, these warriors with winged helmets, this strange otherworldly aura that the paintings radiated? He didn't fit the cultural orthodoxy, and some would maintain that his mysterious death in 1976 was in fact an assassination. What is known is that one day he and a friend were on their way to an exhibition but never arrived. Later their bodies were found near a railway track, allegedly having been struck by a train, but how this could have happened remains unclear.

While he received little exposure during his lifetime, he quickly attained a remarkable posthumous fame, despite the fact that this was still the Soviet era. In September 1977 an exhibition of his work at the Kazan Youth Center drew a large crowd, as did subsequent exhibitions in Moscow. Then in 1978 came the documentary film about him, *Vasiliev from Vasiliev,* by the director Leonid Kristi. Today there is a gallery in

Moscow dedicated to his work, another in Kazan, and his former home in the village of Vasiliev (the same name as his own) is now a small museum.

Vasiliev's work is not alone in its romantic celebration of Russian folk traditions and the ancient Slavic gods and legends. A similar spirit pervades the work of Andrei Klimenko (born 1956), also known under the alias Andriko WenSix. His work is a paean to the beauty, heroism, magic, and mystery of ancient Russia. There are epic scenes from the history of the Scythians and the Varangians, mythical creatures, Hyperborean landscapes and an array of Slavic gods and goddesses. Klimenko's work has achieved wide recognition, both inside Russia and internationally. While living in the United States for twelve years he painted some deliberately grotesque parodies in the style of the surrealists and postmodernists, which nevertheless sold for large sums.[12]

A prolific member of what one might call the folk-romantic school of artists is Alexander Uglanov (born 1960 in Tver), already mentioned in connection with his Hyperborean series, whom I got to know when I was working on my previous book *Beyond the North Wind*. Uglanov has produced a remarkable series of Hyperborean images, another series based on the Atlantis legend, and many works relating to Slavic mythology.

Another artist who celebrates the folk traditions of Russia, but in a much more eclectic way, is Victor Prus (born 1941), a painter, sculptor, designer, and architect with his own distinctive monumentalist style. As a young art student he became influenced by esotericism and the work of Nikolai Roerich as well as that of avant-garde artists such as Malevich. For a time he was an Orthodox Christian, but at some point he left Orthodoxy and joined the neo-pagan movement. Today he is a distinguished looking man of sage-like appearance with flowing white hair and beard and a charismatic personality. While his work strongly features motifs from Russian folk tradition and mythology, he is also fascinated by discoveries in science and in the ideas of Tsiolkovsky and the Cosmists. He professes a philosophy of "all-unity" (*vsyeyedinstvo*), a concept that had already been propounded by the philosopher Vladimir

Solovyov and in fact went back to ancient Greece. It is a perennial attempt to reconcile unity with multiplicity, the oneness of God with the diversity of creation. In Prus's work it is expressed as a kind of "as above, so below" principle and in cultural inclusiveness. While he

Fig. 12.1. *Old Slavic Pagan Ceremony,*
a painting by Alexander Uglanov (see also color plate 9)
COURTESY OF THE ARTIST

insists that each people should know the sources of its culture, and many of his paintings focus on Russian themes, many works combine mythological motifs from many different cultures and regions. In 1980 he issued a *Manifesto on the Unity of Culture*. A few quotes from it are enough to show his grand, idealistic vision for the future:

> Our slogan is the unity of the national and the international in culture. . . . The way of future for art is an integral approach that uses all the methods of all countries, all peoples and all times. . . . Ideally art should uplift a person spiritually, and not stir up animal instincts; it should bring joy and instill a love for humans and nature. . . . Our goal is the birth of a great syncretic art, which embraces the unity of architecture, sculpture, painting, literature, music, theater, cinema and television, based on an integration with philosophy, science, religion and the newest technologies. . . .[13]

Prus's inclusion of architecture in his concept of syncretic art leads me on to the subject of architecture per se. Looking at the modern areas of western towns and cities it is obvious that something has gone profoundly wrong. Never have we had so much technical capacity to create beauty, yet we are busy creating a built environment of unprecedented ugliness. This state of affairs has been searchingly written about by James Stevens Curl in his book *Making Dystopia*. As Curl correctly perceives, the malaise of modernism in architecture has a spiritual and philosophical dimension. The modernist architectural establishment is dominated by what my late friend Ian Hamilton Finlay, the Scottish poet and artist, used to call the "secular terror"—that is a mindset that has no respect for the sacred or the transcendental and no concept of a divinely ordained order or dharma, as it is called in India. It is this omnipresent dharma that, in traditional Indian society, endows even commonplace objects with a certain beauty. The people of the secular terror not only reject such notions but are rabidly opposed to them.

Russia has had its fair share of the secular terror under the Soviets and has not escaped the inroads of modernism in the wake of the collapse of communism. Yet there are some hopeful developments. When Russia took the capitalist road and most architects rushed to adopt a western, corporate style of building, a few of them rebelled and developed a style based on traditional forms. These included a group that was formed at the end of the Soviet era to practice what they called "paper architecture," that is highly fanciful depictions of buildings and townscapes that were never intended to be built, but rather to inspire and stimulate the architectural profession to new creativity. Some of their designs are ultramodern, but others are richly traditional, abounding in domes, arches, rotundas, pillars, and colonnades.

In the new capitalist Russia these architects are now able to gain commissions and their work is seen in a number of recent buildings and urban development projects. One of the most interesting is Mikhail Filippov, who learned about neoclassical architecture by painting detailed watercolors of townscapes in St. Petersburg and Moscow and then progressed to working on actual building projects. One of his creations is the Rimsky quarter in Moscow, an entire city district with crescents, squares, radial axes, and a great variety of different architectural styles, so that the eye is delighted by the continually changing perspective—here an arch leading to a quiet courtyard, there a rotunda with a gazebo or a small park with a café and a children's playground. Another architect of the neoclassical school is Mikhail Belov (born 1956), whose works include a monument in central Moscow to the poet Alexander Pushkin and his wife, the writer Natalia Goncharova. Bronze statues of the pair stand in a circular temple with Doric columns and a roof of gilded tiles, surrounded by a fountain. Belov was also partly responsible for the charming fountain of Princess Turandot, celebrating Puccini's opera of that title. It stands in Moscow's Arbat district in front of the Vakhtangov Theater and features a gilded figure of the Princess by the sculptor Alexander Burganov.

Fig. 12.2. Monument to Alexander Pushkin and his wife Natalia Goncharova in Moscow, designed by the architect Mikhail Belov
WIKIMEDIA COMMONS

SPIRITUALITY AND THE CINEMA

I now turn to a medium in which the Russians excel, namely film, and here the quality of spiritual depth that I have frequently referred to is to be found in abundance. Let's start in the Soviet era with the celebrated director Andrei Tarkovsky (1932–1986). What distinguishes Tarkovsky above all from most western directors is the deep spirituality which informs his work and which comes across clearly in what he has said about himself, his philosophy, and his approach to cinema.

In his autobiographical work *Sculpting in Time* he writes: "It is perfectly clear that the goal for all art . . . is to explain what man lives for, what is the meaning of his existence . . . or if not to explain, at least to pose the question." He contrasts art, which arises out of some deep source within the artist, with science, which depends on a continuous accumulation of knowledge. "Art is born and takes hold wherever there is a timeless and insatiable longing for the spiritual, for the ideal . . . Modern art has taken a wrong turn in abandoning the search for the meaning of existence in order to affirm the value of the individual for its own sake."[14]

In an interview published in *Le Figaro* in October 1986, he talked about the importance of beauty and said of Picasso that instead of glorifying beauty and bearing witness to it, he acted as its destroyer.[15]

Tarkovsky's characters are often tormented, struggling to deal with great metaphysical and religious issues as well as with powerful emotional drives. Perhaps the greatest of his films is *Andrei Rublyov*, about the life of a famous fifteenth-century icon painter. Released in 1966, it is an epic of over three hours containing some of the most memorable scenes in cinematic history. At one point Rublyov chances upon a group of pagans who are celebrating one of their festivals with a mass orgy. He is confronted by an attractive young pagan woman whom he berates for her sinful behavior. She tries to convince him that she and her tribe are merely practicing love as they know it. He is clearly tempted by her but resists and flees.

In Tarkovsky's world there is an underlying layer of the miraculous, which sometimes bursts out in startling ways. A striking example is a sequence in *Andrei Rublyov* in which a teenage boy supervises the casting of an enormous cathedral bell. A huge pit is dug, a clay mold constructed, a row of furnaces built, and a large quantity of copper and silver plate and other metal objects collected for melting. Then comes a series of dramatic moments: when the molten metal is poured into the mold, when the clay is chipped away and the majestic bell appears as though by some miracle of alchemy, then when it is raised by hundreds of men tugging at pulleys, and blessed at the four compass points by Orthodox priests, watched by the local prince and his retinue and a large crowd. Finally comes the moment to test whether it will ring properly. The tension mounts as the huge clapper swings to and fro, at first silently. Then suddenly it strikes the bell, and a deep, sonorous note rings out again and again to a great cheer from the crowd.

It is one of the paradoxes of Russian history that such a powerfully spiritual film should have been made at the time of Brezhnev's decidedly antireligious regime, especially as Tarkovsky's intention was to underline the essential role of the Orthodox Church in shaping Russian identity at a key moment in the country's history. Predictably the film had a difficult passage in Russia. After one initial showing in Moscow in 1966, it was unavailable to Russian audiences until 1971 when a censored version was released. Meanwhile it won great admiration abroad, and an abridged version was released by Columbia Pictures in 1973. Fortunately the full Russian version is now available everywhere.

A more recent film, charged with a similar spiritual intensity, is *Ostrov* (The Island), directed by Pavel Lungin. Released in 2006, it is set in in the 1970s in a small monastery in the bleak, icy environment of an island in the White Sea, close to the Arctic Ocean. The central character is the monk Anatoly, who tends the furnaces that heat the monastery. He has all the characteristics of a fool for Christ. He sleeps on a heap of coals, hardly ever washes, rings the monastery bell when he is not supposed to, and generally behaves like a madman. At the same time he has extraordinary powers. He accurately predicts future events, heals a crippled boy, and drives a demon out of a young woman.

He is revered by the local population and in the end also by his fellow monks, who come to recognize his true holiness.

One of the most remarkable features of the film is the portrayal of Anatoly by Pyotr Mamonov, a former rock musician who converted to Orthodoxy in the 1990s and then lived as a recluse with his wife in a remote village in the Moscow region, where he farmed a plot of land until his sudden death from the coronavirus in 2021, perceived by many as a national tragedy. In the 1980s, as a member of the rock band Zvuki Mu, he worked with the legendary British producer Brian Eno. who described him as "possessed." Speaking of his conversion he has said: "When I was 45, I found myself in an impasse and I kept thinking about those important issues: What are we doing on this Earth? And then I came to faith: the Lord revealed Himself to me. I realized why I was alive."[16] It would be true to say that in the film he plays himself and does so with an intensity that would otherwise be hard to achieve.

The use of nonprofessional actors is also a feature of Alexei Balabanov's 2012 film *Me Too* (the Russian title *Ya tozhe khotchou* means literally "I want it, too"). The film deals with a spiritual quest involving the classic theme of a journey through a wasteland, with deliberate echoes of Tarkovsky's cult science fiction film *Stalker* (1979). The main characters are Oleg, a hippyish musician, Sanja, a bandit, Sanja's alcoholic friend Yuri, Yuri's aging father, and Alisa, a philosophy graduate turned prostitute. Captivated by reports of a legendary "Belltower of Happiness" which is said to be a portal to paradise, they set out for the tower in a car. From the more run-down parts of St. Petersburg the film follows the travelers through bleak suburbs and out into the country to a desolate, Chernobyl-like zone, permanently covered by snow. There they come to the tower, standing on a tiny peninsula surrounded on three sides by water. Three of the travelers reach the tower, which "accepts" two of them, and a flash of light shoots from the roof as each one enters. One is left kneeling in front of the tower, crying out "I want it, too." The bell tower belonged to the ruined church of Zapogast in the Vologda region. Soon after the release of the film in 2013 Balabanov died of a heart attack, and forty days later the tower collapsed into the water.

THE POPULAR MUSIC SCENE AND THE OCCULT

The case of the rock singer turned actor Pyotr Mamonov brings us to the theme of popular music. Here it is necessary to explain that in Russia the term "pop music" does not mean the same thing as in other countries. To Russians it means a specific style of performance that is kitschy and primitive. Typical of the Russian pop scene is the millionaire rapper Alisha Morgenshtern (born 1998), usually known just by his (adopted) surname. Flaunting his admiration for Aleister Crowley, he has the number 666 tattooed on his forehead and once donated 666,666 rubles to a children's charity. Characteristic of his deliberately provocative style is a video filmed in a Catholic cathedral in Italy, where he cavorts about in a white, gold-embroidered priest's robe and skullcap. In no time the whole congregation, including a group of nuns, is jumping about in a frenzy, and the scene dissolves into mayhem.[17] Performers like Morgenstern are in a separate category from what in Russia would be called the rock or underground scene.

While Mamonov's path took him to Orthodoxy, other members of the Russian rock music scene have gravitated eastward or toward the esoteric traditions. A prime example is Boris Grebenshchikov (born 1953), a cult figure of the independent rock stage. His band Aquarium was launched in Leningrad in 1974 but only rose to fame after 1980. As he grew older Grebenshchikov moved into the realm of eastern wisdom and ethnic music. Nowadays he is viewed not only as a musician, but as a kind of wise starets with a Buddhist edge. Many young people turn to him as to a kind of spiritual guru.[18]

Another performer with a messianic aura is Nikita Dzhigurda (born in Kiev, Ukraine, in 1961), actor, singer, and film director, a

Fig. 12.3. Boris Grebenshikov, rock musician and guru
WIKIMEDIA COMMONS

gaunt, bearded figure with shoulder-length hair, whose work often involves defiantly erotic themes. When asked in an interview how his interest in religion, philosophy, and meditation could coexist with his macho image, he answered:

> I immersed myself in spiritual practices, starved and became enlightened. I was looking for myself. And I realized I really love life, my driving force is love. Each person must realize their divine essence in order to become happy. Secretly we are all gods. . . . My adventures are my experience, not a sin, and I, like everyone else, will inevitably return to normal.[19]

Asked by the same interviewer what he thought about the tragic events in Ukraine, he replied: "I am against war, it is like an operation in the body, which we can do without. But how? I believe only through the feminine principle. In general, I am convinced that women should rule the world, as in ancient times. All women are goddesses."[20] Here again it seems we are brought face to face with the "woman clothed with the sun" that we encountered earlier. That a star with such a macho reputation should invoke her in this way says much about the power of this archetype.

The synergy between popular music and occultism that one finds in Russia today reminds me of a similar synergy that existed in the British pop world and had its heyday in the seventies, eighties, and nineties with Crowley admirers like Jimmy Page of Led Zeppelin and the highly innovative group Psychic TV, led by Genesis P-Orridge, whom I knew when I lived for a time in the London district of Notting Hill. Genesis, who died in 2020, was a many-faceted and many-talented person who was also the central figure in a project called "Thee Temple ov Psychick Youth" [sic] (TOPY), which ran approximately for the decade 1982–1992, a remarkable combination of magical order, think tank, artistic movement, social experiment, music studio, publishing operation, and much more. One of the collaborators in the early days of the project was Crowley enthusiast David Tibet, founder of the band Current 93, whom I also knew in those days.

In its magical work TOPY was influenced by, among other things, Aleister Crowley's Thelema, the talismanic magic of the artist Austin Osman Spare, and the "Chaos Magic" of the modern occultist Peter Carroll. The group reached out from the UK via a newsletter and soon had thousands of followers all over the world. Psychic TV split up in the early 1990s but was later reborn as Psychic TV 3. The Temple itself also went through a process of dissolution and rebirth, and various reincarnations and offshoots of it came and went. Two former Psychic TV members, Peter Christopherson and John Balance, went off to found their own band, Coil (1982–2005), which had a similar fascination with magic and the occult.

In Russia the whole movement around Genesis P-Orridge, Psychic

TV, and the Temple of Psychick Youth found an enthusiastic following, and concerts by Psychic TV 3 drew large audiences. After the death of Genesis his mystique lived on in Russia. His magnum opus *Thee Psychick Bible* has been published in Russian translation, and a sanctuary (*kapishche*) of the Temple of Psychick Youth has been created in St. Petersburg, decorated with characteristic images such as Éliphas Lévi's *Goat of Mendes* drawing and the logo of the Temple, a cross with three horizontal arms, the middle one shorter than the other two. In this milieu, along with such visual iconography goes a predilection for Crowleyan and other forms of ritual magic. The music of Coil is also popular in Russia for similar reasons.

The activities of Psychic TV and the Temple of Psychick Youth were partly a protest against the crass materialism and institutionalized greed of the Thatcher years in Britain. Similarly their counterparts in Russia are trying to create an oasis of free creativity, magic, ecstasy, and a spirit of Do What Thou Wilt as an alternative to the prevailing order, which many see as a descent into authoritarianism and crude commercialism after the brief, liberating period of perestroika.

One prominent member of the pop music scene who voiced his discontent with the current ethos in the country was the late Sergei Kuryokhin (1954–1996), an avant-garde musician and composer from St. Petersburg, noted for his virtuoso, high-speed piano playing. He attained a certain notoriety in January 1991 when he appeared on television and announced that Lenin had eaten so many psychedelic mushrooms that he had ended up turning into one. It was of course a jest, but so convincingly done that a number of old Bolsheviks contacted the party office in Leningrad, wanting to know whether it was true that the founder of the Soviet Union was really a mushroom.[21]

During an election campaign for the State Duma (Parliament), Kuryokhin directed a concert in support of the candidacy of Alexander Dugin and dedicated to the memory of Aleister Crowley. There was a moment of silence to honor Crowley's memory, and Dugin read an extract from one of the works of the "Great Beast."[22] It is hard to imagine, say, a British parliamentary candidate quoting Crowley during an election campaign.

In 1995 Dugin and Kuryokhin issued a remarkable joint declaration describing their vision for a transformation of society. Entitled *Manifesto of the New Magi,* it is set out in twenty-two numbered paragraphs, presumably corresponding to the twenty-two letters of the Hebrew alphabet and the twenty-two major arcana of the Tarot. Their starting point is the observation that the modern world is suffering from a crisis of art and politics, both of which have become degenerate, necessitating a new impulse from an independent realm. The manifesto continues:

> This new realm is MAGIC. Magic is not events, things and objects but causes; magic does not simply describe but actively operates. Magic precedes art and politics. Art and politics became autonomous only upon being detached from their magical source. This source has not disappeared but merely slipped away to the periphery from where it exerts indirect influence. Secret societies, lodges and orders have governed history and inspired artists.
> . . . Indirect influence has not been sufficient as politics and art forgot the necessity of constantly appealing to magic. Only the direct, total replacement of art and politics with MAGIC can save the situation.[23]

Tragically Kuryokhin died at the age of forty-two only a year after the *Manifesto* appeared. Dugin, who went on to gain prominence as a writer, philosopher, and political thinker, still stands by what he and Kuryokhin were trying to achieve with that document. He acknowledges that, for those who share its standpoint, it remains a source of inspiration.[24]

THIRTEEN

The Russian Language

June 6 is a special day in Russia, being both Russian Language Day and the birthday of the great nineteenth-century poet Alexander Pushkin, who played a key role in shaping modern Russian. On that day in 2020 President Vladimir Putin delivered a memorable speech via the internet to a conference of arts professionals from various fields. In his speech he said the following words: "For our country the Russian language is more than a means of communication. It unites all the peoples of Russia and is the cornerstone of our national identity, our great heritage, unparalleled in its imagery, clarity, precision, expressiveness, and beauty. These qualities are probably the secret of the greatness and appeal of Russian literature and culture, which delights the entire world."[1]

Russian Language Day is one of six language days established by the United Nations in 2010 to honor the six official languages of the organization, but I would be surprised to hear, say, a British Prime Minister speaking about English with the same eloquence and passion as came through in Putin's speech. As he said, Russian is not just a means of communication. For many—probably the great majority—of Russians it is a national treasure, a precious repository of tradition, imbued with a sacred quality. At the same time there have been periodic efforts by less traditionally minded people to reform the language, and this tug-of-war has continued to the present day. The language,

197

with its special meaning for the Russians, has to be considered when speaking about their mystical quest.

The Russian word for language is *yazik*. In old Russian this word had the meaning that is now conveyed by the word *narod* (people or folk). Hence the word *yazichestvo*, meaning paganism (i.e., the religion of the folk). This underlines the fact that the fate of a people is inseparably bound up with the fate of their language. A language is a container of knowledge, a preserver of culture, and an expression of a worldview. Interfere with the language of a people and you interfere with an essential part of their collective soul.

The Russian language is like a surface that has had many layers of semi-opaque paint added to it over the centuries, leaving parts of all the layers still visible. Fundamental to it is an unmistakably sacred layer from the formative period of the language that remains strongly evident today. Going down to the deeper levels we come to the group of languages stemming from the people whom we now call the Indo-Europeans, who are thought to have inhabited a homeland somewhere in the region between the Black and Caspian seas and to have migrated outward from about four thousand years ago, leaving a linguistic trail reaching from Europe to India.

One branch of the Indo-European language tree, the Slavic branch, produced various sub-branches and sub-sub-branches, eventually leading to the emergence of what might be called proto-Russian during the first millennium CE. To understand the subsequent development of Russian as a national language, we have to glance back at the history of Russia itself, which, like the language, developed in stages. Although historians disagree on some aspects, the generally accepted scenario is as follows. First there was the kingdom established by Viking settlers (the Rus) under their leader Rurik. The Vikings settled initially in Novgorod and then also in Kiev, establishing what later became known as Kievan Rus. By the tenth century the Kievan kingdom extended over a large part of what is now western Russia, but the notion of a Russian nation was initially confined to Kiev and the surrounding territory in what is today northeastern Ukraine. For a long time the inhabitants of the Novgorod region did not consider themselves Russian, and when they went south to Kiev they would talk about "going into Rus." But over time the Novgorod dialect, with its many idiosyncratic words, was amalgamated with the Kievan dialect into what became Russian. Another important influence on Russian came about through the Tatar Yoke, the occupation by the Mongols, also known as the Golden Horde (1287–1480), who were in fact a mixture of Mongols and Turks.

Meanwhile an ecclesiastical language called Old Church Slavonic had been developed. This was linked with the proselytizing efforts of Byzantine missionaries, who shaped it into a language for theological and liturgical purposes. Old Church Slavonic came to be written in an early form of the Cyrillic alphabet, named after the younger of two missionary brothers from Byzantium, Saint Cyril and Saint Methodius, although in fact what they invented was an even earlier script called Glagolitic, and the Cyrillic script itself was devised by disciples of the two brothers. Thus the very letters that modern Russians use to write the language have a religious ancestry, as they are reminded every time they use the word "Cyrillic."

Russian underwent a consolidation after the end of the Mongol rule in the fifteenth century, existing side by side with Old Church Slavonic and strongly influenced by the latter, an influence that increased after the fall of Byzantium to the Turks in 1453 when many scholars and ecclesiastics from Byzantium went to Russia. The interaction between the vernacular Russian dialects and Old Church Slavonic resulted in the creation of what became modern Russian. At the same time Old Church Slavonic continued to exist in parallel as an ecclesiastical and literary language, in a similar way to the continuation of Latin in Western Europe but with the difference that Russian and Old Church Slavonic are much closer to each other than Latin is to any of the vernacular languages. The spirit of Old Church Slavonic, with its religious aura, is still felt in the collective mind of the Russians, inspiring a certain veneration. A language of great purity, that is said not to contain a single crude word, it is still largely used for the liturgy today.

Russian continued to evolve. In 1755 the polymath Mikhail Lomonosov published an influential dictionary that incorporated many Old Church Slavonic words into the regular language. In the early nineteenth century the language was further revolutionized by the poet Alexander Pushkin, who introduced many words and expressions from other languages and gave literary Russian a more colloquial touch. This was the golden age of the Russian language and Russian literature, when Russian was a true language of national self-reflection. This era came to an end with the advent of the Bolsheviks, although the language continued to be cherished among the Russian diaspora.

The expatriate Russian linguist Count Nikolai Trubetskoy, writing in 1927, drew attention to the unusual richness of Russian vocabulary resulting from the Old Church Slavonic element within the language.[2] He lists a whole series of things for which there are two different words, one from Old Church Slavonic and one from everyday Russian. The choice of one or the other can be significant, as the Old Church Slavonic word often has a ceremonial or poetic overtone that is absent from the corresponding Russian term. For example, the English word "girl" is *dyevushka* in everyday Russian but *dyeva* in Old Church Slavonic. Both are cognate with the Sanskrit *deva* (masculine) or *devi* (feminine) meaning a divine or angelic being, but *dyeva* conveys a certain reverence that is missing from the diminutive *dyevushka*.

One unusual feature of Russian affords an example of how language is bound up with the mindset of a people. In Russian the normal polite way to address someone is using the first name and the patronymic (the father's first name)—thus "Vladimir Ivanovich" (Vladimir, son of Ivan) or "Viktoria Nikolaevna" (Victoria, daughter of Nikolai). Even Stalin was often addressed as "Josef Vissarianovich." This usage is extremely rare among European languages, Russian and Icelandic being the main exceptions. The fact that the Russians have retained it shows the importance they attach to family ties and ancestry.

BATTLE OVER A LETTER

At the beginning of the twentieth century an intensely controversial reform of the language was proposed. It involved an initiative to remove the letter ѣ (*yat*), which had the same sound as the letter *e* and was therefore redundant, as well as two other letters considered superfluous. Opponents of the proposal were immediately up in arms. They included many writers such as the Symbolist poet Valerii Bryusov, who argued that the *yat* had an aesthetic quality that the letter *e* did not.[3]

The critic and poet Valerian Chudovsky wrote an article in the literary magazine *Apollo* headed "In Favor of the Letter ѣ," in which he wrote:

> Language is a religion: orthography is its sacred liturgy. Like the heavens above the earth, there must be given to children in their education a feeling of spiritual expanses not created by us . . . there is no path to Pushkin without ѣ, for he lives on the Olympus of the accumulation through the ages, of the unbrokenness of heritage whose symbol and key is the letter ѣ.[4]

There was probably an additional mystique attached to the letter on account of the fact that it incorporated a cross.

In another country such a dispute might have seemed like a storm in a teacup, but not in Russia. The Moscow Pedagogical Society and similar associations in other cities joined in the fray, and the Academy of Sciences appointed a committee to examine the question. The committee decided in favor of the reform, but the implementation was interrupted by military conflicts abroad and the 1905 revolution, and the debate dragged on. It was finally implemented in 1917 by the new Bolshevik government. The War of the *Yat* was over, but the Russian language and its script continued to be a subject of contention between modernizers and conservatives.

After the revolution many of the national languages within the Soviet Union underwent a change from Cyrillic to the Roman alphabet. There was a plan to do the same in the case of Russian, but it was halted by Stalin in 1930. At the time of writing Kazakhstan is in the process of Romanizing its alphabet, and some voices in Ukraine are arguing for the same policy.

One might ask: why get so heated about a script? But a script is not just a neutral medium; it carries a multitude of associations, and its visual impact can sometimes be as important as the text that it conveys. For example, among the Russians of the diaspora it used to be possible to tell a person's political affiliation by whether they used the postrevolution alphabet or the old one including the *yat*. It is understandable therefore that the question of the script arouses such passionate reactions.

RUSSIAN AS A SPIRITUAL LANGUAGE

Turning from the script to the language itself: What makes Russian so special? And can we speak of the language as having a spiritual quality? One thing that is striking when one compares Russian with other languages is its strong family resemblance to Sanskrit, which also stems from Indo-European. Sanskrit in Indian tradition is sometimes called Deva-Vani, the language of the gods, for a number of reasons. At the purely phonetic level Sanskrit is extraordinarily rich, having sixteen vowels and thirty-six consonants, with subtle variations of pronunciation, so that it is extremely pleasing and uplifting to listen to and ideal for poetry and also for the chanting of mantras and sounds to activate different chakras—the centers of energy in the body. Russian, like Sanskrit, also has an unusually large variety of sounds with an alphabet of thirty-three letters, including signs for pronouncing consonants hard or soft, which can alter the meaning of a word. For example *mat'* with a soft t means "mother" whereas *mat* with a hard t means "obscene language." The large register of sounds makes for a resonant quality, which means that Old Church Slavonic, the sister language to Russian, is eminently suitable as a language of ritual. For example, the word *Bozhe* (vocative of *Bog* meaning God), with its ending in a voiced consonant and a long vowel, can be chanted in a rich bass voice in a way that the word God, ending in a single consonant, cannot. Hence, when attending a service in a Russian church one feels all the chakras being activated, which is surely one of the reasons why the Orthodox liturgy is so powerful.

The similarity to Sanskrit is most striking with regard to vocabulary. This is illustrated by something experienced by the Indian scholar of Sanskrit, Prof. Durga Prasad Shastri, who went on a trip to Russia in 1964. When he heard Russian being spoken he had the impression that he was hearing a form of Sanksrit. For example, in his Moscow hotel he was told that his room was number 234, which in Russian is *dvesti tridtsat chetyre* and in Sanskrit is *dwishata tridasha chatwari*. Prof. Shastri was astonished that the two related languages had remained so alike over so many centuries.[5]

The Sanskrit connection can also be seen in Russian words with the root *vyed,* containing the idea of knowledge or wisdom. Hence *vyedat* (to know), *vyed* (you see or you know), *vyedenie* (expertise, competence, or authority). The corresponding word in Sanskrit is *veda* (knowledge of wisdom), and the ancient Hindu scriptures are called the *Vedas.* Russians who cherish the idea that they are heirs to an ancient wisdom tradition are fond of using the word *Vyeda* to refer to this tradition, and the existence of words like *vyedat* are a constant reminder to them of their Indo-European heritage.

Let's turn to how Russians express the cherished concept of their actual native land. In English we usually say just "country" or sometimes "homeland." In France the word *patrie* is somewhat more rousing, as is the German *Vaterland*. But in Russia there are two words for the concept: *rodina* (motherland) and *otechestvo* (fatherland). So for the Russian the idea of the homeland incorporates both parents. It is both the loving, nourishing mother and the stern, authoritative father. Of the two words, *rodina* is the more powerfully evocative. It is often coupled with the word *mat'*, meaning mother. Hence, during the Second World War, there were propaganda posters with the slogan *Rodina Mat' zovyot!* (The Motherland is calling!). There is also the word *strana*, which simply means "country" in the sense of a geopolitical space rather than an emotion-laden concept.

Rodina incorporates the word *rod*, a many-faceted word, possibly cognate with the English word "root." In everyday usage it means "kind" in the sense of category or sort, but it embraces the notions of generation, reproduction, birth, kinship, family, gender, and the like. It occurs in compound words such as *narod* (people or folk), *rodit* (to give birth), *roditeli* (parents), *rodstvennik* (a relative), and *rodovoi* (ancestral) and, as mentioned in an earlier chapter, it is the name of the primal creator deity *Rod* in the Slavic pantheon, to whom all these aspects of life are assigned. So the notions of rootedness, kith and kin, the ancestral land, tribal and family ties—all of these are embedded in the language.

Another deeply rooted notion can be seen in the apparently prosaic word *normalno* (normal). When one Russian meets another on the street and asks "How are you?" the reply will often be *normalno*. This might seem a dull, halfhearted response in comparison with "fine," which would be a standard positive reply in the English-speaking world, but in fact it would seem to reveal something about the Russian character. I asked two Russian friends about this and received two different answers. One explained it to me as follows: The Russians are acutely aware that human experience involves suffering as well as pleasure and believe the art of life is to find the right balance between the two, expressed by the term *zolota seredina* (golden mean), which they often use in everyday speech to indicate this holy grail of balance. So when a Russian says that things are *normalno*, what they mean is "just right" (i.e., the scales of life are poised exactly on the golden mean—a state that Russians value all the more on account of the extremes that they have so often experienced). Russians often make fun of the English habit of saying "fine," which to the Russian ear sounds insincere. My other Russian friend said that the use of the word *normalno* has nothing to do with the Russian character but rather is part of the national post-traumatic stress syndrome caused by seven decades of communism.

One Russian concept that must seem bizarre to the average non-Russian is expressed by the word *vranyo,* meaning telling a lie in such a way that the listener knows it to be a lie. Dostoyevsky writes of this practice as follows: "Courteous reciprocity in lying is virtually the prime condition of Russian society—of all Russian meetings, evening entertainments, clubs, scientific bodies, etc." In such cases, Dostoyevsky says, "only a dull blockhead" will question the truth of what he is being told.[6]

Vranyo proved useful in the Soviet era. Say, for example, the manager of a state-owned factory had to deliver a speech in the presence of the assembled work force and a delegation from the office of the Five-Year Plan. He would speak of record production figures and produce a string of impressive statistics, knowing that his listeners knew that it was all *vranyo*. At the end of the speech everyone would applaud and go away happy.

However, problems could arise when some "blockhead" took a piece of *vranyo* at face value, as in the 1990 film *Cloud Heaven* (*Oblako Rai*). The film concerns a young man called Kolya, who lives in a small, remote town where nothing much ever happens. One Sunday morning he visits his friend Fyodor, who lives with his wife in a tower block. On an impulse Kolya indulges in a bit of *vranyo* and tells Fyodor that he's about to leave for the far east of Russia to start a new job.

Unfortunately Fydor takes him seriously. He calls his wife, drinks are poured, and a toast drunk to Kolya's new life. Word spreads rapidly among the neighbors, and Kolya realizes that he now cannot go back on his story. The neighbors help Kolya to pack his possessions, arrange a new tenant for his rented room, and finally see him off as he departs by bus for the far east with an expression of helpless bewilderment on his face. Perhaps there is a sense in which the neighbors also realize that Kolya's story is a fiction but pretend that they believe it. After all, they live lives of boredom and monotony in a boring, monotonous town. Here at last is a bit of excitement, something to provide endless possibilities for more *vranyo* in the years to come ("Did you hear what happened to Kolya when he got to Vladivostock?").

And perhaps the tradition of *vranyo* helps to explain the Russian genius for storytelling and their disproportionate share of great writers—Tolstoy, Dostoyevsky, Pushkin, Biely, Pasternak, and others. Perhaps it also has something to do with their search for the golden mean. There is a Sufi saying that goes something like this: take a lie, a myth, and a fact, and you get somewhere near the truth. *Vranyo*, the myth, is perhaps the golden mean between the lie and the fact.

I have tried to convey something of the richness and subtlety of Russian and how it is an integral part of the Russian soul. It is therefore understandable that there is much concern in the country about the erosion of the language and the way it is being invaded by English and American words and expressions. Modern colloquial Russian now abounds with such terms as consulting, management, business lunch, voucher, bonus, PR, parking, boutique, gadget, marketing, image, penthouse, high-tech, hype, talk show, press release—not to mention the countless computer-related words that have entered the language. A similar linguistic invasion has happened in New Age circles, where the vocabulary includes terms such as bioenergetics, channeling, master class, relaxation, mantras, chakra harmonization. Each New Age cult has its own jargon, which one assimilates when joining the group and which can shape one's way of thinking, as is usually the cult's intention.

Russia is not alone in facing the challenge of linguistic invasion. France has long had its Académie Française to guard the purity of French, but evidently the need was felt for stronger protection, so in 1994 a law was passed prohibiting unjustified use of Anglicisms and Americanisms in public and official speech under threat of a large fine. Similar measures have been taken in other countries, including Russia, which in 2005 issued a Law for the Protection of the Russian Language, against the opposition of many liberal intellectuals. The law forbids the use of words that do not correspond to modern Russian literary language but allows those words that do not have common equivalents in Russian. In practice it is easy to argue the case for such exceptions, so the law is in fact having limited effect. Iceland, a tiny country with a current population of only about 364,000, has found its own way of dealing with the same problem, namely by finding Icelandic translations for foreign terms. Thus the Icelandic word for "computer" is *tölva* from a word meaning numeral. The example of Iceland shows that even a very small country can protect its language, given determination and a strong sense of national identity, especially when it has a rich literary heritage, as the Icelanders have with their sagas and their *Edda*.

In Russia, with its huge population, encompassing many different ethnic and linguistic communities, the challenge is more complicated. For centuries Russian was the common language of the Romanov empire. Subject peoples in Azerbaijan, Turkistan, or Yakutia used both their native languages and Russian, which played the role of an imperial *lingua franca*, rather as English still does among the countries of the former British Empire. During the communist period Russian was aggressively pushed among all the nationalities of the Soviet empire with the result that many indigenous languages declined or faced extinction. Now the newly independent countries of the former Soviet

208 ❖ The Russian Language

bloc are counterreacting, and many of their citizens, especially the younger ones, prefer English as their second language.

So what are the prospects for Russian as a spiritual language? A Russian correspondent of mine writes:

> In the Soviet time, when millions of educated people were killed, oppressed and driven into exile, the role of the Russian language as an "expression of the soul" declined too. During that time Russian was not a language used to express but rather a language used to hide. It was exactly like Orwellian Newspeak. I have been there and witnessed this, and now I can see the tendency coming back after the short break of Perestroika. The soul of Russia and the Russian language have been badly damaged and corrupted by the tragic events of the 20th century, and we do not know how it will survive the 21st.[7]

English speakers are generally less concerned than Russians about the language issue, being aware that their language has a dominant position as the international *lingua franca*. But the dumbing down of English and a similar creeping tendency toward a kind of Orwellian Newspeak should be matters of concern to all English speakers. Indeed, the significance of Russia's struggle to defend its language as the authentic voice of its soul is something that concerns the whole world.

 **FOURTEEN**

The Russian Diaspora

Diasporas, born of invasion, famine, revolution, or other calamities in the homeland, can prove enriching for the rest of the world. Thus the seizure of Constantinople by Ottoman troops in 1453 led to the flight of Byzantine scholars, some of whom went to Florence, taking with them Greek esoteric manuscripts and sparking off the Florentine Hermetic Renaissance. Similarly, the Chinese annexation of Tibet in the 1950s led to an exodus of the Dalai Lama and other clergy, who spread the teachings of Tibetan Buddhism wherever they went.

Over the centuries the Russian diaspora has been swelled by many different population groups that have sought refuge abroad, including the Old Believers, the radical sect known as the Doukhobors (Spirit Warriors), and the Jewish communities who have fled periodic waves of persecution. The exodus reached a peak during the revolution and the subsequent civil war. The brain drain included some 160 people—philosophers, scientists, engineers, lawyers, priests. and others—who were deported from the country in 1922 on Lenin's orders. They and their families boarded two German steamships at St. Petersburg, which became famous as the "Philosophers' Steamships." These vessels took the exiles to the German port of Stettin (now the Polish city of Szecin), from which they made their way to various European cities to join other members of the diaspora.

They included the philosophers Nikolai Berdyaev and Ivan Ilyin, and the theologian and Orthodox priest Sergei Bulgakov. Later the same year more intellectuals were sent out from the port of Odessa or by train. Thus some of Russia's best minds were shipped away like a load of contaminated waste, but at least they escaped the Gulag or the firing squad, unlike many who stayed behind.[1]

If the ghosts of those writers were able to keep abreast of events in the twenty-first century they would have been most surprised when many of their names, along with others, were on a reading list recommended by President Putin to his regional governors at the 2014 annual meeting of his political party, United Russia. Reflecting on the reasons for this, Gary Lachman mentions Vladimir Solovyov's book *The Justification of the Good,* one of the those on Putin's list, which argued for the concept of good in an absolute sense rather than in the utilitarian sense that has come to prevail in the West. Another name mentioned by Putin was Nikolai Berdyaev who, having started out as a Marxist, came to reject the enforced materialism and egalitarianism of the revolution.[2]

Today there are some thirty million native speakers of Russian living outside the Russian Federation and scattered throughout the world.[3] The enormous diaspora was Russia's loss, but it gave the world writers like Vladimir Nabokov, painters like Marc Chagall, composers like Igor Stravinsky, and ballet dancers like Rudolf Nureyev. It also served as a conduit for esoteric and spiritual movements.

Going back to the nineteenth century, one Russian expatriate stands out particularly in this context, namely Helena Petrovna Blavatsky (1831–1891).* Although of German extraction on her father's side and of mixed ancestry on her mother's, she can be considered Russian, and perhaps only Russia could have produced her. Blavatsky's

---

*For my summary of her life I have relied largely on Sylvia Cranston, *H.P.B. The Extraordinary Life and Influence of Helena Blavatsky,* as well as the entry on her in W. J. Hanegraaff, et al. (eds) in the *Dictionary of Gnosis and Western Esotericism.*

legacy is enormous. More than any other individual she opened up the western mind to eastern spirituality, esotericism, and the world of the unseen, paving the way for the New Age movement, the hippy trail to India, and the practitioners of past-life therapy.

She was born in Yekaterinoslav, Ukraine, of noble ancestry on both sides. Her father, Pyotr von Hahn, was an army officer. Her mother, also called Helena, was a gifted, self-educated woman who became a successful novelist. Because of Pyotr's frequent repostings and her mother's delicate health, Helena's childhood was marked by frequent moves to different cities—Poltava, Odessa, St. Petersburg, Astrakhan . . . It was in Astrakhan, where Russia rubs shoulders with Central Asia, that she came into contact with the Kalmyk people, a Mongol tribe, and with the Tibetan Buddhism that they practiced. This was a sign of things to come. Already as a child she appeared to be destined for an unusual life. Her inner world was full of mystery, magic, fable, the unseen, and visitations from a superior being whom she believed to be her protector. When she was eleven, her mother died.

At the age of seventeen, apparently on a whim, she married the much older Nikifor Blavatsky, but immediately regretted it and took flight. Then began a life of quest and wandering, initially to Turkey, Egypt, France, and England. In London the mysterious protector apparently presented himself to her as a real person called the Master Morya, who, as it later appeared, was one of a group of spiritually elevated beings, the Masters or Mahatmas, living in a hidden abode in Tibet, from which they guided the destiny of the world. More travels followed—to North, Central, and South America, then across the Pacific to India and onward to the north where she made a failed attempt to cross into Tibet. Later, as she claimed, after further travels she succeeded in entering Tibet, accompanied by Morya, and there stayed at the house of another great Master called Koot Hoomi.

Her continued wanderings took her to the United States where,

Fig. 14.1. Helena Petrovna Blavatsky, cofounder of the Theosophical Society
WIKIMEDIA COMMONS

in 1875 in New York, she founded the Theosophical Society together with her friend Henry Steel Olcott and a young Irish American called William Quan Judge. The Society had three aims:

1. To form the nucleus of a universal brotherhood of humanity, without distinction of race, creed, sex, caste, or color
2. The study of ancient and modern religions, philosophies, and sciences, and the demonstration of the importance of such study
3. The investigation of the unexplained laws of nature and the physical powers latent in man

Over the next decade or so Blavatsky and Olcott were constantly traveling around spreading the Theosophical Society message. They established what became the world center of the movement at Adyar in India, where theosophy acquired a substantial following. In Ceylon both of them adopted the Buddhist religion. Eventually Blavatsky settled in London, where she spent her final years in a house in the district of St. John's Wood. When she died in 1891 she left behind an international movement and a body of writing, notably her two major books, *Isis Unveiled* and *The Secret Doctrine.*

These encyclopedic works constitute an extraordinary and often erratic synthesis of religion, philosophy, history, occultism, folklore, archaeology, and much else. What emerges is a great oracular revelation of cosmic laws and the destiny of human beings and the world. According to Blavatsky, humanity, guided by the Mahatmas, is progressing through a series of seven "root races," including the Hyperborean, Lemurian, and Atlantean. The present age is the age of the fifth root race. All through the millennia certain initiates have preserved a secret tradition of wisdom, which lies at the heart of all the world's great religions. Other elements of Blavatsky's teachings include the concepts of reincarnation, karma, and the "astral light," an invisible, all-pervading medium which can affect physical reality and in which all knowledge and experience is recorded.

After Madame Blavatsky's death and following a wrangle over the succession, the Theosophical Society was taken over by the British social campaigner Annie Besant, and the Society spread throughout Europe, America, and other parts of the world. In Russia it was initially banned by the Orthodox Church, flourished briefly in the Silver Age, was banned anew in the communist era, and now is once again active in Madame Blavatsky's homeland.

Over time theosophy gave rise to various offshoots and related movements. Austrian Rudolf Steiner broke away from the Theosophical Society in 1913 to found his own movement, Anthroposophy, which has become influential throughout the world and operates in many spheres including education, art, architecture, medicine, and agriculture. Also out of theosophy came the Arcane School of Alice Bailey, who coined the term "Age of Aquarius," which became a watchword of the New Age movement. Then there were Blavatsky's compatriots Nikolai and Helena Roerich with their agni yoga movement and their reliance on the guidance of the Theosophical Master Koot Hoomi.[4] After the Russian revolution they went via Finland to England where they joined the Theosophical Society and founded their agni yoga school. In 1920 they traveled to the United States where they remained for two and a half years, returning there briefly in 1929.

Roerich's relationship with America was marked by both triumph and disaster. On the triumph side was his successful campaign for a treaty to protect "artistic and scientific institutions and historic monuments" in wartime, usually known as the Roerich Pact. Other achievements were his nomination for the Nobel Peace Prize and the splendid museum on three floors of a skyscraper on Riverside Drive in New York, created for him by his benefactor, the industrialist Louis Horch. Unfortunately he came into conflict with Horch, who dissolved the museum. However, a group of his supporters created a new museum, which now occupies an elegant gray stone house on 107th Street on the Upper West Side. When I lived in New York in the 1990s it was a place I often visited, a haven of serenity and beauty in the hustle and bustle of Manhattan. Around the corner on Riverside Drive is the Master Building, the former home of the original museum. One memento of the Roerich period can still be seen there, namely a block of polished black stone, cemented into one corner on the ground floor and engraved with a circle enclosing the monogram MR, probably standing for Morya, as well three discs arranged in a triangle, as shown on the Banner of Peace, the symbol of the Roerich Pact.

In all of his endeavors Roerich was guided by a belief in humanity's salvation through beauty, as expressed in Dostoyevsky's novel *The Idiot,* where one of the characters, speaking about the hero Prince Mishkin, announces that "the prince says that the world will be saved by beauty."[5] At a time when the very concept of beauty is widely scorned and so much of our built environment is an ugly dystopia,

Dostoyevsky's words and Roerich's life's work offer a different kind of vision for the world.

Another expatriate Russian, almost contemporary with Roerich but a guru of a very different kind, was Georgy Ivanovich Gurdjieff (1877–1949).[6] Not ethnically Russian but of Greek and Armenian extraction, he was born in the Transcaucasus, then part of the Russian empire. As a young man he left home and embarked on a journey of discovery through the Middle East and Central Asia that lasted some twenty years and allegedly culminated in his reaching a secret monastery in the mountains, where he was initiated into a fraternity called the Sarmoung Brotherhood. Here we can recognize a familiar motif from myth and legend: the initiatory journey from which the traveler returns possessing new knowledge. The teaching that Gurdjieff took back with him centered upon the notion that human beings are essentially asleep and need to be woken up. The system he used in order to do this was based in a particular understanding of certain laws and

Fig. 14.2. G. I. Gurdjieff. His system was designed to wake people up from a state of sleep in which humanity is kept.
WIKIMEDIA COMMONS

principles affecting the cosmos and human beings, combined with a highly strenuous program of physical work, mental exercises, and complex dance movements. All of this was designed to "shock" the participants out of their conditioned patterns of thought and behavior and thus enable them to attain mastery of themselves.

When Gurdjieff returned to Russia he made his way to Moscow and gathered a group of pupils. Other pupils soon formed a St. Petersburg group, which included Pyotr Demyanovich Ouspensky. After the Bolshevik revolution Ouspensky emigrated to England, spreading his own version of the Gurdjieff work there, while Gurdjieff went south to the Black Sea region and then to Tbilisi in Georgia, continuing to teach groups of pupils as he went from place to place. As conditions in Russia descended into chaos, he moved to Istanbul and then to France, where he reestablished his teaching center, the Institute for the Harmonious Development of Man, in a mansion at Avon near Fontainebleau, which he occupied from 1922–1933, subsequently operating from a Paris flat where he died in 1949. A number of pupils who went on to disseminate the teaching included John Godolphin Bennett, a former British army intelligence officer, and Olga Ivanovna Henzenberg, who later married the American architect Frank Lloyd Wright.

During the 1920s and '30s Gurdjieff made several trips to the United States, attracting attention everywhere with his arresting appearance—handlebar moustache, shaven head, and large, piercing eyes—and his equally arresting and often abrasive personality. He alienated a potential publisher, Alfred Knopf, by telling him: "First clean house, your house, then perhaps you can have my book!"[7] But there was no lack of Americans who were deeply impressed by him, including Frank Lloyd Wright, and who were eager to carry on his work. Today there are Gurdjieff centers in many parts of the United States, as there are in many other countries, including Russia.

Thus the outward tide of emigration has been followed by a reverse tide, bringing in not so much people as ideas, books, movements, and currents of thought that had been rejected in the Soviet Union but nourished in the diaspora. For the Orthodox community the frequent visits of Archbishop Anthony Bloom, leader of the Orthodox Church in Britain, were of enormous importance in Soviet times. Regarding other spiritual paths, apart from theosophy, the Gurdjieff work, and the Roerich movement, the inward tide includes various movements already mentioned, such as the Eurasianism of Trubetskoy, Jakobson, et al., and phenomena like the *Book of Veles,* which went via the émigré community in San Francisco back to Russia where it became a bestseller. The works of philosophers like Nikolai Berdyaev and Ivan Ilyin are once again eagerly read in Russia and have been expressly recommended by President Putin, as Gary Lachman points out in his book *The Return of Holy Russia.* In this way the diaspora has played a crucial role in Russia's mystical quest.

FIFTEEN

In Search of a Vision for the Twenty-First Century

All of the movements I have looked at have promoted their various dreams and visions, but if we were to look for a grand, overall vision that might inspire the world, what might it be? Perhaps it might include the age-old idea of immortality, which was one of the goals of the cosmist movement. The cosmists may not yet have achieved this aim, but their movement has had important repercussions, so it is worth taking a closer look at them. Cosmism (which in fact was not named as such until the 1970s) stemmed from the nineteenth-century thinker Nikolai Fyodorov (1829–1903), who preached an unusual mixture of messianic religion and radical scientific utopianism. As mentioned earlier, it was Fyodorov's vision that ultimately led to the launching of the Sputnik 1 satellite in 1957 and the space voyage of Yuri Gagarin in 1961. Those achievements were presented by the Soviets as proof of the superiority of communism, and at the same time they caused a panic in the western world and led to the space race. What few people realized was that those feats owed less to communism than to the ideas of Fyodorov and the cosmists, in particular his disciple Tsiolkovsky.

Fyodorov was another of those figures whom only Russia could have produced. He was part saint, part starets, part holy fool, part learned genius. He propounded a vision of such titanic immensity for the future of humankind that some people thought him mad, while others became his devoted followers. As the illegitimate son of Prince Pavel Gagarin and Elisaveta Ivanova, a woman of minor nobility, he could have found a comfortable niche in the world despite the circumstances of his birth. Instead he lived in self-imposed poverty and austerity for most of his life, giving away to the needy almost all of the little money that he earned, dressing in worn-out clothes, subsisting on the most frugal of diets, and sleeping on a humpback trunk with only a book for a pillow.

A polymath with an acute and encyclopedic mind, he lived for many years as an itinerant schoolteacher until he secured a job as librarian at the Rumyanstev Museum in Moscow, now the Russian State Library. A sketched portrait of him in old age shows him hunched over his desk in the library, a bald, gray-bearded sage, eyes gazing into the far distance as though toward some imagined utopian colony in outer space. At the library he had the time and security to develop his extraordinary visionary philosophy, and here he held court with a circle of disciples. Gradually he came to the attention of a wider audience, which included prominent names like Dostoyevsky, Tolstoy, and the philosopher Vladimir Solovyov, all of whom were deeply impressed by him. He published very little during his lifetime, but after his death his followers saw to the publication of his magnum opus, *The Philosophy of the Common Task*.

The "common task" referred to was nothing less than the overcoming of mortality. For Fyodorov death was the central affliction of humanity and need not be inevitable. Moreover, if you could overcome death, you would obviate the need for sexual reproduction, which Fyodorov saw as something that constantly dragged human beings down to the level of the beasts and prevented them from rising to their full spiritual potential. Not content with overcoming death, Fyodorov wished to fulfill the biblical promise of resurrection by recreating all of past humanity from the cosmic dust that constitutes their remains.

To provide sufficient living space for all resurrected people, the earth would be freed from its gravitational orbit and become a spaceship for the exploration and colonization of other planets, where a perfect society would be created, free from death, disease, want, and conflict.

While promoting these science-fiction-like schemes, Fyodorov remained fervently devoted to the Orthodox religion. The "common task" was humanity's God-given destiny. The observances of the Church, its symbols, rites, festivals, and icons, were like windows affording a glimpse of the more perfect world to which we should be aspiring. Moreover, while preaching the kinship of all humanity, Fyodorov assigned the leading role in his project to the Slavs, believing that they, alone among the peoples of the world, had the necessary drive and optimism to carry it through.

In his profound study *The Russian Cosmists,* George M. Young convincingly shows that Fyodorov's ideas can be categorized as "esoteric" according to the definition of that term established by the French scholar Antoine Faivre.[1]

According to Professor Faivre there are four essential ideas that are characteristic of esotericism, which can be summarized as follows: the notion of correspondences ("as above, so below"); the belief in living, animate nature; the importance of the imagination; and the idea of transmutation (as, for example, in alchemy). In addition Faivre posits two secondary characteristics: concordance (i.e., the identification of parallel features in different esoteric traditions); and the notion of transmission (special knowledge being handed down from one age to another).

If we consider Faivre's four main criteria we find that they all fit Fyodorov's vision. Central to that vision is what Fyodorov called *rodstvo* (kinship). This meant not just family ties in the normal sense, but a principle that connects everything in the universe, including ourselves and our ancestors. This is the "as above, so below" principle and fits with Faivre's notion of correspondences. As for the second and fourth criteria, for Fyodorov, each particle of cosmic dust is a fragment of potential life (living nature) and capable of becoming part of a resurrected ancestor (transmutation). Faivre's third characteristic, imagination, is what enables us to envisage the more perfect world that Fyodorov wishes us to create.

Thus Fyodorov's ideas were a combination of esotericism, mysticism, Orthodox piety, utopianism, and science fantasy. It was a heady mixture that, combined with Fyodorov's compelling personality, attracted a devoted following. Among the followers one was to play a historic role—the space travel pioneer Konstantin Tsiolkovsky (1857–1935).

Tsiolkovsky's life story is even more remarkable than that of Fyodorov. Born the son of a minor official in a provincial village some two hundred kilometers to the southeast of Moscow, he became partially deaf at the age of ten through an attack of scarlet fever and consequently was unable to complete his schooling. Educated at home, he became a voracious reader and even as a teenager began to dream of the possibility of space travel. As a penniless youth of sixteen seeking to expand his knowledge, he made his way to Moscow and to the Rumyanstev library, where he joined Fyodorov's circle of pupils. Under Fyodorov's guidance and with access to the library's rich collection, he received the equivalent of a higher education in mathematics, physics, and related subjects. He then became a science teacher in Kaluga province to the southwest of Moscow, where in his spare time he built prototype rockets and spacecraft and wrote papers containing the calculations that would make possible the launching of Sputnik 1 in 1957. During the 1920s and '30s Tsiolkovsky was fêted by the communist regime. As the image of the humble rural schoolteacher and scientific genius fitted perfectly with the Bolshevik notion of a national hero, the esoteric aspects of Tsiolkovsky's thought were conveniently ignored. He shared many of Fyodorov's ideas, such as the possibility of resurrecting ancestors from particles of cosmic dust, but his vision of the ideal society was a kind of benevolent dictatorship by people with superior minds, in which only those who were intellectually and morally worthy would be selected as citizens.[2]

Other people who were influenced by Fyodorov included the philosopher Sergei Bulgakov, the scientist and cleric Father Pavel Florensky (1882–1937), and the geologist Vladimir Vernadsky (1863–1945) who, among other things, popularized such notions as the "biosphere" and the "noosphere." Without adopting Fyodorov's extraordinary space-age vision in its entirety, these people took over some of his core ideas, for example that the cosmos and the human mind are one and that we possess the power and indeed the obligation to engage scientifically and spiritually with the universe and in doing so remake ourselves and open up a world of infinite possibility.

REVERBERATIONS OF COSMISM

The cosmist movement has lived on and branched off in many different directions. Certain aspects of it are found in the Eurasian movement and the ideas of Lev Gumilyov, as well as in the Hyperborean movement. On the face of it there might not seem to be much connection between cosmism and Hyperboreanism until one considers the work of Valerii Dyomin (1932–2006), a leading proponent of the Hyperborean theory. In his 1997 Moscow University doctoral dissertation under the title *Philosophical Principles of Russian Cosmism*, Dyomin presented a holistic way of studying the world, embracing scientific, spiritual, emotional, and philosophical approaches and drawing on a wide range of disciplines from history to archaeology. Thus the cosmist researcher aims to become one with the all-encompassing mind of the universe.[3] It was with the aid of this approach that Dyomin arrived at his conclusions about Hyperborea. Moreover, for Dyomin and others of the same persuasion, Hyperborea represents a lost utopia, a golden age in which humanity was one family with one language, enjoying peace, harmony, prosperity, health, and longevity. In cosmism this past civilization becomes a blueprint for the future.

The progeny of cosmism is manifold, and ideas that once seemed like the wildest of fantasies, such as Fyodorov's resurrectionism, are now taken seriously as, for example, by the proponents of transhumanism, who foresee a future in which we shall essentially be part human, part machine, with enormously extended lifespans. Today there is a museum in Moscow devoted to Fyodorov's life and work, while Tsiolkovsky is commemorated in a museum in his former hometown of Kaluga.

One of the most fascinating initiatives connected with the cosmist legacy is the International Institute for Scientific Research in Cosmoplanetary Anthropoecology (ISRICA), based in Akademgorodok, the scientific research enclave in Novosibirsk, Siberia. Led by Alexander Trofimov, at the time of writing the Institute's program, as described on its website, includes "the study of living matter on planet earth as a cosmo-planetary phenomenon; the investigation of the influence of cosmic factors on the biosphere, the evolution of biosystems and human health; the development and testing of new methods in geoecology, agricultural production, the food industry and health care."[4]

The ISRICA builds on the work of Vladimir Vernadsky and his notion of the noosphere and especially on that of Nikolai Kozyrev (1908–1983), mentioned in chapter 9 in connection with the research of Dr. Olga Kharitidi into the healing methods of Siberian shamans. Kozyrev was a brilliant astrophysicist whose career was interrupted by a ten-year spell in a Siberian prison camp, where there were shamans among the inmates. Spending time with them, he concluded that they had telepathic and other paranormal abilities, which all humanity had once possessed and had the potential to regain. He attributed these abilities to the shamans being in touch with an all-pervading field or etheric fluid, an age-old concept that appears in many cultures. It is what in the Vedic tradition is called *akasha* and what the nineteenth-century French occultist Eliphas Lévi called the "astral light," a term that was later taken up by Helena Blavatsky.

Kozyrev's name is immortalized in the device known as the Kozyrev mirror, which was actually developed not by him but by Vlail Kaznacheev, senior scientist at the ISRICA until his death in 2014. Usually the mirror is a cylinder of aluminum, large enough to accommodate a person standing or lying down. It appears to function as a collector and magnifier of etheric energy, enabling a user to receive messages telepathically from a sender in another mirror in a different location, even thousands of miles away. More than that, it can apparently induce a shamanic state

Fig. 15.1. A Kozyrev mirror, developed by research scientists in Akademgorodok, Siberia. Here the mirror is being tested for its consciousness-expanding properties. (See also color plate 10)
WIKIMEDIA COMMONS

of cosmic consciousness in which one can receive information from past civilizations and from distant bodies in space and even predict future events. It can also be used for healing purposes.

It was a Kozyrev mirror in which Dr. Kharitidi received her revelation about humanity's imminent leap in evolution and about the existence of particular places in the world where it is easier to access other dimensions. According to the findings of Kaznacheev and Trofimov at ISRICA, the earth's magnetic field acts as a kind of veil between us and the cosmos, but there are certain places where the magnetic field is weaker and where contact with the higher dimensions is easier. One of these, according to Dr. Kharitidi, is the Altai region of Siberia, and it is perhaps no coincidence that this is an area with a strong shamanic tradition. Today it is attracting many tourists and New Agers, perhaps drawn not just by the beauty of the mountain scenery, but also by the special energies that the shamans have long been aware of.

Kozyrev also turned his attention to the phenomenon of time. He maintained that time is a form of energy and that certain processes can work backward from the future to the present. His discoveries in this domain continue to have an impact in modern science and to provide explanations for phenomena such as the growth patterns of seashells or the way in which the sap in trees rises in apparent defiance of the law of gravity. In an article on Kozyrev's theory of time, Erik Johansen Stein writes:

> In the years to come Kozyrev will keep on inspiring scientific imagination as well as careful investigations in different areas and disciplines. Hopefully, some mysteries of the World will become more or less solved from this, while at the same time new mysteries will be created as a vital force regenerating the spirit of true scientific exploration unfolding from the marriage between heavenly inebriation and earthly sobriety.[5]

RUSSIA AS AN ARK

The combination of "heavenly inebriation and earthly sobriety" also characterizes another initiative inspired by the cosmist movement, namely the Izborsky Club, a conservative Moscow think tank, founded in 2012 by influential people from academia, journalism, politics, business, the Church, and the military. An idea of the club's agenda can be obtained by looking at its journal, bearing the same name as the club itself. Central to the group's millenarian scenario is the metaphor of a coming global "flood" in which Russia will act as an "ark" to save humanity.

The first issue of the journal, which appeared in 2020, is devoted to the theme of the ark. As the introduction to the issue states: "We are seeing the approach of the Flood—not the biblical one which renewed the ancient world, but a new, invisible flood of information, images, mental chaos and corruption which, from within humanity itself, threatens to choke the last vital springs of the human heart."[6]

The ark project entails a rescuing of the sacred foundations of life. Russia, the author writes, can be such an ark, but would also reach out to other countries and cultures. The world economic crises of the twentieth century were caused by "the arrogance of a narrow community that has given itself the right to dictate to all countries both economic policy and the norms of public life." Western institutions and communities are based on the model of "Faustian man," that is, man who has sold his soul to the devil in return for material benefits.[7]

The basic principles of the ark project include a decisive break with the notion of a common human civilization, which is seen as part of the crypto-colonial agenda of the "flood civilization" with its aim to destroy traditional cultures and values. The ark, by contrast, is open to a multipolar world with fundamentally different approaches to development. The "ark person" rejects the western model of globalization as the only possible path and the one to which there is no alternative. "As long as we live, think and choose there is always an alternative."[8]

In 2021 the Izborsky Club published a collection of essays on the ark project, describing in detail the decline of the West and how Russia can rescue the world. In one passage we read:

> The extraordinary future of Russia in the coming era was predicted by many Orthodox saints. In various ways these prophecies speak of the revival of the faith and of the spiritual authority of Russia, the emergence of a strong leader who will receive the status of a monarch. . . . Note that among these prophecies there is also a direct indication by the Monk Nektarios of Optina that the days before the Flood in the time of Noah are a prototype of our days.[9]

Here again we see that Russian tendency to view historical events as part of a great millenarian scenario.

SIXTEEN

"The Hope of the World"?

If, as many have predicted, Russia is destined to play a special role in the world, then it would make sense to look for the reason first in the Russian character. An interesting statement on this subject is by Yuri Smirnov, whom I mentioned in chapter 11 in connection with the Anastasia movement. Smirnov is a native Russian who spent several years in Australia and New Zealand and therefore can speak from both an outside and an inside perspective. In an article in *New Dawn* magazine he identifies various primary and secondary features of the Russian character. The keywords that he lists include: spirituality, kindness, selflessness, a spirit of communality, traditionalism (e.g., celebration of folk culture and traditions), patriotism, and a recognition of the need for government by a strong sovereign power. He sees Russia as engaged in a struggle to defend its authentic self against outside forces that would impose a different set of values and way of life.[1]

To this assessment we might add Nietzsche's view that strength of will is greatest in Russia. Few peoples could have gone through the horrors of the Stalin dictatorship, the decimation of the Second World War, and the near collapse of the 1990s and rallied to become once again a strong competitor in the global arena unless they had possessed an indomitable will.

Edgar Cayce spoke of the "hope of the world" coming out of Russia. Evidently he had some particularly hopeful development in mind, but he might also have been thinking of the quality of hope itself—as in the biblical triad of faith, hope, and charity. The Russian word for hope is *nadyezhda,* a common first name for women in Russia, which says something about the value that Russians place on this quality. Much of Russian literature highlights the ability to hold on to hope even in the midst of despair. For example, in Solzhenitsyn's novel *One Day in the Life of Ivan Denisovich,* first published in 1962, the hero is sustained by moments of hope even under the appalling conditions in a Soviet labor camp.

To the above qualities I would add the capacity for enchantment, perhaps the most important quality of all—the ability to invest life with magic and mystery. Hence the search for the Firebird's feather, the belief in the wondrous lands of Byelovodye and Hyperborea, the otherworldly paintings of artists like Alexander Uglanov and Andrei Klimenko, the films of Tarkovsky, the writings of novelists like Mikhail Bulgakov, and the respect paid in rural folk tradition to the spirits of nature and domestic spirits like the domovoi.

What about the nearness to God that Rilke spoke of? Certainly among the Russians there is a widespread perception of themselves as an unusually spiritual people, although, as we have seen, they hold a great variety of different opinions as to what that precisely means. Orthodox Christianity is still the predominant religion, and many believe that the Orthodox Church has a special worldwide mission. The strength of Orthodox religiosity was demonstrated in 2020 when a committee was working to revise the Russian constitution, and Bishop Kirill, Patriarch of Moscow and all Russia, put forward a proposal that faith in God be included in the constitution as part of the bedrock of the Russian state. In the ensuing controversy one person who spoke out in support of Bishop Kirill was the Speaker of the St. Petersburg Parliament, Vyacheslav Makarov, who said the following: "I fully and completely support the position of His Holiness Patriarch Kirill. Russia is an Orthodox country, a world power. It is, as we say, the last hope of God on earth. . . . In the 70s they said that there would be no Soviet Union but a variety of seers, sages and so on, and that in 60 years Russia would spiritually rule the whole world. . . . We will live to see this time."[2]

At the same time there are many people who feel that the Orthodox Church has become too subservient to the state. One of my Russian interviewees said that she hoped for the advent of a great spiritual leader, an Orthodox Luther who would reform and renew the religion. She also mentioned that Orthodoxy is having to compete with other religions. Many people, especially in the outlying areas, are converting to Islam. Others are turning to Buddhism and some to Judaism or other faiths.

The millenarian mentality that crops up so often in Russian history is seen in the "flood" scenario of the Izborsky Club, mentioned in the previous chapter. Here again Russia is cast in the role of the world savior, a latter-day Noah who will come with his ark to rescue the sacred foundations of life from being inundated by the mental chaos and corruption spread by modern global media and monoculture.

There is another kind of millennialism in movements of the New Age variety such as Thelema, agni yoga, the Osho movement, the Ringing Cedars movement, and the teachings of modern gurus like Lev Klykov. Speaking to Russians in this milieu, both in the homeland and in the diaspora, I found that there was much talk of a transformation of human consciousness. Irina Egorova, a Russian expatriate living with her Danish husband, Joshua Dharma, in the mountains of Ecuador, sees the Anastasia movement as part of this awakening. She has great hopes for Russia and believes that the Russian diaspora can provide a spark of light everywhere in the world. She spoke of the need for a new paradigm involving a marriage of spirituality, science, and the ancient Vedic tradition. Both Irina and Joshua are teachers in the Art of Living Organization, founded in 1981 by the Indian spiritual leader Sri Sri Ravi Shankar and active in many countries of the world, including Russia.

For a synergy of the kind they envisage there are great possibilities. Russia is fortunate in having various sizeable population groups practicing ancient traditions such as shamanism and Tibetan Buddhism, which miraculously survived the communist years and are now once again thriving. We have seen in chapter 15 some examples of the extraordinarily fruitful collaboration between the shamans of Siberia and scientists like Nikolai Kozyrev, Olga Kharitidi, and the staff of the International Institute for Scientific Research in Cosmoplanetary Anthropoecology in Novosibirsk. Valuable discoveries in medicine, psychology, and other fields have emerged from this kind of collaboration. There is also the example of Dr. Ernst Muldashev's research among the Tibetans and his discovery in the region of Mount Kailas of what he called the Matrix of Life.

So there may be some truth in Spengler's prediction about the emergence of a new culture or the revitalization of an ancient culture in Russia—a culture that can best be characterized by the word "enchantment." An enchanted culture would embrace both religion and science and involve the holistic approach of thinkers such as Vladimir Vernadsky with his belief in the interconnectedness of everything in the cosmos, so that we would recognize ourselves as inseparably embedded in living nature and bearing a responsibility for its well-being. In such a culture the scientist would also be a magus, a poet, a philosopher, a mystic, an artist. . . . There would be an ethos of beauty and respect for tradition. In religion there would be room for both the solemn reverence of Orthodoxy, the visceral energy of paganism and the Sophianic wisdom of the woman clothed with the sun. To put it another way, what Russia has to offer is a re-enchantment of the world in place of the disenchantment that Max Weber spoke of as a characteristic of modernity. Perhaps this is the real transforming gift of which so many prophets have spoken.

Notes

INTRODUCTION: RUSSIA'S MYSTICAL QUEST

1. Nietzsche, *Jenseits von Gut und Böse* [English trans.], section 208.
2. Cohn, *The Pursuit of the Millennium,* 128–29.
3. Cohn, *The Pursuit of the Millennium,* 128.
4. Иванов [Ivanov], *"О русской идее"* ["On the Russian Idea"], 321–27. My translation.
5. Rilke, "Russische Kunst," 3.
6. Massie, *Peter the Great,* 54.
7. Massie, *Peter the Great,* 54.
8. Spengler, "The Two Faces of Russia."

I. TWILIGHT

1. Lachman, *A Secret History of Consciousness,* 47.
2. Ouspensky, *A New Model of the Universe,* 4.
3. Ouspensky, *A New Model of the Universe,* 4.
4. Moore, *Gurdjieff,* 66.
5. Энциклопедический словарь [Encyclopedic Dictionary], "Минцлова Анна Рудольфовна" [Mintzlova, Anna Rudolfovna].
6. Энциклопедический словарь [Encyclopedic Dictionary], "Минцлова Анна Рудольфовна" [Mintzlova, Anna Rudolfovna].
7. Biely, *The Dramatic Symphony* and *Forms of Art.* Introduction, 4.
8. Biely, *The Dramatic Symphony* and *Forms of Art.* Introduction, 7.
9. Biely, *The Dramatic Symphony* and *Forms of Art.* Introduction, 115.
10. Biely, *Petersburg,* 165.
11. Decter, *Nicholas Roerich,* 107.

12. Богомолов [Bogomolov], *Русская литература начала XX века и оккультизм* [*Russian Literature at the Beginning of the Twentieth Century and Occultism*], 281.

13. Богомолов, 280.

14. Богомолов, 299.

15. Богомолов, 299.

16. Богомолов, 378–79.

17. Cousins, "Scriabine and Delville," 358.

18. Godwin, *Harmonies of Heaven and Earth,* 43.

19. Lennhoff and Posner, 1361.

20. Lennhoff and Posner, 1361.

21. McIntosh, *Eliphas Lévi and the French Occult Revival,* 160–61.

22. Aptekman, "In the Beginning Was the Word," 30.

23. Burmistrov, "Kabbalah and Martinism," 3.

24. McIntosh, *Eliphas Lévi and the French Occult Revival,* 220.

25. McIntosh, *Eliphas Lévi and the French Occult Revival,* 220 and Андреев [Andreyev], *Оккултист Страны Советов* [*Occultist of the Soviet Countries*], 16–17.

26. Sabeheddin, "Saint-Yves d'Alveydre and the Synarchy of Agarttha."

27. Godwin, Introduction to *The Kingdom of Agarttha.*

28. Никитин [Nikitin], *Мистики, розенкейцеры и тамплиеры в советской России* [*Mystics, Rosicrucians, and Templars in Soviet Russia*], 30.

29. Andreyev, *The Saint-Petersburg Datsan,* 53 ff.

30. Andreyev, *The Saint-Petersburg Datsan,* 46.

31. Andreyev, *The Saint-Petersburg Datsan,* 60–62

32. Graham, "Rasputin," 2338.

33. Kourennoff, *Russian Folk Medicine,* 21–22.

34. Graham, "Rasputin," 2340.

2. FABLED LANDS

1. For a detailed account of the story see К. В. Чистов [K. V. Chistov], "Легенда о Беловодье" [The Legend of Byelovodye], 116–81.

2. Чистов [Chistov], 146 ff.

3. See Baker, *Heart of the World.*

4. See Moore, *Gurdjieff,* 31.

5. See McIntosh, *Beyond the North Wind.*

6. Андреев [Andreyev], *Оккултист Страны Советов* [*Occultist of the Soviet Countries*], 6.

7. Андреев [Andreyev], *Оккултист Страны Советов* [*Occultist of the Soviet Countries*], 62–63.

8. Андреев [Andreyev], *Оккултист Страны Советов* [*Occultist of the Soviet Countries*], 166.

9. See Андреев [Andreyev], *Оккултист Страны Советов* [*Occultist of the Soviet Countries*], 128 ff for a full account of the expedition.

10. Андреев [Andreyev], *Оккултист Страны Советов* [*Occultist of the Soviet Countries*], 135.

11. Андреев [Andreyev], *Оккултист Страны Советов* [*Occultist of the Soviet Countries*], 137–39.

12. Дёмин [Dyomin], *Гиперборея* [Hyperborea].

13. Андреев [Andreyev], *Оккултист Страны Советов* [*Occultist of the Soviet Countries*], 155.

14. Walker, "Tantrism," 242.

15. Znamenski, *Red Shambhala*, 87.

16. Znamenski, *Red Shambhala*, 91 ff.

17. Znamenski, *Red Shambhala*, 175–76.

18. Znamenski, *Red Shambhala*, 189–92.

19. Prokofieff, *The East in the Light of the West*, 1.

20. Дёмин [Dyomin, *Гиперборея* [Hyperborea].

21. See the video on Muldashev's Tibet expedition, in Russian with English subtitles, available on YouTube.

22. Ashe, *The Ancient Wisdom*.

3. REIGN OF THE ANTICHRIST

1. Jenkins, *The Great and Holy War*, 202.

2. Evdokomov, *Russische Pilger*, 9.

3. Evdokomov, *Russische Pilger*, 199–200.

4. Glazov, *The Russian Mind since Stalin's Death*, 5.

5. Andreyev, *The Saint-Petersburg Datsan*, 67 ff.

6. Andreyev, *The Saint-Petersburg Datsan*, 71–72.

7. Andreyev, *The Saint-Petersburg Datsan*, 79.

8. Никитин [Nikitin], *Мистики, розенкейцеры и тамплиеры в советской России* [*Mystics, Rosicrucians and Templars in Soviet Russia*], 89.

9. See Auction 15, Part 2 at Bidspirit online to view this entry in the auction catalogue.

10. Никитин [Nikitin], *Мистики, розенкейцеры и тамплиеры в советской России* [*Mystics, Rosicrucians and Templars in Soviet Russia*], 89.

11. Никитин [Nikitin], *Мистики, розенкейцеры и тамплиеры в советской России* [*Mystics, Rosicrucians and Templars in Soviet Russia*], 89.

12. Никитин [Nikitin], *Мистики, розенкейцеры и тамплиеры в советской России* [*Mystics, Rosicrucians and Templars in Soviet Russia*], 89.

13. Открытый список [Open List], "Никитин Леонид Александрович" [Nikitin Leonid Alexandrovich].

14. Никитин [Nikitin], *Мистики, розенкейцеры и тамплиеры в советской России* [*Mystics, Rosicrucians and Templars in Soviet Russia*], 34–35.

15. Никитин [Nikitin], *Мистики, розенкейцеры и тамплиеры в советской России* [*Mystics, Rosicrucians and Templars in Soviet Russia*], 263 ff.

16. Савченко [Savchenko], "Солонович Алексей Александрович" [Solonovich Alexey Aleksandrovich].

17. Румянцев [Rumyantsev], "Алексей Александрович Солонович" [Alexey Alexandrovich Solonovich].

18. Menzel, "Occult and Esoteric Movements in Russia," 155–56.

19. Playfair, "Psi Research in Russia."

20. Meleshko, *Lyubimaya Kniga Tovarishcha Stalina* [Comrade Stalin's Favorite Book].

21. Playfair, "Psi Research in Russia."

22. Скляренко [Sklyarenko], "Вронский Сергей Алексеевич" [Vronsky Sergey Alekseevich]; Ковалев [Kovalev], "Великая Тайна Графа Вронского" [The Great Secret Of Count Vronsky]; Соклаков [Soklakov], "Рождение графа Сергея Вронского" [Birth of Count Sergei Vronsky]. See also interview with Vronsky, note 23.

23. Borup, *Sergei Vronksy—The Last Soviet Astrologer*. Video interview available on Vimeo. Accessed March 27, 2021.

24. Kernbach, "Unconventional research in USSR and Russia."

25. Menzel, "Occult and Esoteric Movements in Russia," 151.

26. "Davidashvili, Dzhuna." Available on the All About Heaven website, accessed June 12, 2021.

27. Gordeeva, "Tolstoyism in the Late-Socialist Cultural Underground," 502.

28. Gordeeva, "Tolstoyism in the Late-Socialist Cultural Underground," 503.
29. Lachman, *The Return of Holy Russia*, 349–52.
30. Thubron, *Among the Russians*, 36.
31. Thubron, *Among the Russians*, p. 38.
32. Thubron, *Among the Russians*, p. 38.
33. Clover, *Black Wind, White Snow*, 55.
34. Маланичева [Malenicheva], quoted in "О ВООПИиК" [About VOOPIK].
35. Clover, *Black Wind, White Snow*, 131.
36. Clover, *Black Wind, White Snow*, 130.

4. A HOUSE OF RUMOR

1. Clover, *Black Wind, White Snow*, 186.
2. Дейч and Журавлев [Daich and Zkuravlev], *Память*, 4.
3. Clover, *Black Wind, White Snow*, 165.
4. Национально-Патриотический Фронт [National Patriotic Front], "Information."
5. See the Медиазона [Media Zone] website for an account of Petrov's career.
6. Available on the Арктогея [Arctogeia] website.
7. Дугин [Dugin], "Великая война континентов" [Great War of the Continents]. My translation.
8. Дугин [Dugin], "Великая война континентов" [Great War of the Continents]. My translation.
9. День-ТВ [Den-TV], "О нас" [About Us].
10. Суть времени [The Essence of Time], "Сергей Кургинян" [Sergei Kurginyan].
11. Красная Весна [Red Spring], "Как уходило Небесное Царство" [How the Kingdom of Heaven Left].

5. THE NEW MILLENNIUM

1. Stausberg and Tessmann, "The appropriation of a religion."
2. Belyaev, "Occult and Esoteric Doctrines in Russia after the Collapse of Communism." Menzel, Hagemeister, and Rosenthal, *The New Age of Russia*, 259–61.

3. See Панин [Panin], *Особенности движения телеми в современной России* [Characteristics of the Thelemic Movement in Modern Russia].

4. Crowley, *The Confessions,* 713.

5. Crowley, *The Confessions,* 22.

6. LVXADONAI, Эоны прошлые и будущие [Eons Past and Future].

7. Панин [Panin], 23.

8. My translation and transcription from a video recording on YouTube entitled "Что такое традиция? (Дугин)." [What Is Tradition? (Dugin)].

9. Clover, *Black Wind, White Snow,* 55.

10. Clover, *Black Wind, White Snow,* 55.

11. Sedgwick, "The Case of Alexandr Dugin." Menzel and Hagemeister, *The New Age of Russia,* 289.

12. Sedgwick, "The Case of Alexandr Dugin." 290.

13. Дугин [Dugin], "Без царя в голове" [Without a King]. My translation.

14. Walker, "'Russia's soul is monarchic': tsarist school wants to reverse 100 years of history." Available online at *The Guardian.*

15. Московский Центр Карнеги [Carnegie Moscow Center], "Монархизм в современной России" [Monarchism in Modern Russia].

16. Zarifullin, *The New Scythians.* Unpublished English translation, supplied in digital form by the author.

6. THE STRANGE CASE OF THE *BOOK OF VELES*

1. My translation from Александр Асов [Alexander Asov], *Велесова Книга* [*The Book of Veles*], 235.

2. As recounted by Александр Асов [Alexander Asov] in *The Book of Veles,* 371 ff.

3. My translation from Александр Асов [Alexander Asov], *Велесова Книга* [*The Book of Veles*], 235.

4. See the article "Chariot of the Sun God," available on the Hare Krishna Temple Portal website.

5. My translation from the Russian version in Асов [Asov], 35.

6. My translation from the Russian version in Асов [Asov], 39.

7. My translation from the Russian version in Асов [Asov], 57.

8. See Anatole Klyosov's website for a list of his publications and interviews.

9. Тарянец, Валентинь, [Taranets, Valentin] *Велесова Книга* [*Book of Veles*] (in Ukrainian language).

7. SURVIVAL OF THE OLD GODS

1. Шнирельман, Виктор [Schnirelman, Victor]. *Русское язычество* [*Russian Paganism*], 13–14.
2. Rilke, *Russische Kunst,* 496.
3. See Kleinhempel, "Rilke's Translation of 'The Slovo o Polku Igoreva' ['The Song of Igor's Campaign']," 3–32.
4. Unpublished in English. Text supplied by the author.
5. See the video, "SMITE—God Lore Reveal—Chernobog, Lord of Darkness." Available on YouTube. Consulted May 19, 2020.
6. Alexinsky, "Slavonic Mythology," 294.
7. Alexinsky, "Slavonic Mythology," 297.
8. Dixon-Kennedy, *Encyclopedia of Russian and Slavic Myth and Legend,* 194, 213–15.
9. Fairbairn, *Eastern Orthodoxy through Western Eyes,* 136.
10. Fairbairn, *Eastern Orthodoxy,* 102.
11. Personal communication with the author, May 31, 2021.
12. Kahrs, "Die weißen, reinen Mari," 150–51.
13. Overland and Berg-Nordlie, *Bridging Divides,* 17, 113.
14. Znamenski, *The Beauty of the Primitive,* viii.
15. Eliade, *Shamanism,* 69.
16. Eliade, *Shamanism,* 69.
17. Quoted in Znamenski, *Shamanism in Siberia,* 12.
18. Quoted in Znamenski, *Shamanism in Siberia,* 21–28.
19. Bashkirov, "Gabyshev," 253–68.
20. Quijda et al., "Finding 'Their Own'," 258–72.
21. See, for example, the website of the St. Xenia Orthodox Church, Methuen, Massachusetts, USA.

8. THE NEW PAGANISM: A SPIRITUAL COUNTERREVOLUTION

1. Berdyaev, *The Russian Idea,* 2–3.
2. For a modern digital edition see Zoryan Dołęga Chodakowski *O Sławiańszczyźnie przed Chrześcijaństwem.* Warsaw: Armoryka, 2014.
3. Шнирельман, [Schnirelman], *Русское язычество* [*Russian Paganism*].

4. Quoted in Лапенков [Lapenkov], *История нетрадиционной ориентации,* [History of Non-Traditional Orientation], 98.

5. Ribakov, *Yazichestvo drevnich slavyan* [*The Paganism of the Ancient Slavs*], 1.

6. Асов [Asov], *Velikye taini Rusi* [*Great Secrets of Russia*], 1.

7. Асов [Asov], *Pero Gamayuna* [*The Gamayun Feather*], 1.

8. Родослав, Смагослав, and Рудияр [Rodoslav, Smagoslav, and Rudiyar], "Московская Славянская Языческая Община" [Moscow Slavic Pagan Community].

9. Slavya, "Circle of Pagan Tradition."

10. Veleslav, quoted in Велес Круг [Veles Circle].

11. Зданович [Zdanovich], 1995.

12. Зданович [Zdanovich], 1995.

13. Shnirelman, "Archaeology and Ethnic Politics."

14. See website for Festival of Positive Creation.

9. SAINTS, DOCTORS, AND CUNNING FOLK

1. Bennetts, "Russia has more faith healers than doctors, and many millions believe their troubles can be put right by sorcery." Available at *The Times* UK website.

2. Kourennoff, *Russian Folk Medicine,* 17–19.

3. Iarskaia-Smirnova and Romanov, "Culture Matters," 141–54.

4. Kourennoff, *Russian Folk Medicine,* 39.

5. Kourennoff, *Russian Folk Medicine,* 266–67.

6. Martin Saxer, "Tibetan Medicine and Russian Modernities," 57 ff.

7. Kharitonova, "Folk and traditional medicine." Online article, no pagination.

8. Kharitonova, "Folk and traditional medicine." Online article, no pagination.

10. THE WOMAN CLOTHED WITH THE SUN: RUSSIAN SPIRITUALITY AND THE EROTIC

1. Berdyaev, *The Russian Idea,* 3.

2. Agapkina and Torokova, quoted in Pepel, "Chronicles of Russian Sexual Culture" [*Khroniki russkoi sexualnoi kultury*].

3. Olearius, *The Voyages and Travels of the Ambassadors,* 61.

4. Шестаков [Shestakov], *Русский Эрос* [*Russian Eros*], 7.

5. Solovyov, *The Meaning of Love.*
6. Solovyov, *The Meaning of Love,* 91.
7. Posted on the Russian philosophical website Runivers.
8. Noyce, "Sophia and the Russian Mystical Tradition," 15.
9. Noyce, "Sophia and the Russian Mysterical Tradition," 17.
10. Klevantseva, "Zinaida Hippius."
11. Klevantseva, "Zinaida Hippius."
12. Knyazev, "Russia and the Coming Age," 72.
13. Hetherington, *Myth and Eros in Fin-de-Siècle Russia.*

11. THE PURSUIT OF THE RURAL IDEAL

1. Gordeeva, "Tolstoyism in the Late-Socialist Cultural Underground," 502.

12. THE ARTS AND THE SPIRITUAL IN RUSSIA FROM THE REVOLUTION TO THE PRESENT

1. John Keats, *Ode to a Nightingale* (1820).
2. Yefremov, Kindle edition, position 25. The quotations are my translation.
3. Yefremov, Kindle edition, positions 1553–570.
4. Yefremov, Kindle edition, positions 9088–104.
5. Yefremov, Kindle edition, positions 11200–217.
6. Yefremov, Kindle edition, positions 17001–008.
7. Heller, "Away from the Globe," 193–94.
8. Bulgakov, *The Master and Margarita,* chap. 22.
9. Андреев [Andreev], *Роза Мира* [Rose of the World].
10. Андреев [Andreev], *Роза Мира* [Rose of the World], chap. 1. My translation.
11. Quoted in Культура.РФ [Kultura.RF], "Константин Васильев" [Konstantin Vasiliev].
12. See bio on the website of the design firm Оформитель Блок [Oformitel Blok].
13. Вязовова [Vyazovova], "Проекты Города Будущево" [Projects for the City of the Future].

14. Tarkovsky, *Sculpting in Time*, 36–38.
15. Loupin, "Tarkovsky Parle."
16. Ruvinsky, "Punk Rocker to Holy Fool."
17. Available on MORGENSHTERN's YouTube channel.
18. Кино-Театр [Kino-Teatr], "Борис Гребенщиков" [Boris Grebenshchikov].
19. Альбина [Albina], "Никита Джигурда" [Nikita Dzhigurda].
20. Альбина [Albina], "Никита Джигурда" [Nikita Dzhigurda].
21. Nash, "Lenin was a Mushroom," 63–65.
22. Nosachev, "Influences of Western Esotericism," 183–192.
23. Dugin and Kuryokhin, *Manifesto of the New Magi*, 70–71.
24. Dugin and Kuryokhin, *Manifesto of the New Magi*, 70–71.

13. THE RUSSIAN LANGUAGE

1. Лямин [Lyamin], "Владимир Путин" [Vladimir Putin].
2. Трубецкой, [Trubetskoy], К проблеме русского самопознания [On the Problem of Russian Self-Awareness], chap. 6.
3. Janecek, *Look of Russian Literature*, 14.
4. Janecek, *Look of Russian Literature*, 15.
5. Chulev, "From Sanskrit To Macedonskrit."
6. Dostoyevsky, "A Few Words about Vranyo." My translation.
7. Private correspondence, April 11, 2021.

14. THE RUSSIAN DIASPORA

1. Lachman, "The Philosopher Tsar," 61–62. See also his book *The Return of Holy Russia*.
2. Chamberlain, *Philosophy Steamer*.
3. Figure provided by SIL International.
4. See Jacqueline Decter, *Nicholas Roerich: the Life and Art of a Russian Master*.
5. Dostoyevsky, *The Idiot*. Translated by David Magarshack, 420.
6. James Moore, *Gurdjieff*.
7. James Moore, *Gurdjieff*, 236.

15. IN SEARCH OF A VISION
FOR THE TWENTY-FIRST CENTURY

1. Young, *The Russian Cosmists,* 76–82.
2. Young, 145–54.
3. Dyomin, Valerii Nikitich, biographical entry in online dictionary Энциклопедиум (Encyclopedium).
4. ISRICA, "Международный Научно-Исследовательский Институт космопланетарной антропоэкологии" [International Scientific Research Institute of Cosmoplanetary Anthropoecology].
5. Stein, "Basic Considerations," 703.
6. Виталий Аверьянов [Averyanov and others], "Вводное слово. Ковчег русской Мечты" [Introduction. The Ark of the Russian Dream], 4. Izborsky Club, "Introduction." My translation.
7. Виталий Аверьянов [Averyanov and others], "Вводное слово. Ковчег русской Мечты" [Introduction. The Ark of the Russian Dream], 4.
8. Виталий Аверьянов [Averyanov and others], "Вводное слово. Ковчег русской Мечты" [Introduction. The Ark of the Russian Dream], 4.
9. Виталий Аверьянов [Averyanov and others], "Накануне потопа" [On the Eve of the Flood], 19.

16. "THE HOPE OF THE WORLD"?

1. *New Dawn Magazine,* No. 187 (July–August 2021): 33.
2. Anon., "Россия—последняя надежда Бога на земле" [Russia, God's Last Hope on Earth], in online journal Fontanka.

Bibliography

WORKS IN ROMAN TYPE

Alexinsky, G. "Slavonic Mythology." *Larousse Encyclopedia of Mythology*. London: Paul Hamlyn, 1960, 293–310

Andreyev, Alexander. *The Saint-Petersburg Datsan* (booklet in Russian and English). St. Petersburg: Nestor Historia, 2012.

Aptekman, Marina. "In the Beginning Was the Word: Magical Kabbalah, the Occult Revival and the Linguistic Mysticism of the Silver Age." In Marina Aptekman (ed.), *Jacob's Ladder: Kabbalistic Allegory in Russian Literature*. Boston, MA: Academic Studies Press, 2018,

Ashe, Geoffrey. *The Ancient Wisdom*. London: Macmillan, 1977.

Avalon, Arthur (Sir John Woodroffe), *Shakti and Shâkta*. London: Luzac, 1918.

Baker, Ian. *Heart of the World*. New York: Penguin, 2006.

Bashkirov, M. B. "Gabyshev: Identity at the Intersection of Two Cultures." *Etnograficheskoe Obozrenie,* no. 6 (2021): 253–268.

Berdyaev, Nikolai. *The Russian Idea*. New York: Macmillan, 1948.

Bhaktivedanta Swami Prabhupada, A.C., "Chariot of the Sun God," Introduction to Canto 5, Chaps. 21–22 of the *Srimad-Bhagavatam*. Hare Krishna Temple online.

Biely, Andrey. *The Dramatic Symphony* and *Forms of Art*. Introduction by Roger Keys. Edinburgh: Polygon, 1986.

———. *Petersburg*. Harmondsworth, UK: Penguin, 1983.

Blavatsky, Helena Petrovna. *The Secret Doctrine*. London: Theosophical Publishing Company, 1888.

Burmistrov, Konstantin. "Kabbalah and Martinism: Gregory Mebes and the Occult Renaissance in Russia of the Early 20th Century." Academia.edu, n.d. Available on the academia.edu website.

Chamberlain, Leslie. *The Philosophy Steamer: Lenin and the Exile of the Intelligentsia.* New York: Overlook Press, 2007.

Chulev, Basil. "From Sanskrit to Macedonskrit and vice versa." Available at Internet Archive online.

Churton, Tobias. *Deconstructing Gurdjieff.* Rochester, VT: Inner Traditions, 2017.

"Circle of Pagan Tradition." Available at Slavya online.

Clover, Charles. *Black Wind, White Snow: The Rise of Russia's New Nationalism.* New Haven and London: Yale University Press, 2016

Cohn, Norman. *The Pursuit of the Millennium.* London: Paladin, 1972.

Cousins, James. "Scriabine and Delville." *The Theosophist* 57.4 (January 1936).

Cranston, Sylvia. *H. P. B. The Extraordinary Life and Influence of Helena Blavatsky.* New York: Tarcher/Putnam, 1993.

Crowley, Aleister. *The Confessions,* edited by John Symonds and Kenneth Grant. London: Routledge & Kegan Paul, 1979.

Decter, Jacqueline. *Nicholas Roerich: The Life and Art of a Russian Master.* Rochester, VT: Park Street Press, 1989.

Dixon-Kennedy, Mike. *Encyclopedia of Russian and Slavic Myth and Legend.* Santa Barbara, CA: ABC-CLIO, 1998.

Dostoievsky, Feodor M. [sic],. *The Diary of a Writer,* translated and edited by Boris Brasol. New York: George Braziller, 1919.

———. *The Idiot.* Translated by David Magarshack. Harmondsworth, UK: Penguin, 1978, 420.

Dugin, Alexander and Sergei Kuryokhin. "Manifesto of the New Magi." *New Dawn* 15, no. 3 (2021): 70–71.

Eliade, Mircea. *Shamanism: Archaic Techniques of Ecstasy.* London: Arkana, 1989.

Evdokomov, Michael. *Russische Pilger.* Salzburg: Otto Müller, 1990.

Fairbairn, Donald. *Eastern Orthodoxy through Western Eyes.* Louisville, Kentucky, and London, UK: Westminster John Knox Press, 2002.

Glazov, Yuri. *The Russian Mind since Stalin's Death.* Dordrecht, Netherlands: D. Reidel, 1985

Godwin, Joscelyn. *Harmonies of Heaven and Earth.* London: Thames and Hudson, 1987.

———. Introduction to Marquis Alexandre Saint-Yves d'Alveydre. *The Kingdom of Agarttha: A Journey into the Hollow Earth.* Rochester, VT: Inner Traditions, 2008.

Gordeeva, Irina. "Tolstoyism in the Late-Socialist Cultural Underground: Soviet Youth in Search of Religion, Individual Autonomy and Nonviolence in the 1970s–1980s." In *Open Theology* 3 (2017): 494–515.

Graham, Stephen "Rasputin." *Man, Myth and Magic,* No. 83. London: Purnell, 1971.

Hanegraaff, Wouter J. et al. (eds.). *Dictionary of Gnosis and Western Esotericism.* 2 vols. Leiden: Brill, 2005.

Heller, Leonid. "Away from the Globe. Occultism, Esotericism and Literature in Russia during the 1960s–1980s" in *The New Age of Russia*, ed. Menzel, Hagemeister, and Rosenthal, 193–4. Munich and Berlin: Verlag Otto Sagner, 2012.

Hetherington, Philippa. *Myth and Eros in Fin-de-Siècle Russia: Zinaida Gippius' Sexual Revolution.* Sydney, Australia: University of Sydney, 2006.

Hinze, Oscar Marcel. *Tantra Vidya.* Freiburg im Breisgau, Germany: Aurum Verlag, 1983.

Iarskaia-Smirnova, Elena, and Pavel Romanov. "Culture matters: integration of folk medicine into healthcare in Russia." In Ellen Kuhlmann and Mike Saks (eds.), *Rethinking Professional Governance: International Directions in Healthcare.* Bristol, UK: Policy Press, 2008.

Janecek, Gerald. *The Look of Russian Literature: Avant-Garde Visual Experiments 1900–1930.* Princeton, NJ: Princeton University Press, 2014.

Jenkins, Philip. *The Great and Holy War.* Oxford, UK: Lion Hudson, 2014.

Kahrs, Ulrike. "Die weißen, reinen Mari," in *Heidnisches Jahrbuch 2007.* Hamburg: Verlag Daniel Junker (2006): 131–54.

Kernbach, Serge. "Unconventional research in USSR and Russia." Available at the online archive of Cornell University. Accessed February 14, 2021.

Kharitonova, Valentina I. "Folk and traditional medicine: On the possibility of integrating medical systems, practices and methods in contemporary Tuva." *New Research of Tuva*, No. 4 (2018). Available online, accessed April 12, 2021.

Kleinhempel, Ulrich. "Rilke's Translation of 'The Slovo o Polku Igoreva' ['The Song of Igor's Campaign'] in the Context of His Spiritual and Poetological Development." *Aliter, Journal of the Association for the Investigation of Esotericism and Mysticism,* 8 (2017): 3–32.

Klevantseva, Tatiana. "Prominent Russians: Zinaida Hippius." *Russiapedia.* Available at Russiapedia RT online.

Knyazev, D. N. "Russia and the Coming Age of the Spirit." *New Dawn* (November–December 1999): 72.

Kourennoff, Paul M. *Russian Folk Medicine.* Translated, edited, and arranged by George St. George. New York: Pyramid Books, 1971.

Lachman, Gary. *A Secret History of Consciousness.* Great Barrington, MA, USA: Lindisfarne Books, 2003.

———. "The Philosopher Tsar." In *New Dawn* 15, no. 3 (2021): 61–62.

———. *The Return of Holy Russia.* Rochester, Vermont: Inner Traditions, 2020.

Lennhoff, Eugen, and Oskar Posner. *Internationales Freimaurer-Lexikon.* Vienna and Munich: Amalthea-Verlag, 1980.

Loupin, V. "Tarkovsky Parle." *Figaro Magazine,* October 25, 1986.

Massie, Robert K. *Peter the Great.* London: Abacus, 1992.

McIntosh, Christopher. *Eliphas Lévi and the French Occult Revival.* Albany, NY: State University of New York Press, 2011.

———. *Beyond the North Wind.* Newburyport, MA: Weiser Books, 2019.

Mebes, G. O. *Tarot Majors.* England: Shin Publications, 2020.

———. *Tarot Minors.* England: Shin Publications, 2020.

Menzel, Birgit, Michael Hagemeister, and Bernice Glatzer Rosenthal (eds.). *The New Age of Russia: Occult and Esoteric Dimensions.* Munich and Berlin: Verlag Otto Sagner, 2012.

Moore, James. *Gurdjieff.* Shaftesbury, UK: Element, 1991.

Nash, Charlie. "Lenin was a Mushroom." *New Dawn* 15, no. 3 (2021): 63–65.

Nietzsche, Friedrich. *Jenseits von Gut und Böse.* Leipzig: C. G. Naumann, 1886.

Nosachev, Pavel. "The Influences of Western Esotericism on Russian Rock Poetry at the Turn of the Century," ed. Nemanja Radulović, proceedings of the conference "Esotericism, Literature and Culture in Central and Eastern Europe," 183–92. Belgrade: Faculty of Philology, University of Belgrade, 2018.

Noyce, John. "Sophia and the Russian Mystical Tradition." *History Enlightened,* 23 (2019): 15.

Olearius, Adam. *The Voyages and Travels of the Ambassadors Sent by Frederick, Duke of Holstein, to the Great Duke of Muscovy, and the King of Persia,* translated from the German by John Davies. 2nd ed. London: John Starkey and Thomas Basset, 1669.

Ossendowski, Ferdinand. *Beasts, Men and Gods*. New York: E. P. Dutton, 1922.

Ouspensky, Pyotr D. *A New Model of the Universe*. New York: Knopf, 1961.

Overland, Indra, and Mikkel Berg-Nordlie. *Bridging Divides. Ethno-political Leadership among the Russian Sami*. New York and Oxford: Berghahn Books, 2012.

Pepel, Victor. "Chronicles of Russian Sexual Culture" [*Khroniki russkoi sexualnoi kultury*]. Available at Russian language internet journal *Нож* [Knife] online, August 29, 2017.

Playfair, Guy Lyon. "Psi Research in Russia." *Psi Encyclopedia*. London: The Society for Psychical Research, 2015. Retrieved February 14, 2021

Prokofieff, Sergei O. *The East in the Light of the West*, translated from the Russian by Simon Blaxland de Lange. London: Temple Lodge, 1993.

Quijda, Justine B., Katherine E. Graber, and Eric Stephen, "Finding 'Their Own': Revitalizing Buryat Culture Through Shamanic Practices in Ulan-Ude." *Problems of Post-Communism*, 62:5 (2015): 258–72.

Rilke, Rainer Maria. *Russische Kunst*. In *Rainer Maria Rilke, Sämtliche Werke, Band 10*. Frankfurt am Main: Insel, 1976.

Roerich, Nicholas. *Shambhala*. New York: Nicholas Roerich Museum, 1985.

Ruvinsky, Vladimir. "From Punk Rocker to Holy Fool." *Russia Beyond*, November 10, 2011. Available at Russia Beyond online.

Sabeheddin, Mehmet. "Saint-Yves d'Alveydre and the Synarchy of Agarttha" in *New Dawn* 151 (July–August 2015).

Saxer, Martin. "Tibetan Medicine and Russian Modernities," in Vincanne Adams, Mona Schrempf, and Sienna R. Craig (eds.), *Medicine between Science and Religion*. New York: Berghahn Books, 2010.

Shnirelman, Victor A. "Archaeology and ethnic politics: the discovery of Arkaim." *Museum International*. Paris: UNESCO and Blackwell Publishers, Vol. 50, No. 2 (1998): 33–39.

Skrylnikov, Pavel. "The Church against neo-paganism." August 3, 2018. Available at Rodnovery online.

Solovyov, Vladimir. *The Meaning of Love*. Edited and translated by Thomas R. Beyer, Jr. New York: Inner Traditions International, 1985.

Spengler, Oswald. "The Two Faces of Russia and Germany's Eastern Problems." An address delivered on February 14, 1922, at the Rhenish-Westphalian Business Convention in Essen. First published in Spengler, *Politische Schriften* (Munich, 1932). English translation available at the Wordpress blog, "Besboshnik," entitled "The Two Faces of Russia."

Stausberg, Michael, and Anna Tessman. "The appropriation of a religion: The case of Zoroastrianism in contemporary Russia." *Culture and Religion,* 14, No. 4 (2013). Available online. Accessed December 28, 2020.

Stein, Erik Johansen. "Basic Considerations about N. A. Kozyrev's theory of time," 703. Available at Chronos online. Accessed June 29, 2021.

Tarkovsky, Andrei. *Sculpting in Time.* Austin: University of Texas Press (2003): 36–38.

Thubron, Colin. *Among the Russians.* London: Penguin, 1985.

Walker, Benjamin. "Tantrism." *Encyclopedia of the Unexplained.* London: Routledge & Kegan Paul, 1974, 242–44.

Vernadsky, George. *The Origins of Russia.* Westport, CT: Greenwood Press, 1975.

Young, George M. *The Russian Cosmists.* New York: Oxford University Press, 2012.

Znamenski, Andrei. *Red Shambhala.* Wheaton, IL: Quest Books, 2011.

———. *The Beauty of the Primitive: Shamanism and the Western Imagination.* New York: Oxford University Press, 2007.

———. *Shamanism in Siberia: Russian Records of Indigenous Spirituality.* Dordrecht, Netherlands: Springer, 2003.

WORKS IN CYRILLIC TYPE

Аверьянов, Виталий. [Averyanov, Vitalii.] et al. (eds.). *Русский Ковчег. Альтернативная стратегия* [The Russian Ark: an Alternative Strategy]. Moscow: Nashe Zavtra, 2021.

———. "Вводное слово. Ковчег русской Мечты" [Introduction. The Ark of the Russian Dream], in the online journal *Изборский клуб* [Izborsky Club], No. 1 (2020): 4. Available at Izborsky Club online.

———. "Стратегия «Русский Ковчег»" [Strategy of the "Russian Ark"], special issue of online journal *Изборский клуб* [Izborsky Club], No. 1 (2020). Available at Izborsky Club online.

———. "Накануне потопа" [On the Eve of the Flood], in the online journal *Изборский клуб* [Izborsky Club], No. 1 (2020): 19. Available at Izborsky Club online.

Андреев, Александр [Andreyev, Alexander]. *Оккултист Страны Советов: Тайна Доктора Барченко* [Occultist of the Soviet

Countries: the Secret of Doctor Barchenko]. Moscow: Яица [Yaitsa], 2004.

Андреев, Даниил Леонидович [Andreev, Daniil Leonidovich]. *The Rose of the World*. Updated October 8, 2021. Available at Rozamira online.

Асов, Александр [Asov, Alexander]. *Перо гамаюна* [The Gamayun Feather]. Moscow: Ast, 2013.

———. *Великие тайны Руси i* [Great Secrets of Russia]. Moscow: Ast, 2014.

———. *Велесова Книга* [*The Book of Veles*]. Moscow: Amrita-Rus, 2019.

Богомолов, Николай А. [Bogomolov, Nikolai A.]. *Русская литература начала XX века и оккультизм. Исследования и материалы* [Russian Literature at the Beginning of the Twentieth Century and Occultism. Investigations and Materials]. Moscow: NLO [Новое литературное обозрение], 1999.

Велес Круг [Veles Circle]. Interview with Veleslav, leader of the group Rodolubye. Availabe in the online journal *Велес Круг*, n.d.

Вязовова, Наталья [Vyazovova, Natalia]. "Проекты Города Будущево художника Виктора Пруса" [Projects for the City of the Future by the Artist Viktor Prus]. *Властная вертикаль Федерации* [online pan-Russian socio-political journal], No.8 (2015).

Гумилев, Лев [Gumilyov, Lev]. *Этногенез и биосфера Земли* [Ethnogenesis and the Biosphere of the Earth]. Moscow: Airis Press, 2016.

Дейч, Марк, and Леонид Журавлев [Daich, Mark, and Leonid Zhuravlev]. *Память: как она есть [Pamyat: What It Is]*. Moscow: МП "Цунами," 1991.

День-ТВ [Den-TV]. "О нас" [About Us]. Accessed March 11, 2021. Available at День-ТВ [Den-TV] online.

Дёмин, Валерий [Dyomin, Valerii], *Гиперборея - праматерь мировой культуры* [*Hyperborea, the Original Womb of World Culture*]. Moscow: Veche, 2003.

Дугин, Александр [Dugin, Alexander]. "Без царя в голове, или монархизм без монарха" [Without a king at the head, or monarchism without a monarch]. December 17, 2018. Available at Изборский Клуб [Izborsky Club] online.

———. "Великая война континентов" [Great War of the Continents]. *Арктогея*. Available at Арктогея online.

Ефремов, Иван [Yefremov, Ivan]. *Лезвие бритвы* [*The Razor's Edge*]. Digital edition, Moscow: Zebra E, 2008.

Зданович, Геннадий Борисович [Zdanovich, Gennadi Borisovich, ed.]. *Аркаим: Исслед. Поиски. Открытия* [*Arkaim: Exploration. Searches. Discoveries*]. Chelyabinsk: Kamennoy Poyas, 1995.

Иванов, Вячеслав [Ivanov, Vyacheslav], "*О русской идее*" ["On the Russian Idea"], in *Собрание сочинений* [*Collected Essays*], Vol. 3. Brussels: Foyer Oriental Chrétien, 321–338.

ISRICA. "Международный Научно-Исследовательский Институт Космопланетарной Антропоэкологии Имени Академика В.П. Казначеева" [International Research Institute for Cosmoplanetary Anthropoecology Named After Academician V.P. Kaznacheev]. Available at ISRICA online.

Кино-Театр [Kino-Teatr], "Борис Гребенщиков" [Boris Grebenshchikov]. Accessed June 24 2021. Available at Кино-Театр [Kino-Teatr] online.

Ковалев, Эдуард [Kovalev, Edward]. "Великая Тайна Графа Вронского" [The Great Secret of Count Vronsky]. January 7, 2014. Available at Совершенно Секретно [Top Secret] online.

Красная Весна [Red Spring]. "Как уходило Небесное Царство. Писатель Проханов о премьере спектакля «Крот»" [How the Kingdom of Heaven left. Writer Prokhanov about the premiere of the play "Mole"]. October 18, 2019. Accessed March 12, 2021. Available at Красная Весна [Red Spring] online.

Культура.РФ [Kultura.RF]. "Константин Васильев" [Konstantin Vasiliev]. Accessed January 9, 2021. Available at Культура.РФ [Kultura.RF] online.

Лапенков, Владимир Борисович [Lapenkov, Vladimir Borisovich]. *История нетрадиционной ориентации. Легенды и мифы всемирной истории* [History of Non-Traditional Orientation. Legends and Myths of World History]. Available at RuLit online.

LVXADONAI. Эоны прошлые и будущие [Eons Past and Future]. October 10, 2020. Accessed March 23, 2021. Available at Омниасофия [Omniasophia] online.

Лямин, Евгений. [Lyamin, Evgeny]. Владимир Путин провел встречу с деятелями культуры в Международный день русского языка [Vladimir Putin met with cultural figures on International Day of the Russian Language]. June 6, 2020. Available at 1TV News online.

Максим (Розамира) [Maxim, (Rozamira)], "О нас" [About Us]. 27 April 2019. Available at Розамира [Rozamira] online.

Маланичева, Г.И. [Malanicheva, G. I.]. "О ВООПИиК" [About VOOPIK]. Available at Всероссийское общество охраны памятников истории и культуры [All-Russian Society for the Protection of Historical and Cultural Monuments] online.

Мелешко, Вадим [Meleshko, Vadim]. *"Любимая книга товарища Сталина"* [Comrade Stalin's Favorite Book]. Available on the drfraus Livejournal page. Retrieved February 14, 2021.

Московский Центр Карнеги [Carnegie Moscow Center]. "Монархизм в современной России" [Monarchism in modern Russia]. June 14, 2011. Available at Московский Центр Карнеги [Carnegie Moscow Center] online.

Национально-Патриотический Фронт [National Patriotic Front]. "Information." Accessed March 10, 2021. Available at НПФ «Память» [NPF "Memory"] online.

Никитин, Андрей [Nikitin, Andrei], *Мистики, розенкейцеры и тамплиеры в советской России* [*Mystics, Rosicrucians and Templars in Soviet Russia*]. Moscow: Agraf, 2000.

Открытый список [Open List]. "Никитин Леонид Александрович (1896)" [Nikitin Leonid Alexandrovich (1896).] Available at Открытый список [Open List] online.

Панин, Станислав А. [Panin, Stanislav A.]. *Особенности движения телеми в современной России* [Characteristics of the Thelemic Movement in Modern Russia], presented in 2010 in the Faculty of Philosophy, Department of Religious Studies, Lomonosov University, Moscow. Available at docplayer online, accessed March 23, 2021.

Родослав, Смагослав, and Рудияр [Rodoslav, Smagoslav, and Rudiyar], "Московская Славянская Языческая Община" [Moscow Slavic Pagan Community]. June 22, 2011. Available at Славянская Традиция [Slavic Tradition] online.

Румянцев, Вячеслав [Rumyantsev, Vyacheslav]. "Алексей Александрович Солонович" [Alexey Alexandrovich Solonovich]. Available at ХРОНОС [Khronos] online.

Рыбаков Борис [Ribakov, Boris]. *Язычество древних славян* [*The Paganism of the Ancient Slavs*]. Moscow: Academic Project, 1981.

Савченко, Виктор Анатольевич [Savchenko, Victor Anatolievich]. "Солонович Алексей Александрович" [Solonovich Alexey Aleksandrovich]. Available at ВикиЧтение: 100 знаменитых анархистов и революционеров [WikiReading: 100 Famous Anarchists and Revolutionaries] online.

Скляренко, Валентина Марковна [Sklyarenko, Valentina Markovna]. "Вронский Сергей Алексеевич" [Vronsky Sergey Alekseevich]. Available at ВикиЧтение: 50 знаменитых прорицателей и ясновидящих [WikiReading: 50 Famous Soothsayers and Clairvoyants] online.

Соклаков, Кирил [Soklakov, Kiril]. "Рождение графа Сергея Вронского" [Birth of Count Sergei Vronsky]. February 5, 2012. Available at RIGA CV online.

Суть времени [The Essence of Time]. "Сергей Кургинян, спектакль «Крот» о перестройке: «За их случайною победой роится сумрак гробовой»" [Sergei Kurginyan, the play "The Mole" about perestroika: "Darkness of the grave swarms behind their accidental victory"]. Accessed March 12, 2021. Available at Суть времени [The Essence of Time] online.

Тарянец, Валентинь [Taranets, Valentin]. Велесова Книга [Book of Veles] (in Ukrainian language). Odessa: International Humanitarian University, 2015.

Токарева, Альбина [Tokareva, Albina]. Никита Джигурда: «По секрету—все мы боги» [Nikita Dzhigurda: "In secret—we are all gods"]. May 27, 2015, accessed June 24, 2021. Available at Кубанские Новости [Kubanskiye Novosti] online.

Трубецкой, Николай Сергеевич [Trubetskoy, Nikolai Sergejewitsch]. К проблеме русского самопознания [On the Problem of Russian Self-Awareness]. Paris: Eurasian Publishing House, 1927.

———. Общеславянсий элемент в русской культуре [The Common Slavic Element in Russian Culture]. Original edition, Paris: 1927. Later edition, Moscow: Progress, 1995.

Фонтанка [Fontanka]. "«Россия—последняя надежда Бога на земле». Вячеслав Макаров поддержал предложение патриарха вписать в Конституцию веру и Бога" ["Russia is God's last hope on earth." Vyacheslav Makarov supported the Patriarch's proposal to include faith and God in the Constitution]. December 2, 2020. Accessed June 30, 2021. Available at Fontanka online.

Чистов, К. В. [Chistov, K. V.], "Легенда о Беловодье" [The Legend of Byelovodye]. In the journal Вопросы литературы и народного творчества [Questions regarding literature and folk arts] 35 (1962):

116–81. Published by the Karelia branch of the Academy of Sciences of the USSR. Available at the website of the Karelian Research Centre Library.

Шестаков, Вячеслав П. [Shestakov, Vyacheslav P.]. Ed. *Русский Эрос* [Russian Eros]. Moscow: Progress, 1991.

Шнирельман, Виктор [Schnirelman, Victor]. *Русское язычество* [*Russian Paganism*]. Moscow: BBI, 2012.

Энциклопедический словарь "Литераторы Санкт-Петербурга" [Encyclopedic Dictionary: Literators of St. Peterburg]. "Минцлова, Анна Рудольфовна" [Minclova, Anna Rudolfovna]. Available at Книжная Лавка Писатели [Bookstore Writers] online.

Эткинд, Александр М. [Etkind, Alexander M.]. *Хлыст. Секты, литература и революция [Khlyst. Sects, Literature and Revolution].* Moscow: NLO [Новое Литературное Обозрение], 2013.

Index

Numbers in *italics* preceded by *pl.* refer to color insert plate numbers.